Housing

an environment for living

MARJORIE BRANIN KEISER

Director, School of Home Economics
Montana State University

Macmillan Publishing Co., Inc.

NEW YORK

Collier Macmillan Publishers

LONDON

Dedicated to

Gladys, who believed . . .

Macmillan Publishing Co., Inc.
866 Third Avenue, New York, New York 10022

Collier Macmillan Canada, Ltd.

Library of Congress Cataloging in Publication Data

Keiser, Marjorie B
  Housing.

  Includes bibliographies and index.
  1. Architecture, Domestic. 2. Architecture—
Environmental aspects. I. Title.
NA7125.K44 1978   728   77-1259
ISBN 0-02-362230-X

Printing: 1 2 3 4 5 6 7 8   Year: 8 9 0 1 2 3 4

Preface

THE bird builds a nest, the bear seeks a cave, and the bee creates a hive—all for protection, promotion of growth, and reproduction of the species. But human shelter has another purpose: it becomes the site of abiding affection and a source of identity. Von Eckhart calls this "a sense of place."[1] The house also serves as a symbol of personal achievement, making it an appropriate status symbol.

Each person has a different concept of the most desirable place to live. Architects, builders, and the many workers in the housing industry design and construct houses to fit public taste and preferences. The individual seeks a comfortable environment to facilitate his daily activities, and information that will enable him to gain the best quality of living for each housing dollar he spends. Unfortunately, there is no formula that can be universally applied. Housing standards or codes relate to structural requirements for construction techniques or materials, with little or no attention to the life style the building will provide.

The book is divided into five parts. Part One examines the environmental factors that influence housing design. Parts Two and Three study trends in home construction, past and present, with emphasis on the American housing market for the 1970's. Part Four discusses the financial and legal aspects of housing. In Part Five, the concluding section, we look toward habitats of the future, on land, sea, and outer space.

The drawings and photographs were selected to illustrate housing principles and alternatives with the hope that these will suggest solutions to the reader.

M. B. K.

[1] W. Von Eckhart, *A Place to Live* (New York: Delacort Press, 1967).

iii

Acknowledgments

MANY people helped with the development of this book. My thanks go to the Director of the Montana Agricultural Experiment Station, Dr. J.A. Asleson, who not only offered periodic encouragement, but also support. The editorial help of John D. MacKellar and Allan Smart of the Montana State University Publication and News Services was invaluable.

All of the illustrations and most of the photographs were made by my husband, Robert L. Keiser. Without his expertise and patience, this book would never have become a reality. Then there were the editorial reviewers, whose comments and critique were especially appreciated. They include June H. Carpenter of Mississippi State University and Mary Wallace Crocker, formerly of Texas Tech University, now with Memphis State University. Last of all, to the faculty and staff of the School of Home Economics at Montana State University, for their understanding of my conflicting schedule with the university and the publisher: thank you.

M. B. K.

Contents

introduction

A Definition   3

PART ONE
environmental influences

Influences of the Biophysical Environment   9

Influences of the Sociopsychological
Environment   30

PART TWO
influence of the
macro-environment: the exterior

PART THREE
influence of the
micro-environment: the interior

The Space for Living 123

Space for Personal Activities 136

Space for the Work of the Household 150

Consumer Assistance 302

PART FIVE
the future of housing

The Future of Housing   317

Sources of References   330

Index   347

introduction

Suppose that it were possible to invent an imaginary architecture. Suppose that we could think of architecture as a process for perfecting the earth. . . .

Arthur Drexler

1

A Definition

HOUSING plays an important role in the life of each individual. Its cost may require up to a third of a person's income over his lifetime. Its physical quality may facilitate or restrict everyday activities, and may even affect physical and mental health. Its location may determine social and economic opportunities as well as reflect social and economic achievements.

The housing industry plays an important role in the political, economic, and social order. It produces approximately one fourth of our national wealth, and it provides employment for hundreds of thousands of people who are involved in the construction of new houses, the manufacture of components and supplies, the financing and maintenance of homes. Housing plays a significant role in the use of energy, the design of transportation networks and communications systems, and the delivery of community services. So important has housing become in the political process that the U.S. Department of Housing and Urban Development was established in 1966.

Although definitions of housing vary, most describe a building, or part of a building, designed for occupancy by a single family or individual. The assumption is that each individual has the right to choose a personal style of living and to express that choice in the design characteristics of the place in which he lives. Housing has also been described broadly as "interior and exterior space," and specifically as

the nursery in which a child spends its formative years, the bath in which the essentials of cleanliness are taught, the structure containing these rooms, the street on which the structure belongs. . . .[1]

[1] R. Neutra, *Survival Through Design* (New York: Oxford University Press, Inc., 1951), pp. 24–25.

3

For most living organisms, the environment is a well-defined place in which the organism grows and reproduces. The longer the organism lives in these surroundings, the more perfectly attuned to them it becomes. Each organism's key to survival seems to lie in meeting change with change. Those organisms that fail to adapt are unlikely to survive.

Human beings, like other organisms, evolve by adapting to the environment. Natives of the tropics, for example, are likely to have more pigmentation in their skins than do natives of frigid climates. But, partly because there are biological and physical limits to their adaptability, and partly because they possess a creative intelligence denied to other species, human beings also build artificial shells for protection from unfriendly environments.

The development of sociological and technological skills has made human survival possible in an amazing variety of environments. Human habitats have been built on land, in water, and even in outer space. So refined have their building techniques become that human beings have come to disregard the natural environment completely. But the magnitude of man's manipulations of the environment is such that it can produce changes in the environment itself. By the mid-1970s it has become clear that a more synchronous relationship between human shelter—housing—and the environment is essential.

A systems approach may help to explain these environmental relationships. The human being can be compared to a "rubber band"

FIGURE 1-1 The Human System.

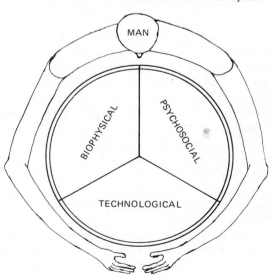

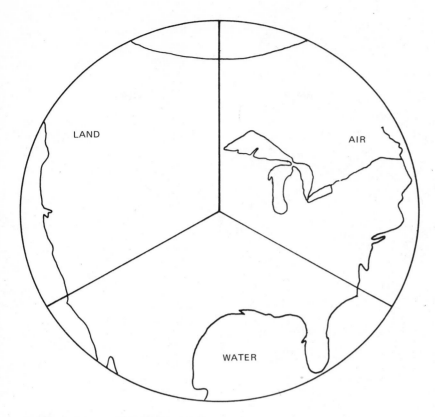

FIGURE 1-2 The Environmental System.

holding together the biophysical, psychosocial, and technological factors of the environment, permitting each factor to expand or contract. If the system were in equilibrium, each of the factors would be equal in importance and size. In reality, however, the significance of any aspect of this environment varies with man's knowledge and understanding of it.

Nature, another system, can be thought of as being composed of three equal and essential factors—land, water, and air—held together by a "rubber band" called earth. Nature is the macro-environment in which the human system is located, so that all the factors in each system tend to influence one another.

Housing is yet another system composed of three parts—structures, communities, and networks of communications and services—held together by the "rubber band" of human habitation. The housing system is located between the human system and the natural system, and is influenced by the factors in both. Housing, then, is best understood as an environment for living. See Figs. 1-3 and 1-4.

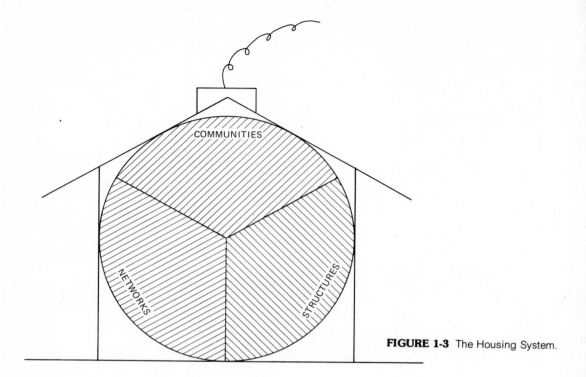

FIGURE 1-3 The Housing System.

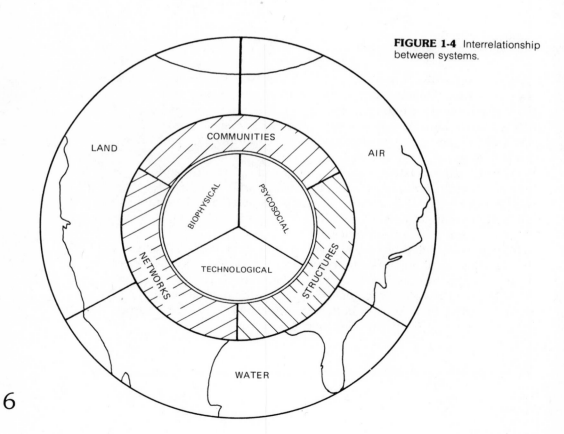

FIGURE 1-4 Interrelationship between systems.

6

environmental influences

Each generation has its own rendezvous with the land. . . . We are all brief tenants. . . . We can misuse the land and diminish the usefullness of its resources, or we can create a world in which physical affluence and affluence of the spirit go hand in hand.

Stuart Udall
The Quiet Crisis

2

Influences of the Biophysical Environment

THE biophysical environment includes climate, geography, and the waste products of metabolic and manufacturing processes. The characteristics of each locality determine the structure developed as an environment for living.

Many primitive human beings chose caves as their first shelter. Caves provided security, warmth, and company—and an atmosphere that encouraged a perception of the natural environment as an enemy to be conquered. But other primitive people perceived nature as a friend with which to live in harmony. A bowerlike structure or tent enhanced this perception though it afforded little protection. Contemporary man wants both protection from, and communion with, nature. The problem is to strike a balance between control of environmental forces and a sensitivity to nature.

CLIMATE

The chief characteristics of climate are solar energy, temperature, precipitation, humidity, and wind. Each influences and controls the others and all are regulated by altitude, distribution of land and water, mountain barriers, and ocean currents. Climate determines the length of the growing season, the type of vegetation, and even life itself. Inevitably, it influences housing. Some people build several places to live, erecting separate structures to correspond to seasonal weather conditions—such as a winter igloo and a summer tent. Others move a portable dwelling from one location to another. Most people, however, have one dwelling that is modified to provide protection from all types of weather. Most of these structures were created in an economy of

9

scarcity that left little margin for error, and they reflect a high level of performance. As Louis Kahn remarks

> . . . many of the huts were native made. They were all alike and they all worked. There were no architects . . . ; how clever was man who solved the problems of sun, rain, wind.[1]

The modern architect has the advantage of scientific data concerning solar angles, number of days of sunlight, and ranges of temperature, humidity, precipitation, and wind. Correct orientation and design of the house can reduce energy needs and costs as well as improve selection of materials and construction methods.

Physical Geography

The earth's contours have a dynamic effect on climatic conditions. The relationship between land masses and water, as well as the many sorts of irregularities of terrain, produce distinctive types of soil, vegeta-

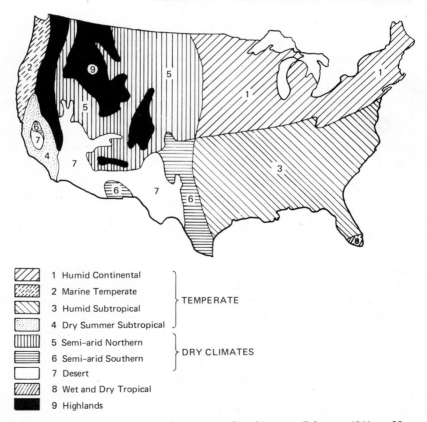

FIGURE 2-1 Climatic conditions in the United States.

1 Humid Continental	⎫	
2 Marine Temperate		
3 Humid Subtropical	⎬ TEMPERATE	
4 Dry Summer Subtropical	⎭	
5 Semi-arid Northern	⎫	
6 Semi-arid Southern	⎬ DRY CLIMATES	
7 Desert	⎭	
8 Wet and Dry Tropical		
9 Highlands		

[1] L. Kahn, "A Statement by Louis Kahn," *Arts and Architecture*, February 1961, p. 29.

tion, and animal life. Most of the United States is located in the temperate zone, where westerly winds, summer rains, and winter snow prevail. Some arid regions exist in the western interior and a few southern states have tropical characteristics.

Solar Energy

The sun provides a continuous flow of energy to the earth in the form of heat and light. The earth's rotation and slope, as well as its slightly elliptical course around the sun, are responsible for the length of night and day and the progression of the seasons. Clouds or pollution can alter the intensity and duration of this energy.

Most of the time, the sun has a beneficial effect on man and his dwelling. Its light adds zest to living; its heat provides physical comfort. Dwellings designed to maximize these blessings during long, cold winters are desirable. Even the Eskimo's igloo had a window of

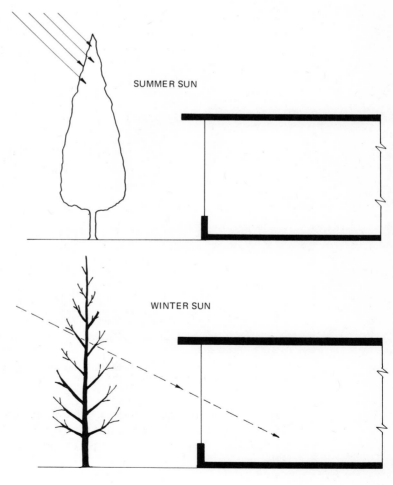

FIGURE 2-2 A tree will protect the interior from the summer sun but permit passage of the sun's rays in the winter.

SUMMER SUN

WINTER SUN

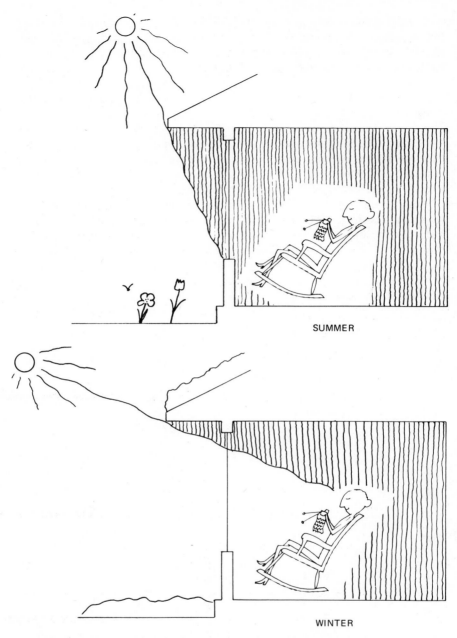

SUMMER

WINTER

FIGURE 2-3 A properly designed overhang will protect the interior from the summer sun and permit additional warmth in the winter.

ice or skin directed toward available sunlight. In most of the United States, openings or outdoor activity areas should be oriented to the south. The larger the openings, the greater the warmth derived from the sun.

During the summer, protection may be needed from the sun. Trees, bushes, and shrubs can block or at least filter the sun's rays. Their effectiveness is determined by the relationship between the size and shape of the plants and their distance from the building. Deciduous trees lose their leaves in autumn, thus allowing the warming rays of the winter sun to reach the dwelling. Artificial devices can achieve the same effect. For example, a roof beyond the building's walls blocks the rays of the hot summer sun but, properly designed, will permit the entrance of the sun's warmth in the winter. Other architectural devices include stationary and adjustable fins or louvers, awnings, and jalousies.

FIGURE 2-4 Architectural devices that provide sun protection.

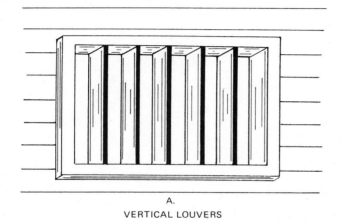

A.
VERTICAL LOUVERS

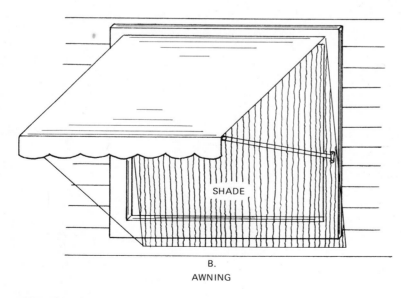

SHADE

B.
AWNING

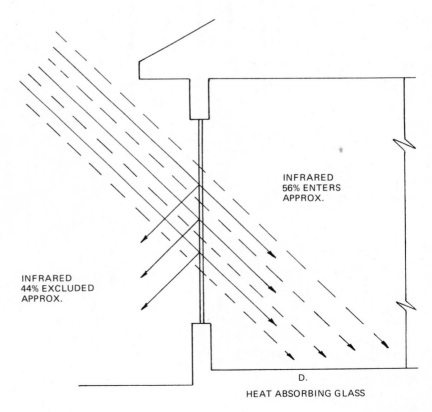

Fig. 2-4 (cont)
Architectural devices that provide sun protection.

C.
LOUVERED WINDOW OR JALOUSIE

INFRARED
56% ENTERS
APPROX.

INFRARED
44% EXCLUDED
APPROX.

D.
HEAT ABSORBING GLASS

14

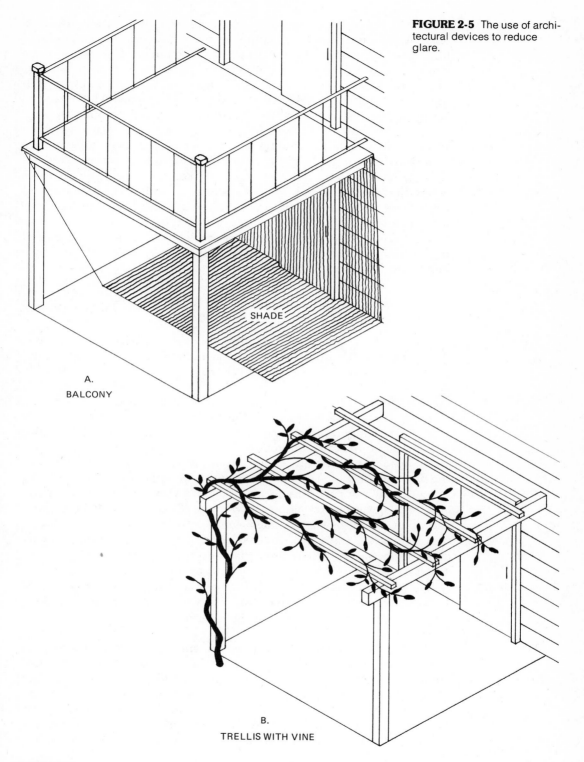

FIGURE 2-5 The use of architectural devices to reduce glare.

SHADE

A.
BALCONY

B.
TRELLIS WITH VINE

CHAPTER 2
INFLUENCES OF THE BIOPHYSICAL ENVIRONMENT

Ground radiation, which can cause both heat and glare, is more intense when there is no vegetation or ground cover. Windows placed high above the ground help impede reflection of glare within the structure. Landscaping and architectural devices—such as shaded arcades and walkways, porches and terraces, bushes and trees, or trellises with climbing vines—reduce glare. In the tropics, where most of the potential discomfort is caused by glare, the elimination of windows and the use of permeable materials can reduce glare while increasing air circulation. Sunlight also affects a structure's decorative features. Brilliant sun highlights the shallow fluting and delicate design characteristic of architecture in the southwestern United States where the air is clear and the sun's rays short and direct. Deep indentations are necessary to give design shadow and shape in locations that have less sunlight. Decoration of this type is prevalent in areas with a high concentration of industry (which causes air pollution) and in northern climates (where the sun's rays are weak or obscured by a high concentration of clouds).

Atmosphere

The atmosphere, a colorless, odorless mixture of gases that surrounds the earth, has three factors that affect human comfort: temperature, humidity, and wind force and direction.

Temperature. Because the metabolic process produces heat, a certain amount of heat loss is necessary for the human being to feel comfortable. High temperatures, by preventing heat loss, cause discomfort; low temperatures cause discomfort by inducing too rapid a loss of internal heat. Air temperatures vary from the severe cold of the Arctic to the intense heat of the desert (a range of approximately 261°F. or 127.5°C.); in any particular locale, they also vary with the time of day and with elevation. Dwellings in warmer climates tend to be colorful and open, rambling—sometimes even sprawling—in style, characterized by outside stairways, covered arcades, shaded porches, and gardens, terraces, and courtyards that encourage outside activities. In contrast, houses in colder climates tend to be more compact and protected: doorways are covered to protect visitors from storms, vestibules have double doors to prevent both inward and outward flow of air, and stairways are located in the interior.

Humidity. The water vapor of the atmosphere ranges from zero to 4 per cent by volume. Relative humidity (the ratio between the actual amount of water vapor present and the amount possible at a certain temperature) determines the rate of evaporation of body moisture, an important factor in human comfort. Hot humid air retards evaporation, making the individual feel more uncomfortable than when the air is hot and dry; cold humid air seems especially penetrating.

When heat is accompanied by high humidity, there is usually little daily or seasonal variation in temperature, heavy rainfall, and intense radiation. The primary need in such a climate is to lose body heat. There is little to be done but increase ventilation. Open buildings made of low-heat-retention materials like bamboo encourage air circulation and reduce heat build-up. Long, narrow structures with many windows (or with low-walled surrounding gardens) separated by wide streets also encourage heat loss and reduce ground radiation. Raised floors permit air flow beneath the structure and may also provide protection against floods, insects, and rodents.

The roof should protect the structure from both intense sun and torrential rain. It may be shaped like a parasol, sloping steeply to shed water rapidly. High ceilngs permit storage of cooler air but can be a disadvantage in colder climates or seasons because they increase the amount of air that must be heated. Reflective materials retard solar radiation and avoid heat build-up and subsequent reradiation. Condensation can be reduced by building the exterior walls and roof of materials that permit air to circulate through them. Moorish architecture, for example, developed openwork screens to provide shade and cross ventilation without sacrificing privacy.

FIGURE 2-6 Cliff dwellings in Arizona.

When the air is relatively dry, wide fluctuations of temperature can occur. A structure built in such a climate should be designed to block or at least delay the transfer of heat. Its components should be thick, and the building compact in shape—a sphere or, more usually, a cube. The most common design in a hot, dry climate is a low, thick-walled building set close to other buildings on narrow streets. Another way to retain heat is to cover or partially cover the structure with earth. Homes built into cliffs (as is the southwestern United States) or underground (as in China, Egypt, and Israel) apply this principle. The energy crises has created renewed interest in such methods of increasing heat retention. Heat build-up may be avoided by the use of white and light-colored exteriors to reflect the sun's radiant heat, and by separating the cooking area from the rest of the dwelling. Antebellum homes in the southern United States usually had separate cookhouses. Heat invasion can also be reduced if windows are few, small, and high-set. Windows are essential, however, if the hot air accumulated within the structure is to be exchanged for the cooler air outside. A significant drop in temperature for a sufficient length of time induces air movement; if windows are opened as temperature falls and closed as it rises, as much cool air as possible will be trapped within the structure. If there are only short cool periods—or none at all—more comfort is achieved by keeping the windows open all the time.

Open areas such as courtyards or patios, around which rooms can be located, help to reduce discomfort from heat. Greenery, shade, and running water lower ground temperature, reduce radiation, and promote air currents. Such areas can also be used for meal preparation. More important, they provide psychological relief through the appearance of shade, a bright spot of color, or the soft music produced by the sound of falling water. Opinions on roof design for hot climates differ. A flat roof provides a cool place to eat and to sleep, but a steep pitched roof of light color will reflect heat and keep the interior cooler. Humidity has less effect on efforts to keep warm than on efforts to keep cool. If the goal is to retain heat within the structure and keep out cold, the structure should be designed to capture solar heat. In most of the United States, this means orienting windows and doors to the south. Insulation also helps to prevent heat loss, as do multiple-story units, which reduce the ratio of roof to living space. Snow accumulation on the roof and in air spaces (such as those between ceiling and roof or those achieved by double-construction methods) and materials that do not transfer heat readily also help to retain heat.

Moisture.   Water in its many forms—vapor, rain, snow, hail, dew, and frost—can be destructive to buildings. Many materials are damaged by moisture. During construction, moisture may cause individual parts to expand, and the shrinkage that results after they dry creates structural cracks and warping of floors and doors. Damage from rain can be reduced by an overhanging roof, a double roof or double walls, and the use of moisture-resistant materials for exteriors.

18

Primitive structures often had thatched roofs overhanging mud walls whereas contemporary wooden roofs are protected with asphalt shingles. Expansion of materials because of moisture absorption can be an advantage: during rainy seasons, the materials expand, keeping interiors dry; during the dry season, they contract, permitting air circulation. Although snow on the roof provides extra insulation, it is important that the roof be strong enough to sustain the weight and steep enough to encourage rapid run-off.

Wind. The movement of the air (wind) transports heat from lower to higher latitudes, moisture to land masses, and equalizes pressure. It is important to know how to increase its benefits and reduce its potential for damage.

In cold or very dry climates, the best policy is to discourage the wind. In the northern hemisphere, where winter winds come from the

FIGURE 2-7 Examples of primitive windbreaks.

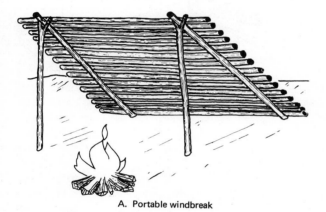

A. Portable windbreak

B. Stationary windbreak

FIGURE 2-8 Use of a wall or tree for wind deflection.

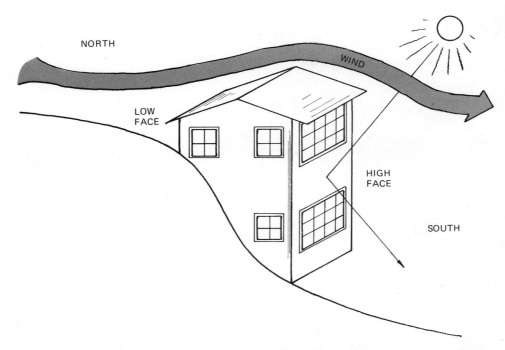

NORTH

WIND

LOW FACE

HIGH FACE

SOUTH

FIGURE 2-9 Placing a multilevel dwelling on a hillside helps to protect it from the wind.

north, it is best to have shorter, well-insulated walls with few windows facing that direction. When this is not possible, devices to control wind should be employed. Primitive men tied groups of branches together and placed them in the direction of the prevailing wind to block or direct it. Modern landscape architects suggest breaking the wind's force with a hedge of tall bushes or short trees, which deflect the wind, allow the passage of air, and yet beautify the premises.

Other devices, such as walls or windpoles, can be substituted provided that they are designed so as to permit some air passage and constructed of materials that do not cause glare.

Structures should be built on spots most protected from the wind. The windward wall of the dwelling can be sheltered by a hillside or it can be designed to be lower than the others. Another solution is partly to submerge the house in the earth, like the sod houses built by American settlers.

The shape of the house can deflect the wind. This is the advantage of the hemispheric igloo, the Mongol's yurt tent, and the modern dome-shaped house. A roof that slants into the wind can also help reduce the wind's effect. In Normandy, this principle was so refined that the roof came to resemble a ship's hull with the bow end into the wind and the stern or square end on the lee side. Low eaves (as in the A-frame) can direct the wind and encourage a snow blanket for added

FIGURE 2-10 Hemisphere or dome shaped house offers only slight resistance to the wind.

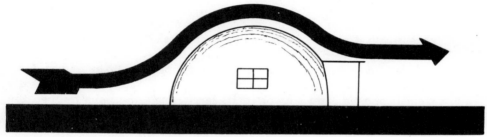

FIGURE 2-11 Roof design used to deflect and direct the wind.

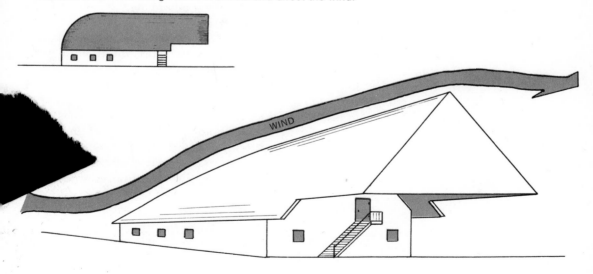

 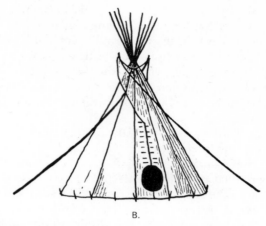

A.   B.

FIGURE 2-12 The flaps of the teepee used for wind control. A. Open flaps permit breezes to enter. B. Closed flaps prevent cold wind from entering.

insulation because its steep roof causes the snow to slip off and collect underneath. Curved doorways or entrances also provide protection, as do shrubs, projecting walls, or porches.

In hot and humid climates, advantage should be taken of any natural air movement. The Plains Indians had two flaps at the top of the teepee: opened, and supported by large poles, the flaps trapped the cool breezes of the hot summer; drawn together, they shut out the wind and rain of winter.

Large bodies of water induce breezes during the sunlight hours. Those areas of the dwelling that are used most often during the day should be oriented toward such breezes. At night, the wind comes from the land, and sleeping areas should face in this direction. The same principle can be applied in mountain regions: living areas should be oriented toward the daytime upslope or valley winds; sleeping areas, toward the nighttime mountain breeze.

Locating a room between a sunny and a shady court will increase its coolness: as the warm air rises from the sunny court, the cooler air of the shaded one will be drawn toward it—and, in passage, cool the room between. If a court has high walls, devices can be added to create suction and cause cross-ventilation.

Wind is sometimes destructive. It need reach only sixty miles hour to tip over a trailer or mobile home. Additional bracin anchoring will counteract the pressure caused by high wi corners of the dwelling can be attached to a poured concre an auger-type anchor screwed at least five feet into the g

FIGURE 2-13 (opposite) Houses should be oriented to take advantage flow. A. The daytime breeze comes from the sea and valleys. B. The dov breeze blows at night.

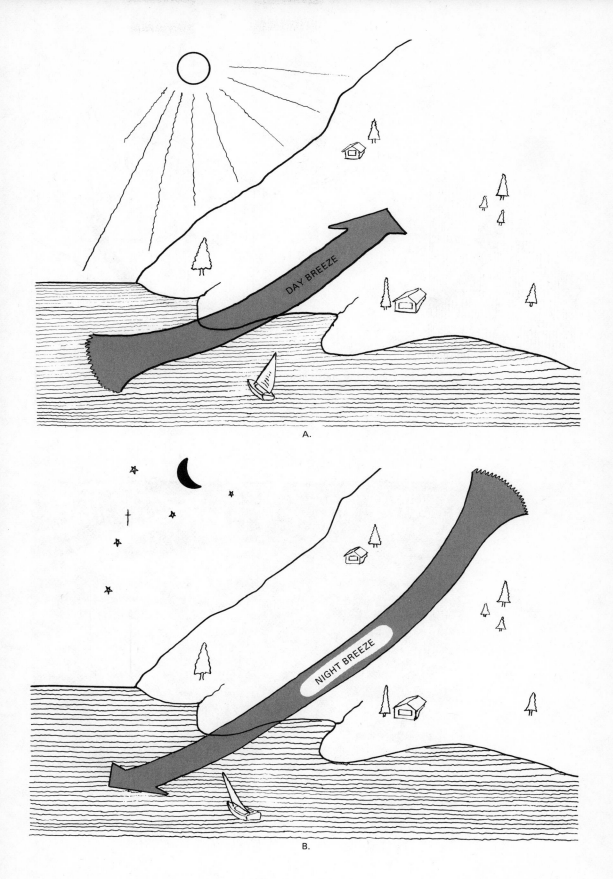

A.

B.

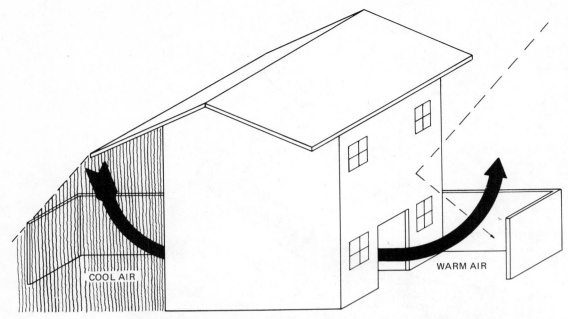

FIGURE 2-14 Inducing movement of air by placing a room between a sunny and cool court.

A.

FIGURE 2-15 Inresidence Shelter from Extreme Wind. A. (opposite) indicates construction in a central location; B. the finished appearance. Courtesy E. W. Kiesling, Professor Department of Civil Engineering, Texas Tech University.

B.

mobile home lacks internal bracing, straps with a breaking strength of 4,800 pounds or more can be wrapped around it. Hurricanes and tornadoes cause people to seek safety in underground wind cellars. The cost of constructing a wind-resistant house is prohibitive, but a small interior room accessible to all parts of the house may be made wind-resistant.

SITE

Each site is intrinsically suited to certain uses—a fertile valley is ideal for agriculture, whereas mountainous terrain may support forests or recreational facilities. When land use is planned to be complementary to prevailing physical conditions, the process of living can be more comfortable, more attractive, and more economical.

Contemporary technology makes it possible to gouge out lakes, level mountains, and to recontour land according to human desires. But a house may be planned to merge with the landscape, so that it seems to be a natural part of the physical environment. Contemporary site planners try to create dwellings that harmonize with the natural environment and with the lives and activities of those who inhabit them.

The View. The view from the windows of a dwelling may have a beneficial or deleterious influence. A view of nature in all its majesty is priceless: it can create a sense of liveliness and richness of experience, and may even be beneficial to the eye by causing it to refocus from a near to a far object. An objectionable view reduces the viability of the location. Large windows should be located toward pleasant scenery, and imaginative landscaping should be used to block less acceptable vistas.

The more beautiful and interesting parts of the site should be used for outdoor living, but there are no hard and fast rules. It is usually desirable, for example, to locate a house at the top rather than at the bottom of a hill, but other locations may permit a closer relationship between the view and the viewer.

Topography. Topography describes the "face" of the land—hills and valleys, mountains and plains. Topographical features are formed by the glaciers that have gouged out the land, by the flows of lava or water that have swept over it, by the winds that have blown against it and created alluvial plains that stretch toward the sea. The contour of the land is a crucial influence on the problem of drainage.

Good drainage is inherent in a steep, sloping site. Such a site usually assures, in addition, a beautiful view, privacy, and cool breezes in the summer, but it may also give rise to practical problems. Water may run off so swiftly that it causes soil erosion; snow or ice can render a steep drive unusable; flat areas for parking or outdoor activities may be difficult to plan and construct. Hillsides are a favorite haunt of squirrels, gophers, and groundhogs and these animals may undermine terrain, pavements, and lawns. In general, the choice of a steep lot entails higher improvement costs for the grading of land, the drainage and siting of the building.

The most valuable construction site is flat land. A house built on flat land requires fewer changes of level, enjoys easier access to outdoor activity areas, and entails less expensive construction methods. But if a flat area is low-lying, swampy, or marshy, it may present other disadvantages: excellent breeding places for insects, a high water table, or rock formations near the surface, any of which can add to development costs. If the level land is close to a river or stream, the danger of flooding must be considered. A land survey can determine whether the risk of flood is high. Good drainage can reduce the risk and prevent any moisture problems.

The ideal building lot, however, is one with gently rolling terrain. Such a lot provides natural drainage that will divert water from the house, and prevent soil saturation. This helps to preserve desirable site features while assuring convenient access to and around the building and lot.

Soil. With proper drainage, almost any soil can be acceptable for construction. The ideal soil for a residential site has effective drainage, no restricting layers, no danger of flooding, and a low water table. Rock formations close to the surface render a site less desirable, as does the presence of soft clay, loose silt, water-bearing sand, swamp, peat, or mulch. By the same token newly filled areas or former dump areas should be avoided.

Most building codes are designed for average soil conditions within the district, but conditions within a given district may vary widely. Soils are rated according to their suitability for various uses and such ratings may help in estimating building costs. Soils that are waterlogged less than half the year, for example, may be classified as having a moderate limitation for good drainage; those that are wet over half the time are classified as having severe limitations. Problem soils with moderate limitations can be rendered usable through special planning and design, usually at a moderate cost. (For other guidelines, see Table 2-1.)

Vegetation.   Plants, trees, and shrubs help to create a pleasing landscape. The Federal Housing Administration minimum property standards require that every house have at least one shade tree, preferably to the southwest. There are thousands of kinds of vegetation, each with its own advantages. Woody deciduous plants, which lose their leaves during the winter months, include many flowering trees and shrubs as well as shade varieties. Evergreens, which retain their leaves the year round, usually have needlelike foliage, but some have broad leaves. Annuals and perennials are valuable for their blossoms and growth habits. Trees and plants come in many shapes—tall, short, spreading, upright, trailing. Some appear to advantage in groups; other need to stand alone.

A site with native plants or trees is ideal. The vegetation creates a pleasant microview and prevents soil erosion. When trees are de-

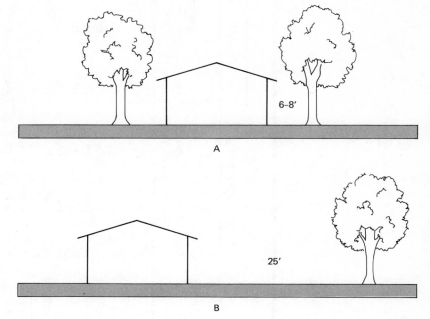

FIGURE 2-16 Two theories of the best relationship between a house and plantings. A. the "nestled" appearance achieved by placing trees close to the building; B. the distance believed to be required between the dwelling and trees to prevent damage.

6–8'

A

25'

B

TABLE 2-1   Ratings for Various Soil Types in Relation to Residential Buildings

| Typical Name for Soil Type | Fill Soil | | | | | | | | | | Undisturbed Soil | | |
| | General Characteristics | | | | Special Characteristics (Hydrologic Reaction) | | | Use | | | Foundation | | Drainage |
	Sta-bility	Perme-ability	Corrosion Potential	Ability to Compact	Pack	Expand	Frost	Founda-tion	Drain	Frost	Dense Hard	Loose Soft	
Bedrock	Ex	NS	Ex	VP	NS	NS	VP	Ex	NS	VP	Ex	Ex	NS
Coarse Grain													
Gravel	Ex	Ex	Ex	Ex	Ex	VP	Ex	Ex	Ex	Ex	Ex	Ex	Ex
Gravel/Sand	VG	VG	Ex	VG	Ex	VP	Ex	VG	Ex	G	Ex	NS	Ex
Gravel/Silt	Med	G–P	Ex	G	VG	P	G–Ex	G	VG	G–VG	VG	VG	VG
Gravel/Clay	F	VP	VG	G	G	F	G–VG	G	VG	F–Med	G	Ex	VG
Sand	G	Ex	Ex	Ex	Ex	VP	Ex	VG	Ex	VG–Med	Ex	VG–Ex	Ex
Sand/Silt	F–G	G–P	Ex	G	G	F	G	VG	Ex	F–VP	VG	VG	VG
Sand/Clay	F	VP	VG	G	G	F	G	Med	NS	F	G	VG	VG
Fine Grain													
Clay/Silt	P	G–P	VG	F–G	G	F	G–Med	F	NS	P–VP	G	G	VG
Clay	P	VP	G	G	Med	Med	G	F	NS	F–P	G–VP	G–Med	VG
Organic Silt	P	G–P	G	F	F	G	G	P	NS	P–VP	G–VP	G	VG
Inorganic Silt	P	G–P	VG	F–G	F	G	G–Med	VP	NS	VP	Med	G	VG
Inorganic Clay	VP	VP	G	F–G	F	G	G	P	NS	VP–F	Med–P	G–VG	NS
Organic Clay	VP	VP	G	F	F	G	G	VP	NS	VP	F–VP	Med	NS
Loam	NS	NS	Med	NS	NS	NS	VG	NS	NS	NS	F	NS	NS

RATINGS: *Ex*-Excellent, *VG*-Very Good, *G*-Good, *Med*-Medium, *F*-Fair, *P*-Poor, *VP*-Very Poor, *NS*-Not Suitable to Use
These are comparable only within vertical columns.

Adapted from *Engineering Soil Classification for Residential Development.* FHA Bulletin No. 373 (November 1961), pp. 13–37.

stroyed in preparation for building, all too often nothing but subsoil remains. The landscaping of stripped areas is neither simple nor inexpensive, although it may be immensely satisfying.

Good landscaping takes into account family needs as well as the physical features of the land. Plants define activity areas, delineate traffic patterns, screen or protect, shade and enhance. The choice of vegetation is determined by individual taste—and by prevailing soil, sun, and moisture conditions. Neat slow-growing plants improve with age and provide a pleasant sight. Trees planted close to the house will eventually give the effect of nestling it between them, but tree roots can create drainage problems, rob nutrition from cultivated plants, or keep a lawn from acquiring that even texture that results from uniform exposure to sun.

Pollution.   The pollution of the natural environment by the discharge of waste products into air, water, or soil is more severe where there are high concentrations of population. Pollution is not a problem unique to our time. The citizens of ancient Rome complained of soot on their white togas; nineteenth-century Londoners endured an almost continual smog from the burning of coal with a high sulfur content; before the automobile, horse manure made city streets unusable for pedestrians who did not wear high boots.

The ill effects of modern pollution can be noted in the increased number of deaths caused by respiratory diseases, the stimulation of aquatic weeds caused by rising water temperature, and the spread of diseases caused by improperly treated solid wastes. Some pollutants, such as radioactive waste, carry potential harm not only to present but also to future generations.

Since human survival depends on the maintenance of an ecological balance, reduction of pollutants is essential. Visual pollution is the most easily treated: offensive sights can be hidden from view by imaginative landscaping. Noise can be deflected or absorbed. Agricultural pesticides and other chemicals can be used with increased discretion. The Clean Air Act of 1970 holds promise for decreased smoke pollution, and public health officials have established standards for treatment of solid waste. Whether these measures will be effective depends on the strictness with which they are enforced in the years to come.

SUMMARY

The biophysical environment is a major influence on housing design. Adverse weather conditions provided the original impetus for the creation of artificial shelter. Houses designed to adapt to and harmonize with their natural settings tend to be more efficient and effective than other houses. If the natural setting is to be maintained, pollutants must be eliminated or sharply reduced.

Influences of the Sociopsychological Environment

HE culture of the society—the sociopsychological environment—encompasses all socially transmitted forms of behavior and beliefs. Basic psychological needs of people—the need for security, the need for communication, the need for identity—are constant, but the manner in which they are fulfilled changes almost imperceptibly. The complex phenomena that constitute cultural change have profound consequences for house design.

FAMILIES AND HOUSEHOLDS

The most basic, complex, and sensitive human relationships are those of the family. There are many family patterns. The extended family, for example, encompasses several generations. The most common family pattern in the United States is the nuclear family, composed of a single pair and their offspring. Other social groupings recognized in the U.S. Census as "households" include individuals living alone and individuals who (though not related by kinship ties) share a common residence and share responsibility for domestic functions.

Families and other households have similar goals. They all seek an environment in which the group can thrive. A household is a place for seclusion, solace, and companionship. Within this protection, the group maintains its identity and sense of place. The size of the group, and the values, ages, and occupations of its members, influence the physical structure and its location.

30

Size

Industrialization, reduction in infant mortality, and a rising awareness that the world is finite in space and resources have rendered population growth less desirable. The development of contraceptives has made it possible for couples to limit the number of their offspring. It is not surprising to find there has been a steady decline in family size in the United States for the past several generations.

Reduced family size has had a concomitant effect on the size of the family dwelling. The need for bedroom space is reduced, so there will be a need for fewer bedrooms in each dwelling. Less space will be needed for other activities as well. Eating areas can be reduced in size and since smaller cooking vessels and fewer table appointments are required, less storage space is needed. With fewer people involved, less space is required in areas used for work or leisure activities. Smaller homes are replacing the large houses popular at the turn of the century.

Values

In the final analysis a constructed environment reflects the civilization that planned and built it and, in turn, influences the future development of that society. As Brannfels suggests, Versailles was designed to symbolize the position of Louis XIV in the state, the simple farmhouse represents a family that maintains itself by working the land.[1] Morris and Winter conclude that what most Americans equate with the good life is a single-family detached dwelling congruent with income in a safe neighborhood with a good school for their children, well-maintained streets, and a homogeneous population.[2] The degree to which these needs are met determines the degree to which families are satisfied with their living situation.

The design of the individual dwelling is also important. Signals that a dwelling no longer fulfills the family's needs begin with small, almost indiscernible, changes—a new shelf in the cupboard or a light switch by the door—and then proceed to more significant changes—a doorway to improve traffic patterns, the addition of a room or of a swimming pool. The decision to move is often determined by the local housing supply and the family's ability to pay. From 18 to 20 percent of the population change domiciles each year; at least as many more would like to do so.

An early study of Beyer, Montgomery, and Mackesey shows the effect of values on housing decisions. Such values, of course are con-

---

[1] W. Brannfels, "Institutions and Their Corresponding Ideals," *Quality of Man's Environment.* (Washington, D.C.: Smithsonian Institute Press, 1968).

[2] E. W. Morris and M. Winter, "Theory of Family Housing Adjustment," *Journal of Marriage and Family,* February 1975, p. 82.

tinually changing and developing, and are, furthermore, often adapted to available choices.

Occupation, Education, and Income

Americans value education because it has tended to widen occupational choice. Occupation, in turn, determines income—and since more money can buy better education, education, occupation, and income are seen as mutually dependent. As people move from one income group to another, their values tend to change too.

When most Americans lived on family farms, farmhouses tended to have large areas for preparing meals, making butter, baking bread, and preserving food. As farming developed into a business, the need for such space was replaced by the need for office space. As more and more people, owing to increased education, find employment in service occupations and professions, the need for work space decreases within the dwelling unit.

Life Cycle

The family life cycle begins with the formation of a family or a household and includes the coming of children, their entrance in school, their departure for a life of their own, and the death of one of the adult partners. The life cycle of the family—which varies with the particular family—is a major influence on housing needs.

Today's newlyweds tend to be young—many of them still in school. Simple housing arrangements smooth their transition into family life, and so a small apartment in a large complex or an older single-family home is the usual newlyweds' choice.

From the birth of the first child (between eighteen months and three years later) to the birth of the last child (between the fifth and twelfth years of marriage), major housing adjustments occur. More space is needed for children to sleep and to play, and for privacy for both parents and children; a well-planned work area expedites meal preparation; children require sturdy furnishings. The search for a "good" neighborhood, considered a symbol of success, also influences housing decisions.

During the school years, children develop their own friends and values, and the needs of each child may or may not coincide with those of siblings or parents. Both parents and children desire more privacy, and more space for entertaining and for hobbies, so that during this period household facilities are stretched to their fullest.

Between the time children leave school and the time they leave home for marriage or careers, they spend much time at home. During this period, the beauty and the location of the home have a high priority. A few families move to larger homes; others make improvements on existing ones.

When all the children have moved, parents can look forward to ap-

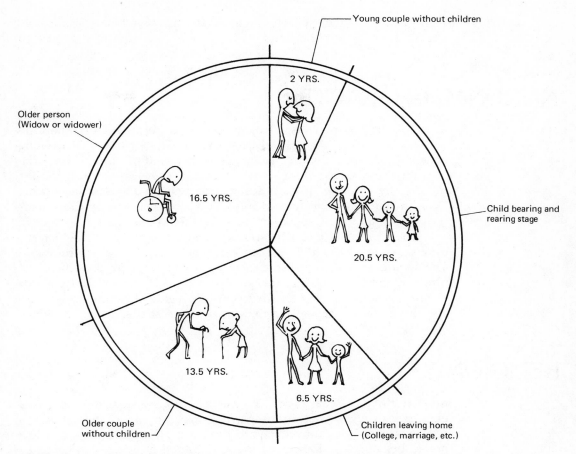

FIGURE 3-1 Typical time periods in the family life cycle. Adapted from Handbook for the Home, U.S.D.A. Yearbook, 1973 (Washington, D.C.: U.S.G.P.O.), p. 7.

proximately ten to fifteen years of privacy, and—for one or the other—several years of solitude. New interests and friendships outside the family may increase the older couple's social life, and their new critical need may be not for bedrooms but for leisure areas. The modernization of work areas tends to reduce labor and to permit time for new activities. The prospect of entertaining friends at mealtime increases the emphasis on commodious, gracious eating areas. In general, homes for older couples are remodeled to provide privacy, extra sanitary facilities, and controlled temperatures. Although income may decrease with age, two thirds of the senior citizens in the United States maintain their own households.

Seldom do people plan their total life environment. Certain careers require frequent relocation. But even people who do not move with their jobs can expect to make at least one major move. The rest of the time, they simply adjust to their living environment. Since neighborhood ties are important, making people loath to move every time their needs change, what is needed is an expandable-contractable structure, or a neighborhood that provides more than one type of home.

NATIONAL CHARACTER

There was a time when oceans and mountains formed natural barriers and created strong regional distinctions in life styles, and in housing styles as well. The unfenced front yard is believed to express American openness; the fenced garden with protective gate, English reserve; the harem, the extreme privacy desired for women in Moslem society. Even the current trend toward informality is illustrated by the substitution of a family or recreation room for the Sunday parlor.

Political practices and education influence the manner in which individuals cope with the problems of creating a living environment. The uneducated are less able to judge or to improve conditions. A powerful government can designate the use of certain materials or techniques for housing construction, segregate dwelling types into specific areas, or legislate minimum levels of shelter for its constituents.

RELIGION

Most cultures are characterized by a belief in the supernatural. Some authorities suggest that buildings were first devised as shrines. Many religious rites are connected with fire, and Hocart suggests that the house began as a shelter for fire.[3] Elaborate structures came to be built—temples for the living, and tombs for the dead. In some societies, the family house was considered a temple in which daily worship was held and household spirits resided. The domestic deity was most likely to dwell in the hearth fire. To walk or step there was considered an offense and, in the Aztec world, walking on the hearthstones of the 'old god' presaged death. Because of its religious significance, the house was periodically purified. Spirits were especially active in the spring, and a rigorous cleaning at that time was believed to rid the house of unfriendly spirits. Cooking, childbirth, and death caused impurity. Hence meals were seldom prepared within the structure; menstruating women were expelled; childbirth signaled the need for purification rites; and death required the destruction or abandonment of the house. This last practice was both expensive and wasteful so, eventually, dying persons were removed before they died, and the dwelling was symbolically "destroyed" by extinguishing the house fire.

In some cultures the house is viewed as a miniature world. If the

---

[3] A. M. Hocart, *Progress of Man* (London: Metheun and Co. Ltd., 1933), p. 69.

world is believed to be round, houses are more likely to be round; when it is seen as flat or square, houses tend to be rectangular. (This practice is demonstrated in the four-cornered world of the Mayans and the circular one of the Sioux.) In some cultures, parts of the house symbolize aspects of nature: the floor, the earth; the walls, the horizon; the roof, the arching sky. (Pawnee earth lodges are a good example.)

In some cultures, it was deemed important that the house not interefere with a local spirit's home. In Japan, where gods are believed to live in stones and trees, the stony, forest-covered mountains were reserved for the gods, and human dwellings were constructed in the valleys. Rituals to establish whether the gods favored a house site were also important. The Polynesians had various rituals designed to test whether a site was auspicious, while other cultures sought divine sanction by offering sacrifices on the house site or consecrating the ground with holy water. Ground-breaking ceremonies are a modern vestige of such rituals.

After the location was chosen, the house had to be oriented properly. The Crow Indians placed their teepees so that the door faced east and the four major poles marked the cardinal points of the compass. In other societies, dwellings were oriented according to astronomical rules or the direction of environmental forces. The Japanese, for example, do not locate the entrance, the kitchen, or the toilet on the northeast/southwest axis.

The status of the inhabitant often determined the material of which the dwelling was made. Houses for the living were made of perishable

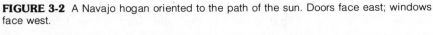

FIGURE 3-2 A Navajo hogan oriented to the path of the sun. Doors face east; windows face west.

wood; those for the dead or for the gods, of enduring stone. Usually the latest innovations and rarest materials were reserved for the most prestigious persons in the society.

Human sacrifice was often mandated to protect royal or sacred buildings from unfriendly spirits (animals or fowls were sufficient for ordinary citizens). Victims might be buried alive under foundation stones, and in Peru, the fetus of a human being or a llama (depending on the family's status or the degree of protection required) was placed underneath the threshold to help prevent the entrance of unfriendly spirits.

The idea that some corners or sides of a house are sacred or lucky is common. In Fiji, the east wall is reserved for the chief, while the position next to the center pole of the Crow teepee is the place of honor. In other cultures, the most propitious positions are reserved for the husband and wife (for example, the master bedroom), then for guests in decending order of importance, then for children according to age, and last for other relatives. In some cultures the most dispensable person, often a mother-in-law, is given space at the entrance.

INDIVIDUALS

Each individual develops a system of values that influences decisions about the living environment. In addition, individual's social role or roles may place other demands on the living environment.

Relationship to Human Needs

Cooper has suggested that shelter is the basic human need, followed by the need for security, the need for comfort and convenience, the need for socializing and self-expression, and finally the need for aesthetic satisfaction.[4] These parallel the hierarchy of psychological needs developed by Maslow. Others describe basic environmental needs as those conditions that support physical as well as mental health.

Physical Needs.   Each society determines the amount of light, heat, and sound required for health and happiness. Some cultures have a high tolerance to smell, cold, or noise, whereas others go to surprising lengths to avoid them. Most authorities agree that sanitation has a high priority because unsanitary conditions—lack of pure water and/or accumulation of human waste—result in illness, often of epidemic proportions. Although up-to-date plumbing and disposal systems have reduced these problems, poor housing facilities continue to contribute to a high rate of illness and, sometimes, death. Inadequate

[4] C. Cooper, *Easter Hill Village: Some Implications of Design* (New York: The Free Press, 1975), p. 211.

toilet facilities help the spread of respiratory infections. Poor washing facilities contribute to all types of skin diseases.

Protection from animals, evil spirits, and other human beings have historically been important to physical survival. Religious rites, developed to keep away evil spirits, have affected housing design, as has already been indicated. A fire at the cave entrance deterred wild animals, as screens on windows or doors now prevent the entrance of undesirable animals and insects. During the Middle Ages, walls or moats protected towns from marauding bands. Protection from modern war weaponry—radioactive waste, fire, flood, blackouts, air and water pollution—is a problem to which housing design must respond. Rising crime rates stimulate a desire for defensible space: low buildings, small units, fences, benches, and area lighting help to provide some protection.

FIGURE 3-3 A well-planned housing development which provides opportunity for surveillance by interspersing open space, low and high rise buildings. Courtesy of Metropolitan Life.

The lowest priority among physical needs is given to comfort and convenience. Human reponses vary: people can rest lying down, sitting, squatting, or even standing on one foot. Each method calls for a particular housing design. To accommodate chairs, dwellings had to be enlarged, windows were set higher, and new construction methods and materials were developed to provide a level floor. At present, the increasing complexity of the woman's role and the lack of household help have focused new concern on the design of kitchens, where the majority of household work is done.

Psychological Needs. The key to psychological survival is privacy, which provides an opportunity for withdrawal, self-reliance, solitude, quiet contemplation, or concentration. Privacy can be achieved by physical isolation, or by providing barriers against the sight and sound of others. Kira describes three kinds of privacy: being heard but not seen; being seen but not heard; being neither heard or seen.[5] The degree of privacy considered desirable or essential influences the location of various rooms, doors, and windows, and the number of people for whom a room is designed. It has also been suggested that lack of acoustical privacy between parents' and children's baths and bedrooms may be a factor in producing psychoneurosis.[6]

Buildings can be designed to be attractive to human beings (anthropophilic) and to foster human relationships (socio-petal), or they can be alien to humans (anthropozenic), forcing them to disperse (sociofugal). Osmond believes homes should be "highly anthropophilic as well as socio-petal" because this helps family members to interact with one another.[7] Chermanoff, on the other hand, claims that physical insulation is the only way to fulfill the need for relaxation, concentration, contemplation, and healthy sensuousness.[8] Others claim it is sufficient if people are permitted to control the physical and visual access to their private living space. If entrances are located too close to one another, for example, the feeling that,"every one is on top of one another," limits the individual's ability to obtain privacy. Ideally, the main entrance should be approached through a semiprivate zone, such as a yard, a porch, or a patio. In multifamily units the fewer the doors opening off one corridor, stairway, or balcony, the greater the sense of privacy.

Noise disrupts privacy and is a common cause for complaint in multifamily units. Among the most frequent offenders are people who bang doors, carry on loud conversations in communal areas, or turn

[5] A. Kira, *The Bathroom* (New York: The Viking Press, Inc., 1976), pp. 164–65.

[6] J. D. Barkley, "Room Space and Its Relationship to Mental Health: Some Observations of a Relocation Officer," *Journal of Housing*, March 1973, pp. 132–133.

[7] "The Psychological Dimension of Architectural Space," *Professional Architecture*, April 1965, p. 160.

[8] S. I. Chermanoff and C. Alexander, *Community and Privacy* (Garden City, N.Y.: Doubleday & Company, Inc., 1963, p. 70.

38

up the volume on television and stereo sets. Sounds with meanings attached are more annoying than those that are unintelligible. Background noise is tolerable until it is necessary to be heard over it. Older people are more sensitive to sound than younger ones, and the hard of hearing are more sensitive than those with normal hearing.

Overcrowding can cause mental stress. Hall believes people are limited by what they think they can do in a given space and by what they regard as the critical distance from other human beings.[9] Culture and background determine the individual's sense of critical distance. People of Italian, French, Spanish, Russian, and Middle European background tend to enjoy physical contact and to conform to critical distances at the lower end of the scale. People of English, German, Belgian, Scandinavian, or Dutch background tend to need more space around them, to enjoy solitude, and to conform to critical distances at the upper end of the scale. Stress may occur when people of different critical distances come together. Those with short critical distances appear pushy and obtrusive; those with long critical distances appear cold and aloof.

Stress arises when there is insufficient room for the number of people or activities involved. Because definitions of "insufficient space" vary, it is difficult to determine the point at which overcrowding begins. Regulations to prevent overcrowding are usually based on objective measures such as the number of persons per room or the number of functions incorporated in an area. But what seems to be crucial is an allotment of space that assures a healthy density, good interaction, a proper amount of involvement, and a continuing sense of identification. Moving people from relatively crowded quarters to more spacious ones has not always been successful: physical health is often improved, but social pathologies—neurosis, delinquency, and divorce—may increase.

TABLE 3-1   Critical Distance Scale for Various Types of Contact

Type of Contact	Voice Level	Physical Contact or Involvement	Distance Required (Feet)
Intimate	Whisper	Close together	0–1½
Personal	Low to moderate	Touching or holding hands	1½–4
Social	Conversational	Arm's length	4–12
Public	Loud, often magnified	None	Over 12

From *The Hidden Dimension* by Edward T. Hall. Copyright © 1966 by Edward T. Hall. Reprinted by permission of Doubleday & Company, Inc.

[9] E. T. Hall, *The Hidden Dimension* (Garden City, N.Y.: Doubleday & Company, Inc., 1966), pp. 111–16.

Social Needs

Most people like to live in small groups and to visit friends. Lack of human contact has been known to cause depression and even exacerbate suicidal or homicidal tendencies. Human relationships among neighbors are fostered by homogeneity, similarity of life styles, or similarity of stages of family life cycles. In such cases, neighbors are more supportive, helping one another with household tasks, child care, and emergencies. If too many families are clustered together, on the other hand, the high density of children may prove troublesome.

Proper location of buildings fosters friendships and a sense of community. People find an opportunity for interaction while situated on their own territory (walk, porch, or backyard) or a familiar common ground like a parking area, a laundry room, or a recreation area. Neighborly contacts are promoted by dwellings grouped around a common open space or shared facility—a central mailbox or a road junction. Those living in the center of a development often have more friends than those who live on its fringes. Conversely, shared entrances or walkways cause many unwanted meetings and often become a source of complaint.

Poor housing can lead to pessimism, passivity, dissatisfaction, and cynicism. Improved housing raises pride in the neighborhood, and people often feel their life position has been improved, even though their aspirations remain unchanged.

When people have a sense of place, their tendency is to improve, not destroy, the environment. A sense of place insures continuity of the group and its activities and provides the individual with familiar surroundings and a framework for doing things. People who are forced to move frequently try to reproduce this sense of belonging by furnishing each new home with cherished personal belongings.

The house also serves as a symbol of social status, and the exterior reflects the way the individual wants to be perceived by others. The self-made business man or woman tends to choose a dramatic "display" home, while people in the helping professions—health, legal, instructional services—more often select quieter, inward-looking styles. The interior provides a more intimate view, preserving the person's past and giving promise of a future.

Western culture places a premium on originality. The need for personal uniqueness is reflected in the desire to have one's own house different from the others on the block. This difference might be provided by small details—color, doorway design, fences, or landscaping.

Aesthetic Needs.   Beauty in the living environment lifts the spirit but is usually low in priority among human needs. Some consider beauty synonymous with aesthetic design, which, in turn, is often confused with "good taste" or fashion. Actually, good design is a quality independent of personal taste or popularity.

Although there is no single formula for making buildings beautiful, aesthetically pleasing buildings cannot evolve in an intellectual or spiritual vacuum; they must communicate the spirit of the culture. Good housing design integrates historical heritage, natural resources, and acquired skills.

Many subscribe to the theory that for a building to be beautiful, form must follow function. But while function may be dominant, it cannot control housing design. Since the house serves as the setting for a slow process of growth, maturation, and aging, the structure should enhance the lives of the occupants and fulfill their present and future needs.

Although beauty is often ordered, regulated, and predictable, it is more experienced than understood. Its effect is demonstrated by the Maslow studies in which participants rated more highly faces of people seated in a beautiful room than those of people seated in rooms considered average or ugly.[10] As Berenson describes it,

> [Beauty is] that fitting instant when the spectator is at one with the work he is looking at. The two [building and spectator] become one. Time and space are abolished in a moment of mystic vision.[11]

Relationship of Role to Environment

Individuals assume various roles differentiated by age, sex, and task. Those roles may be supportive or conflicting, dominant or subservient. Each role, however, interacts with the built environment.

Wife.   In many societies, it is believed that a woman should marry and bear children, finding status and identity in her husband's work and position. In some cultures, separate quarters protect and isolate her. Rich families provide separate rooms; poor ones, separate corners. Windows, doors, and other openings are located and designed to discourage intruders. To expedite the work of the household, the women's quarters include the kitchen and storerooms. As women gain more educational and employment opportunities, spouses are increasingly sharing work responsibilities both inside and outside the family group. Cooperation is promoted when work space provides room for more than one and when leisure facilities are designed for activities enjoyed by both wife and husband.

Efficient and convenient room design is most important to the wife-mother, companion-partner role. Also important are proper symbols of the socioeconomic class to which the family belongs, enough floor space properly divided to foster the full emotional and cultural development of the children, and an atmosphere and appearance that can be used creatively.

---

[10] A. H. Maslow and N. L. Mintz, "Effects of Aesthetic Surroundings: I. Initial Effects of Three Aesthetic Conditions Perceiving 'Energy' and 'Well Being' in Faces," *Journal of Psychology*, April 1956, pp. 247–54.

[11] B. Berenson, *Aesthetics and History* (Garden City, N.Y.: Doubleday & Co., Inc.), p. 93.

Husbands. Traditionally, the husband's role had a higher status in society than the wife's. In an agrarian society, his work did not isolate him from the other family members, but in an industrialized society, the husband is separated from the rest of the family because his work is no longer accomplished at home. Constant reminders of his family membership are left behind—his chair at the head of the table, his shaving kit, his hunting and fishing gear, his tools, and usually his easy chair. He often considers his house evidence of his ability to earn. In that case, its location, size, style, and appointments are important to him.

As social attitudes change and the husband assumes reponsibility for more of the work of the household, his lack of time and skill encourages his interest in mechanized work areas. Increased responsibility for child care has made him more aware of space needed by children, and in general changed his attitudes about space allotment in the home. The family room and arrangements that facilitate communication with other family members are now considered a necessity, and less space is reserved specifically for guests.

Infants. Until an infant is about a year old, it needs continuity. The bed can provide continuity as the infant is relocated—in a car, a house, or a vacation cabin. Most authorites recommend a separate room for infants, but one located near to parents to provide maximum convenience and supervision. The infant's belongings can be incorporated into the parents' storage space; a separate storage cabinet, McCullough estimates should be 84 inches high, 84 inches wide and 24 inches deep. [12] Out of doors, the child needs a sunny spot protected from the wind.

Preschoolers. Psychologists agree that preschool experiences are significant. A two-year-old, whose main interest is in the world of things, is experimenting with and learning about the surrounding world. Although nothing is really safe from the toddler, and the child is safe from nothing dangerous, it is crippling to cut the child off from all types of environmental experiences. The playpen is not appropriate, so gates above stairs and between rooms may direct activity. The child enjoys the water sports of the bathroom, and favorite play areas may include the kitchen and the workshop.

By the time children are able to dress themselves and play alone, they show both sociability and independence. They like to visit their parents' bedroom, so the parents might find a lock on the door desirable. To encourage independence, suitable storage (lower than 48 inches from the floor) should be available to the child. When the child is very young, hooks are preferable for clothes but later, when muscle coordination develops, rods for hangers may be installed.

[12] H. E. McCullough, Household Storage Units. Circular Series C5.1, Small Homes Council, *University of Illinois Bulletin*, January 1953, p. 12.

Preschoolers are attracted to spaces where they can act out fantasies. They like to build "forts" and "offices" and to experiment with "caves" under the kitchen sink. The fireplace holds special magic. They are eager to help with firebuilding and then herd the rest of the family around so everyone can enjoy the "pictures" in the flames.

Outdoors play space should be sheltered but sunny. Very young children like to play close to a frequently used entrance. Enclosed play spaces make young children feel more secure and discourage older children from disturbing them. Fencing material and design should facilitate adult supervision and make quick access possible.

Middle Childhood. The years between babyhood and adolescence are characterized by alternating periods of extreme messiness and neatness. Neatness will be encouraged by ample storage space. Tip-out bins that provide easy access for younger children can, by the addition of a lock, become a place for a teen-ager's valued possessions. A convenient out-of-sight storage unit is a roll-about that fits under the bed.

Children, like adults, need a private place in which to follow their own inclinations, to study, to think. Children who live in crowded conditions with too many adults fail to develop independence or a sense of individuality; they tend to have few illusions about people and to exhibit signs of aggressiveness. Children react to overcrowding by spending more time out of doors and studying less.

Children are the chief users of public residential areas. But, although America prides itself on being child-oriented, little effort is spent on planning children's outdoor play areas, most of which are characterized by standard tubular steel play equipment or some type of playing field. Some children are uninterested in organized group games; they prefer to fantasize or even to play alone. Western European adventure playgrounds encourage children to learn about nature by providing places to dig, to light fires, and to build. A pathway system provides a safe area for cycling and skating.

Adolescents. The adolescent strives to be accepted as an adult by both peers and parents. Adolescents tend to be awkward and to be concerned about their own appearance and that of their living environment. Indoor social space permits teen-agers to entertain friends without adult interference and without impinging on the privacy of others. The space should be located near a food-preparation or food-storage area. In multifamily units, recreation rooms should be accessible by bike, car, or public transportation and should contain a refreshment bar or dispenser. The car is a significant artifact in many teenage cultures: work space, a cupboard with a lock for tools, and washing facilities facilitate its repair and maintenance.

Teen-agers like to flirt, to show off, to see and be seen. Most of this socialization is informal, occurring after school and at night. Areas where teen-agers congregate—street corners, major pathways, intersections, parking lots, and game areas—should be well lighted. Because adolescents are faster and rougher than younger children, their outdoor activities should be separated or scheduled at different times. A recreation area is enhanced by benches for conversation during rest periods, or as a place for onlookers, special friends, and parents to meet.

Elderly.   The number of senior citizens is increasing. The elderly do not have the income, tastes, needs, interests, problems, or expectations of younger persons. For some, old age is marked by social, economic, and physical dependency. But many senior citizens expect to have a comfortable place to live and the leisure to do as they choose, and most desire to live independently and to care for themselves. Unfortunately, most physical environments are designed for younger, stronger people—and the costs of remodeling a home may be too high for many older people.

When forced to move, older people feel uprooted and helpless. Moving in with relatives may reduce self-esteem, and give rise to tension or unhappiness caused by uncongenial relatives, crowded conditions, and annoyances with small children.

Failing physical capacity complicates the process of living. The need for company is less important than the need for space to display memorabilia. About 20 per cent of the old need custodial care; the remainder need physical surroundings that facilitate movement and self-care. In many ways, the physical environments needed by the elderly can be compared to those needed by the handicapped, and architectural features for one will aid the other.

In general, housing for the elderly should provide security, independence, involvement, and privacy. Basic design characteristics include a size small enough to be easily maintained but large enough to prevent overcrowding. Safety features can help compensate for diminishing sense of balance, acoustical control helps make sleeping areas quiet; large windows offer more light and sun as well as broader horizons; automatic controls on equipment facilitate operation; and higher temperatures compensate for reduced circulation. Economic restrictions may prevent elderly citizens from living in their accustomed style, and houses may be allowed to deteriorate to the point of dilapidation. Financial assistance would enable the elderly to have a place of their own in which to entertain in their own way and to dream of the past while remaining an integral part of the community.

SUMMARY

Buildings reflect the general culture. Heritage, traditional resources and skills and domestic, political, and economic policies as well as the individual's needs and role influence and are influenced by the living environment.

The major domestic institution is the family. Its size is directly related to the size of the dwelling required—if more people are living together, more space is needed.

The stage of the family cycle correlates with the age of the group members. If the needs of each are not satisfied family members respond by spending more time outside the home. Aging is accompanied by reduced physical abilities, which often require a reconsideration of the location and design of housing. If the home is to be supportive, it must conform to individuals' priorities and characteristics, so that current needs are accommodated and future ones anticipated.

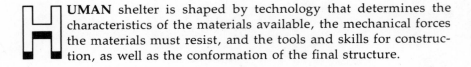

Influences of the
Technological
Environment

HUMAN shelter is shaped by technology that determines the characteristics of the materials available, the mechanical forces the materials must resist, and the tools and skills for construction, as well as the conformation of the final structure.

ARCHITECTURAL DRAWINGS

An architectural drawing interprets a design for the consumer and provides all the information needed for construction. Drawings are made to scale (usually a quarter of an inch to a foot), and the scale is indicated on the drawing. A symbol showing the north point indicates the position of the house in relation to the path of the sun, suggesting which rooms will have sun and which will not. (Other common symbols are shown in Figure 4-1.)

Preliminary Drawings

Usually two types of drawings are developed—preliminary and working drawings. Preliminary drawings of the proposed design include realistic sketches or perspectives and sometimes a scale model of the size, shape, and appearance of the finished house. Preliminary drawings include floor plans or a horizontal section of the house, viewed from directly above at a point approximately four feet above the floor. They also show such features as walls, partitions, doors, windows, electrical switches and lighting fixtures, directions in which doors and windows open, and any built-in furniture (kitchen cabinets for example) that are to be supplied as part of the building contract.

46

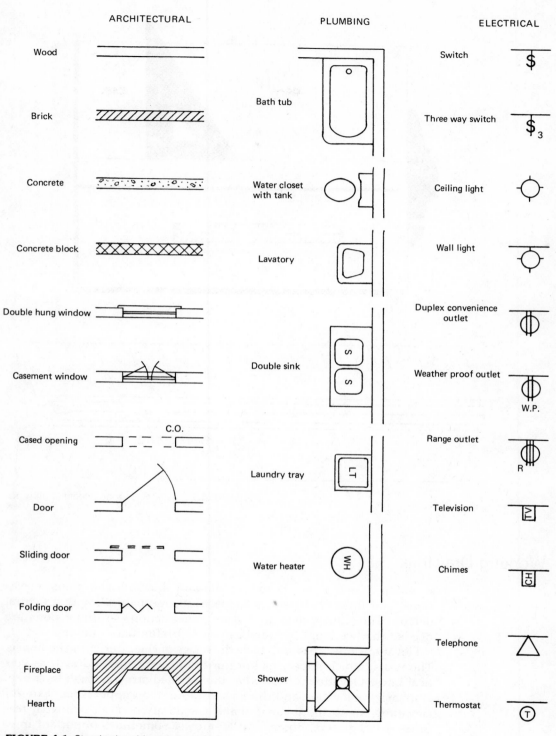

ARCHITECTURAL		PLUMBING		ELECTRICAL	
Wood		Bath tub		Switch	$
Brick				Three way switch	$₃
Concrete		Water closet with tank		Ceiling light	
Concrete block		Lavatory		Wall light	
Double hung window				Duplex convenience outlet	
Casement window		Double sink		Weather proof outlet	W.P.
Cased opening	C.O.			Range outlet	R
Door		Laundry tray		Television	
Sliding door				Chimes	
Folding door		Water heater		Telephone	
Fireplace		Shower		Thermostat	
Hearth					

FIGURE 4-1 Standard architectural symbols.

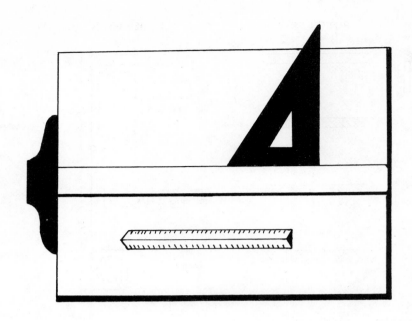

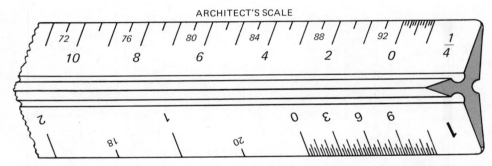

ARCHITECT'S SCALE

FIGURE 4-2 Basic tools for architectural drawing.

Working Drawings

Working drawings are in exact scale and illustrate site plans, elevations, and floor plans, and also electrical, mechanical, and structural details. Their purpose is to specify construction; so dimensions are needed that were not included as part of preliminary drawings.

Elevations are "head on" scale drawings of the exterior of the house. The walls (which appear as lines of the floor plan) are drawn as vertical lines. Elevations show what the finished structure will look like, emphasizing location and dimension rather than appearance. Exterior elevations show the general shape and location of all principal features—roof, gutters, doors, and windows. Sometimes important interior walls are also shown in elevations to indicate the location of win-

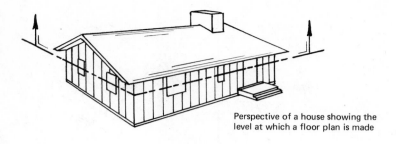

Perspective of a house showing the
level at which a floor plan is made

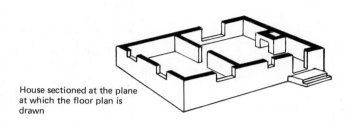

House sectioned at the plane
at which the floor plan is
drawn

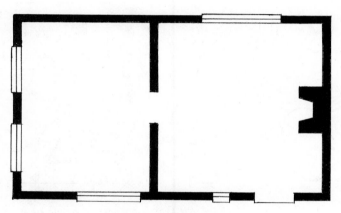

Floor plan of the first floor

FIGURE 4-3 Development of a floor plan.

dows, doors, shelving, built-in cabinets, and radiators or heating vents.

The section drawing cuts through the plan or elevation to show construction and materials. For example, it might show the general shape of a fireplace and how it is to be located in an interior wall.

Detail drawings show isolated construction features, drawn on an enlarged scale. They usually include a vertical elevation, a plan or sectional cut of a special feature or area of the building that does not conform to standard building procedure. Detail drawings specify construction of stairs, windows, balconies, and porches. Unless sufficient

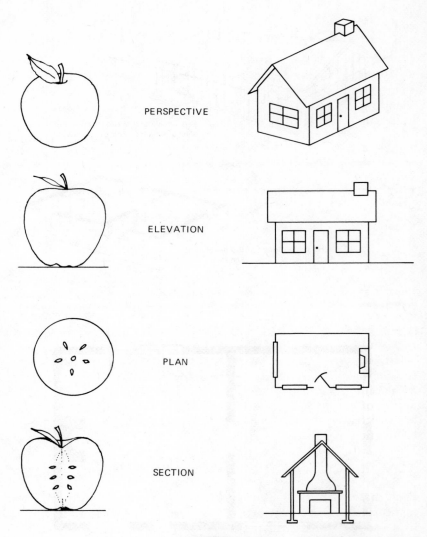

PERSPECTIVE

ELEVATION

PLAN

SECTION

FIGURE 4-4 Types of architectural drawings.

detail drawings are included with the working drawings, the builder does not know exactly what is expected.

Specifications

Accompanying the drawings are specifications for materials, legal considerations of the project, insurance required, and various directives about the quality of the workmanship. The ultimate success of the structure depends on the completeness, simplicity, and accuracy of all these drawings and specifications.

MATERIALS

Construction materials were once limited to those available in the local environment. Religion, fashion, prestige, and tradition influenced their selection. Modern technology creates material to meet very demanding requirements. (Table 4-1 lists some common construction materials.)

TABLE 4-1   Common Construction Materials

Type	Example
Natural	
Organic	Wood, fiber, sod, reeds, bamboo, leaves
Metals	Wrought iron, steel, aluminum, copper, zinc, pewter
Masonry	Brick, stone, adobe
Cast or Molded	Concrete, cement tile, plaster
Man-made	
Plastics	Paint, vinyls, asphalt, linoleum, glass, fiberglass, polyesters
Prefabricated	Sheet rock, wall paneling, plywood, Formica, fiberboard

A great variety of materials allows the designer to consider many new building forms, but this has increased the complexity of material selection. Ideally, the material chosen is that which can best fill the indicated need. In practice, materials are often selected on the basis of availability, cost, local building codes and regulations, and the availability of workmen skilled in their use. In the final analysis, materials are selected on the basis of their physical, aesthetic, architectural, and economic properties.

Physical Properties

Each material has inherent characteristics that determine its performance under various structural conditions (see Table 4-2). Strength, heat and moisture resistance, and sound absorbency are valuable characteristics because they affect human health and safety. Durability, upkeep and maintenance, adaptability, and necessary preprocessing are also important characteristics because they affect cost. If special processing, skilled labor, or special equipment is required for construction, the cost will be higher.

Wood

Because of its physical properties, wood has been the material most often used for house construction. It is relatively strong: cut with the grain, it resists pressure. It is relatively durable, and it is versatile (four basic building materials are made from wood—dimension lumber, plywood, laminated timber, and fiberboard). Most important, wood can be easily worked with relatively simple tools. Wood does

TABLE 4-2

Physical Properties of Common Construction Materials

Physical Property	Material					
	Organic	Masonry	Casted/Molded	Metals	Plastic	Pre-fab
Strength	Poor–good	Good–excellent	Excellent	Good–excellent	Varies according to type	Designed to specification
Absorbency Moisture	Absorbs liquids, expands, must be sealed to prevent decay	Very little reaction	Very little reaction	Usually coated to prevent rust	Very little	"
Heat	Insulator Combustible	Absorbs Fire resistant	Absorbs (color) Reflects heat Fire resistant	Expands Conditioner Melts	Thermo setting Withstands higher temperature than thermo-plastic combustible	"
Sound	Absorbs	Reflects	Reflects	Transfers	Varies	"
Insect Resistancy	Subject to infestation	Impervious	Impervious	Impervious	Varies	"
Durability	Temporary	Permanent	Permanent	Permanent	Permanent	"
Adaptability	Very	Average	Above average	Difficult Sophisticated equip.; trained personnel to fabricate	Designed for use	"
Workability	Easy to work	Some skill required	Finisher and special equipment required	Varies according to product	Varies according to type	"

52

have disadvantages: it is susceptible to decay and insects, easily damaged by fire, and affected by changes in humidity. Some of these disadvantages, however, can be mitigated by relatively simple treatments.

Concrete

Another commonly used building material is concrete, a fluid mixture of cement, stone or slag, sand, and water that can be poured into molds. When it hardens to rocklike consistency (as it soon does) it is strong, fireproof, vermin-proof, watertight, and rot-resistant, and therefore ideal for footings and foundations. Concrete reinforced with steel bars or tenons is stronger still. But concrete has some disadvantages, too. It is heavy and difficult to form and finish. The molds may cost as much as the concrete itself. Highly skilled workmen are needed to assure a uniform, finished surface. Precast concrete, though less strong and more expensive, is usually more uniform—and also more versatile, because so many materials can be used for molds.

Metals

Structural steel is a commonly used building material in the United States. Relatively inexpensive, it—in relation to volume and weight—is claimed to be the strongest low-cost building material. Nonferrous metals and their alloys, softer than steel, are easier to work. Metals, however, are highly susceptible to moisture and heat. Although they have been used successfully for the construction of mobile homes, their use on the building site is limited to minor items: doorknobs, hinges, faucets, pipes, spouts, furnaces, radiators, screens, insulation, ducts, and wiring.

Nonmetals and Plastics

Plastics and nonmetal materials are often used in construction. Glass is appropriate for windows and doors because it transmits light, heat, and pleasant views. Improperly placed, however, glass can allow passage of too much heat, wind, cold, or noise. It is susceptible to cracking and breaking under wide variations in temperature. New formulations have improved the insulating and reflective properties of glass and reduced its relative weight, thus increasing the usefulness and desirability as a building material.

Plastics, another useful building material, can be made lighter than aluminum, clearer than glass, or stronger than steel. The many varieties of plastics promise new versatility in construction and design. Plastics are usually classified according to their reaction to heat. Thermosetting plastics, solidified by heat, cannot be remelted after molding; thermoplastic plastics, softened by heat, are more workable. Most

TABLE 4-3   Common Building Plastics

Plastic	Physical Property	Building Use
Cellulose	Withstands moderate heat and sub-0° temperature; good insulator	Pipes and tubing
Epoxy	Resists weather and corrosion	Protective coating; bonding agent for wood, metal, glass
Polyester	Hard and rigid; resists acids, salts, solvents	Translucent skylights, roofs
Polystyrene	Will crack on impact; resists water	Wall tiles
Vinyl	Resists water, oil, food, common chemicals; withstands 130°F. heat; good insulator	(For indoor use only) Wall and floor coverings, electrical wiring, and plugs

Adapted from A. Friedmann, J. F. Pile, and F. Wilson, *Interior Design: An Introduction to Architectural Interiors* (New York: American Elsevier Publishing Co., Inc., 1976), pp. 33–35.

plastics are resistant to insects, moisture, and rot. Plastics for construction should be carefully selected (see Table 4-3).

Aesthetic Properties

The texture, character, and color of building materials add visual appeal. The qualities of any material may be masked or enhanced by a coat of paint. Traditional materials can be simulated by finishing techniques, or by synthetic products. The use of synthetics to simulate natural materials, deplored by those who believe a material should be "honest," may have begun as an attempt to create symbols of luxury and status at lower cost; it has continued, however, because synthetics have superior properties. (Water, for example, has no discernible effect on Formica but leaves a stain on marble or wood.)

Some materials add aesthetic appeal to buildings. Massive materials (the stone in pyramids) suggest permanence, strength, or durability. Light, transparent materials suggest openness and informality.

Natural building materials, earth-colored, blend with the environment and are psychologically reassuring. Manufactured products often reproduce the color range of natural materials. Natural color can be altered by paint or stain—a necessary preservation process for wood, but a practice that only adds to maintenance costs for those materials that do not require preservatives. Stone, brick, and tile have decorative properties.

Brick, the oldest of the manufactured materials, is most often used because building codes frequently favor it. The small scale of bricks has a softening effect, especially when used on a large surface. Most bricks retain the color and character of the clay or shale from which they are made. Their texture ranges from smooth to rough, depending upon the finish process. The mortar that bonds the bricks can be made

54

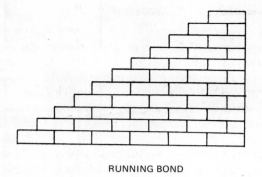

RUNNING BOND

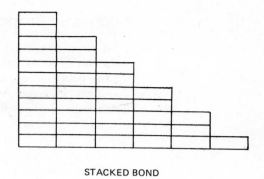

STACKED BOND

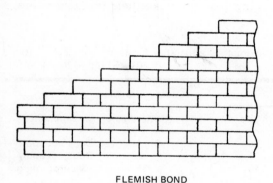

FLEMISH BOND

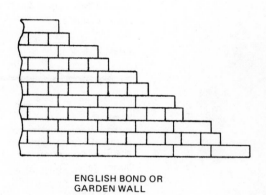

ENGLISH BOND OR
GARDEN WALL

FIGURE 4-5 Patterns created by brick bonds.

to blend or contrast in color. The way in which bricks are joined adds to the decorative effect.

Wood comes in many colors and textures; exposed to the elements, it turns a muted gray. The design of its natural grain can be emphasized by acrylic stain or covered with paint. Wood creates harmony between structure and environment, making it an obvious choice when such a blend is desired.

Architectural Properties

Imported materials can be out of keeping with the local landscape or life style. Stucco and tile, for example, seem appropriate for a Mediterranean landscape. Log cabins match the simple life of the American pioneer. Materials like brick or stone convey formality and permanence. Sleek metals suggest mobility and speed—and because they are used for mobile homes, they are also associated with transiency and impermanence.

Economic Properties

Cost often has a high priority in the selection of construction materials, and the cost of any material is influenced by its availability, and by the processing, labor, and maintenance it requires (see Table 4-4). Wood, for example, must be milled into structural lumber; bricks must be mixed, shaped, and baked; stone must be cut or carved; metals must be rolled or molded; and synthetic materials must be manufactured.

Local availability helps to determine cost. Wood can be obtained almost everywhere in the United States, but brick manufacture is limited to certain areas, and some plastics are processed in only one plant in the country. The longer the distance from the source to the site, the higher the price of the building material. Over the past twenty years, the relation between cost and distance has been reduced because manufacturers have averaged shipping costs to make their products more competitive.

TABLE 4-4   Approximate Comparative Costs for a Wall 8' × 10' (Based on 1976 prices)*

Material	Costs in Dollars		
	Inherent	Structural	Maintenance
Studded Frame Skeleton	$ 15	$ 11	Does not apply
Plywood Subsiding	23	8	Does not apply
Concrete, 6" Thick	45	35	(Waterproofing below ground) $7
Exterior Finishes			
Horizontal 5/16' × 12' Masonite Lap Siding	26	15	$11
Vertical Cedar Siding 8"–10" Wide	55	22	$11
Plywood, for Simulated Board and Batten	30	10	$11
Cedar Channel Board	37	10	$11
Cedar Shakes 1/2" × 3/4" × 24"	34	30	None applied
Aluminum Simulated Lap Siding	27 (unpainted) 43 (painted)	12 12	$13 None applied
Steel Siding	25 (unpainted) 41 (painted)	12 12	$13 None applied
Brick Veneer Single Course	93	134	None applied
Cement Block	58	89	None applied
Native Stone	215	375	None applied
Travertine	235	300	None applied

* Inherent costs were determined by the amount of material required for the exterior surface. Structural costs were based on local labor rates. Maintenance costs include the cost of materials purchased to seal the surface of the wall plus labor. No attempt was made to account for regional variation, which can be very great.

The labor required for use of a particular material also influences its cost. The more skill required, the greater the cost of the labor. Stone usually requires the most experienced craftsmen and can therefore be relatively expensive.

Some materials require more maintenance than others, but the maintenance costs for any material may be increased if the product is not locally available. Organic materials—subject to fire, weather, and insects—require constant maintenance (thatch roofs, for instance, have to be replaced often). The perishability of wood can be reduced by paint or stain, but many houses are permitted to stand for years without the benefit of this protection. Some believe that leaving wood unpainted allows it to "breathe"; others contend that the greyness of unpainted wood, embellished perhaps by lichens and moss, makes a house picturesque or "honest." (Adjacent property owners sometimes fail to appreciate this natural antiquing process.)

TOOLS AND CONSTRUCTION

There are as many approaches to the construction of a house as there are sites and styles. Construction can be viewed as a purely technical matter, limited only by available tools and techniques. But some stress "honest construction," in which structural aspects of the building are integrated into the design whereas others consider an unblemished interior and exterior finish more important.

Structures are built to define and enclose space. A building must be designed to withstand tension, compression, and shear. The structure must also resist the forces of nature—gravity, wind, pressure, or vibration. Its final form depends on which system is chosen to overcome these forces.

Early construction methods involved piling sticks or stones on top of one another. These were kept in place through the friction of stone on stone or log on log, and by the weight of the mass against the earth. Organic materials, mixed with water, were used to seal cracks or hold the rubble together. Brick manufacture initiated new building techniques. Each subsequent improvement in either tools or techniques had its effect on the building process.

For centuries frame construction was the basic method of building, especially in the United States. A cellar or foundation was dug, and the chimney stack erected. Trees cut at the site were hewn and smoothed for the frame. The skeleton was assembled, secured with mortise and tenon, and raised to an upright position.

Industrialization brought important changes to American construction. By 1865, new methods of joining materials were said to enable a man and boy to "attain the same results that twenty men could using the old-fashioned mortised and tenoned joints."[1] By 1910, precut

[1] S. Giedion, *Mechanization Takes Command* (New York: Oxford University Press, Inc., 1948), p. 288.

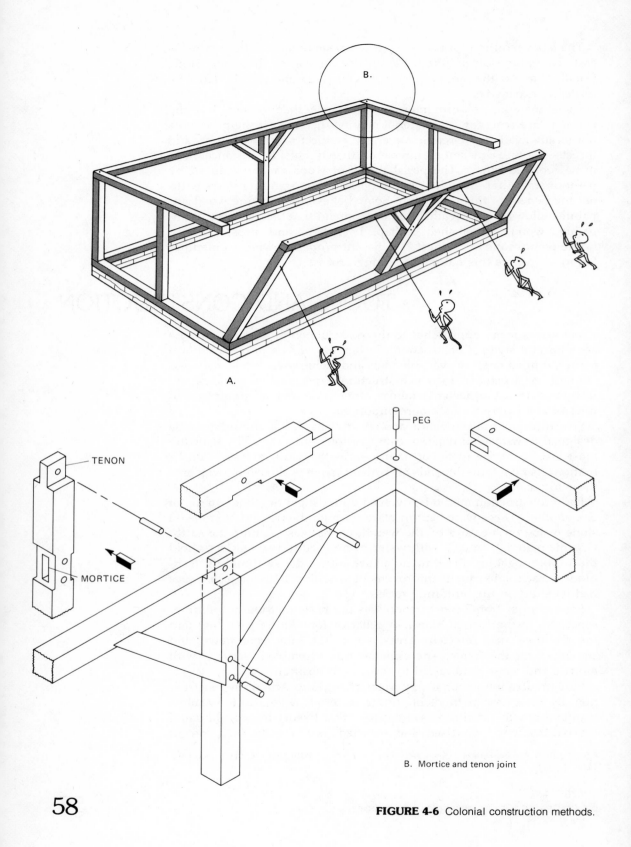

B.

A.

PEG

TENON

MORTICE

B. Mortice and tenon joint

FIGURE 4-6 Colonial construction methods.

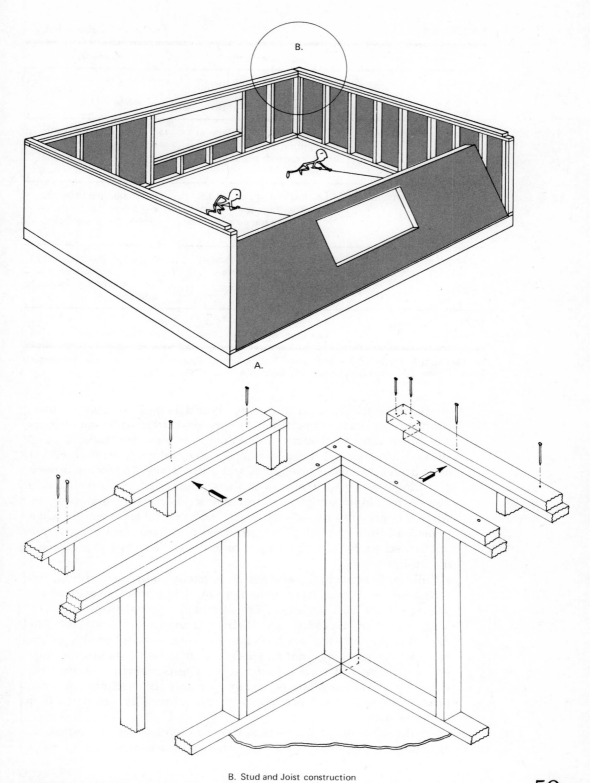

B. Stud and Joist construction

FIGURE 4-7 Typical modern frame construction.

TABLE 4-5   Design and Labor Changes

House Type	On-site Work	Off-site Work
Log Cabin	Lay foundation, fell trees, shape and fit logs, hew planks for roof, etc.	
Balloon Frame House	Lay foundation, cut and fit lumber, construct windows, door, other elements, finish	Mill lumber, manufacture hardware
Conventional Frame House (1930s)	Lay foundation, cut and fit lumber for shell, install factory-made components, finish	Mill lumber, manufacture hardware, cabinetry, windows, stairs, wallboard
Package House	Lay foundation, assemble prefabricated parts	Design and fabricate set of building components for shell, plumbing, windows, and storage
Mobile or Sectional House	Lay foundation	Fabricate house

Adapted from A. Friedman, J. F. Pile, and F. Wilson, *Interior Design: An Introduction to Architectural Interiors* (New York: American Elsevier Publishing Co., Inc., 1976), p. 270.

lumber had become available. After World War II, an acute housing shortage spurred the development of preconstructed walls, roof trusses, and other exterior elements (for other examples, see Table 4-5). Of all the industrialized housing techniques developed, most acceptable have been component assemblies and utility cores. The former involve prefitting doors and windows to their frames and prefinishing cabinets. A minimum utility core provides access runs for plumbing and wiring; larger ones include the entire bath or kitchen assembly. Component assemblies and utility cores tend to reduce costs because production schedules can be changed and less skilled labor is required at the building site.

Building codes, the problems of financing and distribution, and consumer resistance have impeded the widespread use of industrialized housing systems. To stimulate acceptance, the U.S. Department of Housing and Urban Development, in Operation Breakthrough, invited producers of housing systems to design and erect houses (ranging from single-family, detached dwellings to high-rise apartments) at nine selected sites. The experiment showed that relatively unskilled laborers, using assembly-line techniques, could produce manufactured houses to be transported by rail or truck to building sites.

On the other hand, the method imposed limitations. The house, for example, is limited to a size that can fit in a railroad car or truck.

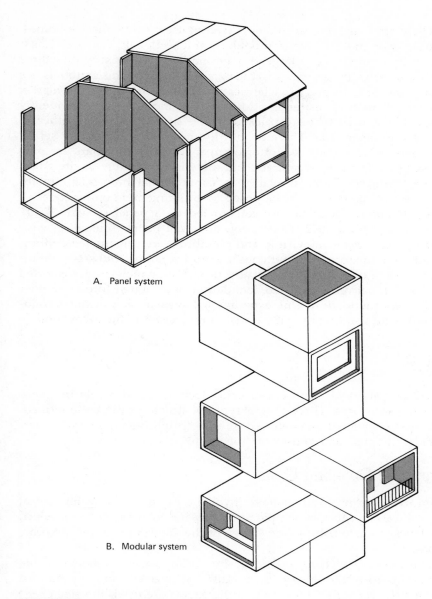

A. Panel system

B. Modular system

FIGURE 4-8 Industrial housing construction.

Structure and materials had to be selected to withstand both building stresses and the rigors of transportation and handling. To prevent infiltration by rodents, rain, ground water, and road dirt, protective coverings were needed—yet the coverings had to be disposed of at the site. Because snow, rain, and high wind at the site can halt construction, temporary storage is needed for the unit as well as for the specialized equipment needed for on site construction.

There are four types of industrialized houses: single mobile homes, double-wide mobile homes, modulars, and sectionals. For such housing to be competitive, a large enough market must exist within three hundred miles of the manufacturing plant. Man-made materials are more amenable to precision fabrication, but do not have the market appeal of natural materials. Multifamily modules are frequently stacked in blocks that are trucked to the site and fitted together in various arrangements. Three or four living units a day can be set on foundations and made ready for occupancy. Since modulars are purchased on a fixed-price contract, and there is a minimum of site work, cost is reduced. Their similarity to conventional houses eliminates many problems that might be posed by building and zoning codes.

Single-family sectionals are constructed by a panel system; 37,717 were produced in 1972. Floor, roof, and wall panels (including windows, doors, electrical wiring, and plumbing) are constructed and finished on both sides. Wood frames are most common, but steel, aluminum, concrete, and plastics are also used. The panels are transported to the site, set on a prepared foundation, and bolted to one another and to the foundation. One experimental system even includes foundation panels so that the only on-site preparation is the excavation.

STRUCTURES

The materials, tools, and construction techniques available influence housing structures. Three general types of structures can be identified: a basic unit (sometimes referred to as a "primitive" dwelling), "vernacular" homes, and houses of "the grand design."

Primitive Dwelling Units

Primitive dwelling units usually involve a minimum of technological sophistication. Most are simple, uniform, and temporary. They reflect, however, an astonishing knowledge of the environment and its processes.

There are two characteristic designs. One serves a nomadic life style. Because the living unit must be erected and dismantled frequently, no nails, glues, or binding agents are used; the size of the shelter depends on the method of transportation. Building materials typically include poles or hides. The second primitive type is more permanent, usually designed to serve the needs of an agrarian culture. It might typically include stuccoed walls to keep out the weather, and often a fireplace for warmth.

The main purpose of the primitive dwelling unit is to shelter the inhabitants from the weather and to provide protection. Because the design is determined by the local availability of materials and the prevailing beliefs and traditions of the society, there is strong resistance to change. A one-room design is customary, and larger struc-

A. Log cabin

B. African hut

C. Mexican fisherman's shelter

FIGURE 4-9 Primitive dwelling units.

tures are simply multiples of the basic unit. The size and decoration are usually determined by the status, number, and skill of the occupants. Most of these dwellings are located near natural sources of water.

Housing of this type is found in some highly developed technological societies: in the camping tents or log cabins used by outdoor enthusiasts; in the public housing built for the economically deprived or for special occupational groups.

Vernacular Homes

Folk or "vernacular" dwellings, built by craftsmen as family shelters, were built around the Acropolis, the Roman Forum, the Egyptian temple, and the Gothic cathedral.

The vernacular home reflects tradition as well as the tastes of the builders and the occupants. Its chief characteristic is versatility within a standard type. Standardized outlines and main features are combined with details added and adjustments made to suit the occupants. Interior space can be divided according to use: a stable, a room for weaving or sewing, a workshop or office, sleeping areas for various members of the family, an area for cooking and eating. The vernacular house has few aesthetic pretensions. To be successful, the vernacular home must be socially valid and within the economic limits of the majority; it must also be healthful for the occupants, and must require minimum maintenance.

Houses of the Grand Design

Houses of the grand design are built, to individual specifications and tastes, by a team of specialists. Such houses include the house of the chief of a primitive tribe, the castle of the lord of the manor, the palace of the king, the showplace of the American industrialist. Constructed of materials more permanent than those used for other types of structures, many have remained intact, to the gratification of the anthropologist and the delight of antiquarians.

Materials for such houses are selected for beauty rather than practicality. Designs tend to be complicated, with unusual roof styles, much ornamentation, and careful landscaping. The occupant is responsible for costs as well as for upkeep and maintenance (usually carried out by others).

SUMMARY

The level of technology in a society determines the design and construction of housing.

Architectural drawings—essential to communication between the

A. A development
tract

B. A resort retire-
ment community
centered around
business and recre-
ational areas, Sun
City, Arizona. Cour-
tesy of Del Webb
Inc.

FIGURE 4-10 Vernacular homes.

A. A castle in Bavaria

B. Moorish palace in Spain

C. The Nevada governor's mansion

D. Chief's house in Fiji

FIGURE 4-11 Houses of the grand design.

consumer, the designer, the builders, and the craftsmen—should be complete, simple, accurate, and to scale.

Contemporary buildings can be made from a wide variety of materials. Selection is influenced by the cost of the material and by its physical, aesthetic, and architectural properties. Prefabrication reduces price but limits design and choice of materials.

There are three types of houses: primitive, vernacular, and custom-designed. Primitive houses are simple in design and structure. Vernacular houses—development or tract houses, for example—are built to satisfy the needs of the "average" person. A very few houses are custom designed to fill individual desires. They are usually large in scale, elaborate in decoration, and complex in construction.

the influence of the macro-environment: the exterior

built to last and to be lovely . . . with such differences as might suit and express each man's character and occupation and partly his history. . . .

John Ruskin
Seven Lamps of Architecture

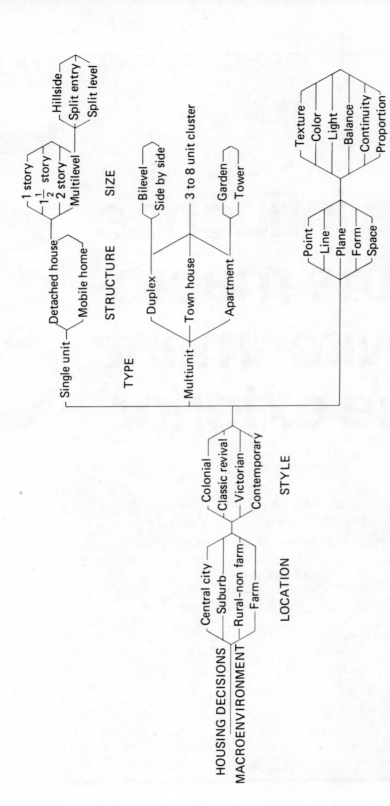

5

Housing Clusters

ALTHOUGH human beings are born as individuals, they live in clusters and survive as a group—most small groups (families) are part of larger groups (clans, tribes, nations). The societal group gives aid in times of crisis, contributes to the socialization of the young, and upholds traditional standards. Social class—defined by income, education, and occupation—often determines the amount and purpose of this interaction. Members of lower classes tend to seek more aid from neighbors than do members of upper classes, perhaps because they need more help to survive. On the other hand, all—young and old, married and single, rich and poor—are interested in the common territory occupied by the group.

Most people tend to cluster where work, education, health services, communication with others, and other social amenities are available. These resources form the focal point of the modern neighborhood. In the United States, there are two general types of cluster: one is the community of not more than 10,000 people that is referred to in the U.S. Census as "rural"; the other is the large central city and its suburbs, identified as "standard metropolitan statistical areas" (SMSA).

Each cluster gives rise to distinctive dwelling designs. Central cities accommodate large numbers in limited space. High-rise multifamily dwellings are typical of the city, whereas single-family dwellings are more common in rural areas.

RURAL HOUSING

The chief occupation of people in rural areas is agriculture. A farm today is defined by the U.S. Census as plots of ten acres or more from

71

which sales of farm products amounted to $50 or more in the preceding calendar year, or plots of fewer than ten acres from which sales of farm products amounted to $250 or more in the preceding calendar year. Any other living unit in the open country or in a village is designated as a rural nonfarm unit.

In 1790, 95 per cent of the population lived in rural areas dotted with small villages where the farmer could obtain community services and sell farm produce. By 1970, approximately 32.6 per cent of the population was listed as living outside the standard metropolitan statistical areas. Only about 5 per cent lived in small towns and villages and 26 per cent were living in the open country. Farm units are characterized by fewer numbers of bathrooms and more bedrooms, and they have a larger proportion of household equipment such as washers, dryers, and food freezers. Nonfarm units, on the other hand, that have been built after 1968 tend to have more than one bathroom and space for two cars.

Mobile homes are popular in rural areas, accounting for 10 per cent of housing in these areas in 1974. Community services tend to be limited: in cities there is, on the average, one doctor for 700 people; in rural areas, there is one doctor for approximately 2,100 people. Even so, between 1970 and 1973, more people migrated to the country than remained in the cities (see Table 5-1). The number of houses outside standard metropolitan statistical areas increased by approximately 14 per cent, a greater gain than that shown for housing in the central cities.

A viable rural community requires an adequate mix of community services and employment opportunities. The clean air and lovely views that brought the urban newcomer do not always compensate for

TABLE 5-1   Migration from Major Cities—1970–73

City	Loss in Population
New York City	305,000
Los Angeles	119,000
Chicago	124,000
Philadelphia	75,000

Adapted from "Big City, Small City," *House and Home*, September 1975, p. 22.

the lack of good schools, libraries, police and fire protection, good streets, or adequate health and sanitation facilities. Many services tend to cost more in rural areas than do similar services in more densely settled areas. Unfortunately, development planning in rural areas is limited: it emphasizes the attraction of new business to the neglect

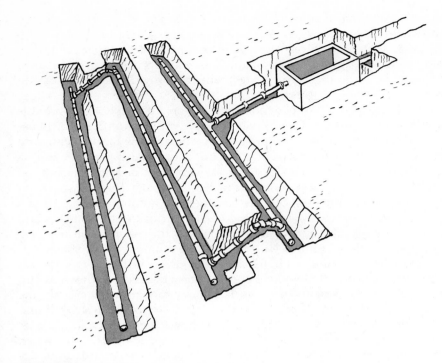

FIGURE 5-1 An individual sewage system.

of additional social amenities. A time lag between the influx of new people and the collection of new tax monies based upon increased property values intensifies the problem.

A safe water supply and an efficient sewage disposal system are not found in every rural area. Fifty million people in the United States depend upon individual water supplies. Waterborne diseases caused by surface contaminants occur sporadically, but mechanical and chemical equipment that might eliminate the contamination are not recommended for individual systems because of the high risk of equipment failure. Almost as important as the cleanliness of water is the quality of the service. An average household requires 2.08 gallons of water per hour. In addition, water pressure should not fall when individuals compete for water use. Many rural houses have a low-yield well that requires an intermediate storage system (a lake or pond, or the more common steel or fiberglass tank).

Approximately 25 per cent of the new houses under construction in rural areas depend on individual sewage disposal systems—septic tanks or cesspools. Health experts estimate that 50 per cent of the individual systems do not work properly owing to limitations of soil, system capacity, or installation. Much of the environmental legislation in recent years has been designed to improve this situation. Most helpful are the loans that enable property owners to join together to provide adequate water and sewer service. (Priority is given to smaller communities that need to restore a deteriorating water supply, or to improve, enlarge, or modify an inadequate water or sewer system, or to merge facilities to improve management and provide more economical service.)

Social scientists often overlook rural poverty because it is more diffuse and less apparent than urban poverty, yet most of the poor housing in the United States is located in rural areas. Low farm prices, crop failures, depression, and debt reduction during the period between the two World Wars, as well as postwar shortages of materials and rising costs prevented normal farmstead replacements. The farmstead has a low priority in the farm budget—of the more affluent rural families 9 per cent live in substandard houses. About a third of the substandard units, mostly rental units or those for which there is no cash rent, are occupied by black families—a vestige of the plantation and sharecropper era when the landlord housed farm laborers. With the mechanization of agriculture, the workers are no longer needed but they remain, and neither the tenants nor the landlords can afford to repair the houses. When the tenants move, the shacks are often destroyed and the land cultivated. Encouraged by development projects and more lenient loan policies, rural housing is slowly improving. It is estimated that from 1960 to 1970 the number of owned substandard units declined from 2.8 to 1.2 million, whereas the number of substandard rental units declined from 2 to 1.8 million units during the same period.

The rural environment offers more space and privacy as well as a closer association with nature and the opportunity to raise animals, to take part in outdoor activities or simply to enjoy the more relaxed atmosphere. The elderly in rural areas seem more satisfied with their community and express greater happiness and less fear than the elderly in the city. There are disadvantages, however, fewer social services are available, and children must travel greater distances to school.

Any discussion of rural housing is incomplete without special attention to the farmstead, which is both a place of business and a residence. A rise of ground with good surface drainage and enough slope for sewer and drain lines will insure a safe and adequate water supply. Animal enclosures or septic tanks should not be near wells lest they contaminate the water supply, nor should they be in the path of prevailing winds lest the odor (especially in summer) carry to the house. Some authorities recommend shrubs and fences around house and lawn in order to screen other farm buildings. Usually the farmhouse is located near the public road with a drive wide enough for cars and machines to pass, park, and turn around. It is also convenient to have a service yard where feed and equipment can be stored.

Farming activities place additional requirements on the interior design. Space is needed to transact business, to keep records, to store home-produced foods and supplies, and to accommodate water system and fuel storage tanks. A separate entry is often required for workers to reach indoor processing and dressing centers without tracking through the remainder of the living area.

URBAN HOUSING

The history of the city is as old as the history of man. Cities grew as people clustered together to work, to seek protection against a common enemy, or to exchange goods and services. Older cities are approximately thirty kilometers apart—a convenient day's travel afoot or on horseback.

At some time in its history, almost every American city has been a "boom" town. Located on harbors and major waterways, these communities were often the link to the world left behind. Because many American towns were established in the 1800s, the typical townscape is predominantly Victorian with a railroad station at its hub.

Comfort, opportunity, and growth are the main attractions of the city. Aristotle said that men came to the city to live, but they stayed to live the good life. Those from the farm came because life on the land was difficult and provided few luxuries. During the Middle Ages, a serf who could escape to the city and remain for a year gained the status of a free citizen. Urban "freedom" today might be interpreted as the opportunity for cultural and personal enrichment. When urban population growth is rapid, houses are built everywhere, sometimes wisely but more often indiscriminately. The high concentration of population in the metropolitan area gives rise to two chronic urban housing problems: city slums and urban sprawl.

Central Cities

Industry and commerce generate the wealth of the central city. The most common urban pattern involves a series of concentric residential circles around a central business core. As the core expands, it absorbs the residential ring and brings a new type of activity or use to the buildings. A new residential ring forms at the outer edge. Eventually there are many rings around the central core.

Cities usually grow because businesses or industries do. As industry expands, the need to accommodate the rapid growth conflicts with the need to maintain environmental quality. The best solution would permit both needs to be met. More often, however, a filtering process occurs, and residential areas change character. Some home-owners convert their dwellings to office or business space, to private schools, to nursing homes, or to special facilities needed by urban res-

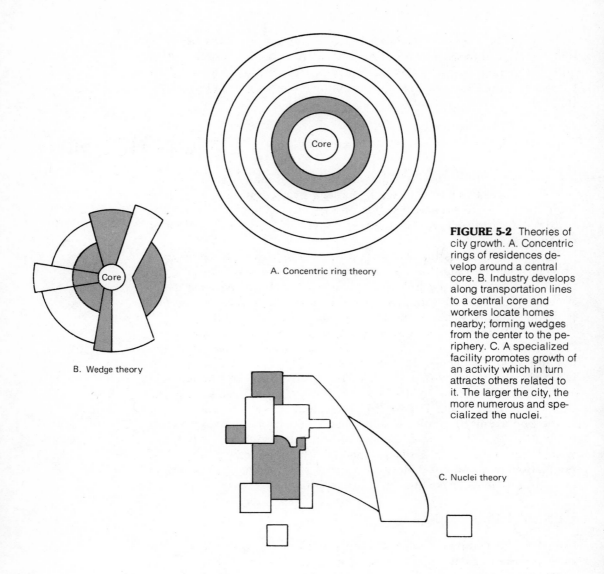

A. Concentric ring theory

B. Wedge theory

C. Nuclei theory

FIGURE 5-2 Theories of city growth. A. Concentric rings of residences develop around a central core. B. Industry develops along transportation lines to a central core and workers locate homes nearby; forming wedges from the center to the periphery. C. A specialized facility promotes growth of an activity which in turn attracts others related to it. The larger the city, the more numerous and specialized the nuclei.

idents. Others retain residential features but increase density so that more families can be housed. Low-income families, minority groups, and elderly citizens who desire to live near their work, who lack the means to acquire a more adequate living unit elsewhere, or who simply do not wish to change their life styles, occupy the converted family dwellings. Subtle changes result from the increasingly crowded conditions. Houses fall into disrepair because the occupants are unemployed, ill, poor, or simply indifferent. Property values decline, taxes increase, structures deteriorate and decay, and crime invades the neighborhood. The incineration of large amounts of solid waste and the movement of additional automobiles help create air pollution; increased amounts of ashes in waterways lead to water pollution.

All people—even those within the metropolitan district—want cleaner air, less noise and dirt, and inexpensive transportation to jobs and schools, and to shopping and recreation centers. In 1970, approximately 33 per cent of the population in standard metropolitan statistical areas lived in central cities. Approximately 48 per cent of the living units (as compared to 59 per cent of the metropolitan area as a whole) were owner-occupied. In New York, only 24 per cent of the population lived in owned units.

There is evidence of renewed interest in the central city. The 1970 U.S. Census showed an 11 per cent rise in available housing. This could have been encouraged by decreasing energy supplies that increased the cost of commuting and revitalized interest in mass transit systems. In addition, the high cost of new suburban housing forced people to appreciate the value of existing houses in the city.

Several plans have been suggested to reverse urban deterioration. For example, since one out of every five Americans moves yearly, higher-income persons could be encouraged to move by the construction of more new units in their price range. As these better units are occupied, a chain of moves could eventually leave the lowest-quality units vacant. Those empty units that met minimum standards could accommodate increasing population; the rest could be demolished to create sites for new construction. New units could be designed to accommodate increased densities.

A second response to urban decay is slum clearance and urban renewal. Legal restrictions often hamper these efforts, however, and this approach also necessitates double funding: present occupants must be relocated and the builders compensated. Former residents rarely return to a redeveloped area because it no longer fits their economic status or because they are satisfied with their new location.

A third plan involves attracting new residents to structurally sound older houses. The young professional who desires to be within walking distance of work and shops is encouraged by a homestead plan to which a house repossessed for nonpayment of taxes is given to anyone who will improve its condition and occupy it for a prescribed period.

But a rise in urban population does not insure increased socialization. A person can be as lonely in the crowded city as in the empty countryside. Central cities do offer proximity to business and commercial activities as well as to cultural and educational advantages. They also create pools of specialized people and groups, an advantageous situation for certain professionals.

Suburbia

The development of suburbs is attributed to Americans' preference for home ownership. Even in the eighteenth century wealthy city residents moved in the city's periphery for quiet, better air, comfort, and space. Some time between 1910 and 1920, when the United States was transformed from a rural to an urban nation, the fringe area experienced the most growth. Early transit lines were helpful in opening the suburbs to the middle class by providing inexpensive and relatively rapid transportation. After World War II, federal programs encouraged the trend by lowering down payments and interest rates for home buyers. At the same time the income tax structure encouraged home ownership for the middle class and made it difficult for the upper class to hold idle land. Technological advances such as septic tanks provided a more adequate method of sewage disposal than the old-time cesspool and new mass construction methods lowers costs, permitting more houses to be built more rapidly. New household appliances reduced housekeeping tasks; new homes supplied with such appliances became more desirable than older homes.

The urban scene also changed. Public transportation and housing deteriorated; land costs rose; manufacturing or service industries encroached upon residential areas. The work week shortened, making more time available for family, friends, hobbies, and group activities. As two cars became more common for American families and made them more mobile, vast new suburban developments amalgamated large portions of former farm and woodland, country villages, and even the nearby industrial towns.

An expanding middle class contributed to suburban growth. In 1960, two of every three new houses were built in the suburbs; by 1970, 24.5 per cent of the population was living outside the central cities but within the standard metropolitan statistical areas. Initially the refugees from the overcrowded city found space and greenery at low cost. Developers laid out homesites, installed sewers, and built streets. Moderate- or low-cost houses were built by the dozens, hundreds, and even thousands in vast development tracts. Generally there was little to make one subdivision distinguishable from another. Because the land was leveled, no genuine landmarks survived. Adjacent lots gave an appearance of spaciousness but failed to provide the security of the city or the privacy, freedom, and expansiveness of the country. The arrangement of houses and the direction of the streets often had little relation to land contours. Vegetation was stripped to permit more efficient and inexpensive building techniques, and the new plantings added as part of the development were ineffective as sun or wind protection.

Some suburbs are attractive but most exude uniformity. Building codes often specify interior conveniences. These represent a considerable improvement, especially in comparison to the slum, but as Burchard says,

> [But] something is still missing from this new suburban aesthetic; something of beauty, something of humor, something of informality, something of surprise, something in short of nature.[1]

[1] J. E. Burchard, "The Urban Aesthetic," *The Annals of the American Academy of Political and Social Science,* November 1957, p. 117.

Suburban populations are mobile. Newcomers are young and may move again if family size or income increases, or if careers take them elsewhere. Those most satisfied with suburban living are agricultural workers and factory workers. They are motivated by a desire for a cleaner, healthier environment than that offered in the city, better schools, or the chance to be near the "right" sort of people. Lower land costs, lower tax rates, and cheaper rent are appreciated by the lower middle class.

Much of the suburbanization has been uncoordinated. A new subdivision that springs up on hitherto unimproved land strains both public and private enterprise. Taxes rise to provide schools and other facilities, creating a heavier burden on property owners than anticipated. Recently, the tendency has been to discourage growth. Bond issues to provide facilities are frequently defeated simply because more facilities bring more people. Some communities have enacted ordinances to prevent growth until appropriate facilities are made available by the developers. This raises the cost of houses, and often pricing low- and moderate-income families (especially the young) out of the market. In others, a moratorium that may last for months and even years halts new hookups to existing systems. These seem more numerous in California, the industrial Midwest, the Northeast, and Georgia and Florida.

Suburban living is the choice for persons who desire to be near the city but not in it. Lower land values and lower densities provide more space for children. But commuting to and from work, and transporting children to and from activities, can be exhausting and costly. Tract houses are designed for profit, not excellence. People who purchase them are likely to be similar in income, age, and occupation. Although this similarity has certain advantages, it can also lead to boredom and loss of identity and privacy.

PLANNING AND DEVELOPMENT

Much of real estate law is based on the idea that each property owner should be able to conduct any activity he wishes as long as it does not adversely affect neighbors. The most successful communities find a way to serve both business and individuals to determine land use in order to produce the best quality of life for all. Community planning is one way to accomplish this.

Such planning is not new. In Colonial America, a central village green was allotted to government buildings and churches; family dwellings were placed around them, with farms at the outer fringe. Another pattern, the "gridiron" design, used by William Penn, had straight streets crossing one another at right angles, and open areas in which residents could live closely together without crowding. L'Enfant patterned the nation's capital after Versailles, with streets radiating from and encircling the Capitol. (Jefferson is said to have complained that specifying the distance a house could be placed from the street would make for "disgusting monotony.")

Laws to control the use of land within the city were introduced at the turn of the twentieth century. Plagued by overcrowding, and encouraged by a beautification movement created by the Columbian exposition, city fathers adopted regulations that determined the height of buildings and their location on the lot. The goal was to provide more sunlight and air, but gradually the emphasis shifted to efficiency. Industry, commerce, government, and residential areas were separated, as were various types of residential dwellings in order to control occupation densities and restrict the location of multifamily buildings. Currently zoning is being suggested as the method to provide clean air as well as more direct control of development and design through grants-in-aid to local governments for long-range continuous, comprehensive community programs by the U.S. Department of Housing and Urban Development.

Mistrust of government intervention, fear that professional planners will not understand the services a community wants and needs, and general apathy have slowed the regulation of public and private property. Nevertheless, the idea that land is a limited resource and its use must benefit all citizens has gradually been accepted.

Building Codes

Building codes establish minimum standards and specifications for materials and methods used in construction. Designed to assure healthy, safe, and sanitary conditions, they specify the number and placement of stairways, exits, or doorways, and the installation of plumbing and electrical systems. Sometimes they attempt to legislate good taste by including regulations about appearance—roof style, or maximum height. Building codes are formulated and enforced by local government, usually the municipality.

Complaints against building codes are widespread. Some fear that such codes inhibit creativity, that antiquated provisions inhibit innovation. Many codes prohibit mobile homes, prefabrication, and mass production techniques that could reduce costs per dwelling unit. Lack of uniformity among municipalities (especially where a large number of small continuous autonomous units exist) can increase construction costs. (The New York metropolitan district, with over 500 separate jurisdictions, is a good example.) Still another problem is the lack of well-qualified local officials, and the lack of training programs. Members of planning boards are often susceptible to political influence, and local enforcers can be arbitrary.

The Douglas Commission, assigned by the U.S. Department of

80

Housing and Urban Development to study building codes, found that such codes existed within 59.5 per cent of the standard metropolitan areas and 36.8 per cent of the communities outside these districts—a total of 96.3 per cent of all United States cities and towns. Of these, 78.1 per cent had adopted the National Electrical Code. Complaints concerning lack of uniformity, lack of clear standards, or proliferation of provisions were confirmed. Local codes bore little relationship to those suggested by Model Code organizations, and contained no provision for annual updating. Only 15 per cent of all municipalities and townships had building codes that were reasonably up to date. As a result, Operation Breakthrough was introduced to stimulate re-evaluation of building codes, to prevent protection of products, unions, or local economic interests, and to emphasize performance standards rather than types of material or construction. To date, seventeen states have adopted new codes.

Housing Codes

Housing codes deal with the use, occupancy, and maintenance of existing buildings. Major alterations require a permit and must meet current building codes. Regulations are designed to assure sanitary conditions, proper ventilation, sunlight, safety, and to prevent overcrowding. To date legislation has been relatively ineffective but has served to increase public awareness of the need for healthful, safe, living environments.

Only communities forced by the need for federal funds have established housing codes. Enforcement is difficult, for people resist being told how to live, or how to care for property, and inspectors may or may not be objective. Notice of violations is forwarded to both owner and occupant, along with a request that the condition be corrected. If this does not occur, legal remedies are enforced. Sometimes social pressure mandates action.

Zoning

Zoning is designed to regulate land use, to ban industry and commerce from residential areas, and to separate different types of living units. (Petitions for exception, however, are often granted.) Benefits accrue for those in residential areas: the exclusion of industrial or business operations reduces the risk of fire and explosion, excessive noise, lighting, vibration, pollution, and traffic. But stereotyped development, with houses of uniform age, price, size, and design can also result.

Zoning standards are controlled by local government, whose emphasis on specifications rather than performance standards can restrict innovation. Moreover, zoning can be an exclusionary device. Much zoning stems from a desire to retain an open semirural environment, to avoid the substantial local tax increases that seem to accompany large-scale or low-income residential development. It also stems from the dislike or fear of the people who might occupy the new residences. For the most part, zoning regulations specify what can or can't be done; not effective use land.

The establishment of minimum lot sizes (making large-scale projects unprofitable) is most common. A more subtle device (with similar effect) is the setting of frontage or setback requirements. Another approach is to restrict or ban multifamily buildings or mobile homes, in the belief that these attract large, low-income families whose presence raises school taxes and reduces neighborhood quality. In reality, mobile homes are often purchased by very young or by elderly couples who impose little strain on community and educational facilities.

Subdivision Plats

A subdivision is created any time raw land is divided into two or more parcels of less than ten acres for the purpose of present or future construction. Many authorities believe that control of the raw land offers the best hope for channeling future growth. Adequate control requires the synchronization of residential development with development of adequate utilities and social services. Minimum standards must be set for safe and efficient sewage disposal; for sufficient pure water; for improved access to permit passage by police, fire trucks, and ambulances; for adequate public utilities; and for lot sizes, soil conditions, and topography amenable to residences.

A good traffic system is essential for a good subdivision. All streets should cross at right angles, avoiding jogs and multiple crossings. The primary concern should be to provide access to residents and needed services. Local streets should lead to others that redistribute traffic to major arteries. As a rule, neither local nor collector streets should enter arterials at less than 800 feet. This ruling permits traffic to flow along the arterial road and reduces the number of points at which accidents can occur.

The goal of the street and lot design should be to maximize convenience, and to minimize accidents, congestion, and loss of time and money. The most traditional pattern, the gridiron-rectilinear based on William Penn's model, features straight streets crossing each other at right angles and forming rectangular lots. Little adjustment for land contour is possible; front and side yard requirements are common; and unless residences vary in type and size, a monotonous appearance results.

The curvilinear plan emphasizes the contour of the land. Streets can be located along natural drainways, avoiding the need for drainage

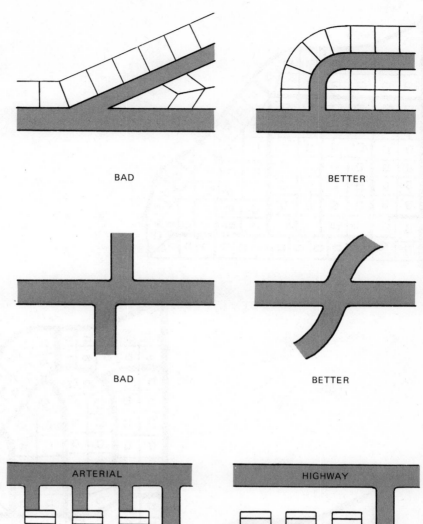

BAD

BETTER

BAD

BETTER

ARTERIAL

LOCAL

HIGHWAY

STREET

FIGURE 5-3 Alternate street designs showing examples of poor and improved planning.

BAD

BETTER

easements. Cul-de-sacs, loops, or even courts (see Figure 5-5) permit more interesting house groupings, reduce traffic, and increase safety for children.

The cluster concept, which seeks to group residences, is based on the number of people the land should accommodate rather than on the

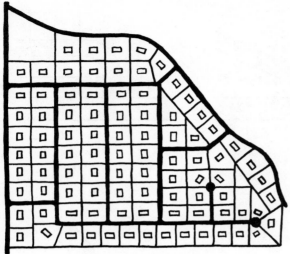

A. Rectilinear subdivision plan

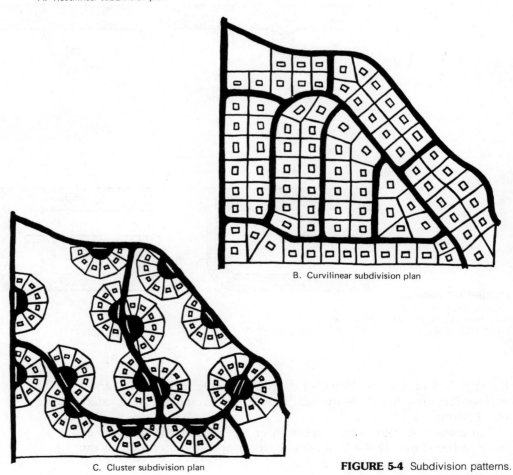

B. Curvilinear subdivision plan

C. Cluster subdivision plan

FIGURE 5-4 Subdivision patterns.

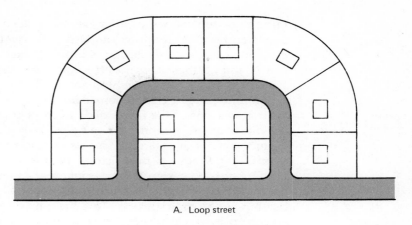

A. Loop street

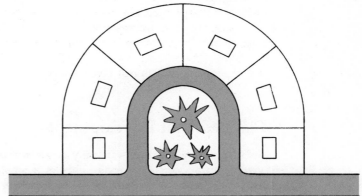

B. Court street

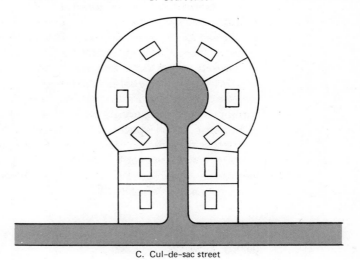

C. Cul-de-sac street

FIGURE 5-5 Street designs for curvilinear subdivisions which promote safety.

minimum dimensions of a single lot. It makes possible diversity in site, architectural groupings, and the preservation of natural and topographic features. If the design is properly executed, economy in street length and utilities as well as freedom from traffic can be achieved.

The question of ownership, administration, and maintenance of common areas is a critical consideration for any subdivision. Several alternatives exist. One is the dedication of common areas to the community as a part, permitting use by the public at large. Sometimes the municipality is unwilling or unable to adopt this alternative owing to insufficient funds or insufficient maintenance personnel. A second possibility is to assign the common space to an organization of local home owners, whose purchase or rental of property entails membership in the organization. This has proved the most successful approach, provided that legal agreements establish the area's use so that common properties are really designed for the use and enjoyment of all residents. The third method is the establishment of a private club that retains title to the common space and makes facilities available, for a fee, to residents of the subdivision. This method has exclusionary overtones and is not often successful.

Planned Unit Developments

Subdivision planning is usually governed by economic rather than environmental considerations. This is a wasteful practice. The 1974 energy crisis led to recognition of the need for improved planning. It was found that central city dwellers, because they use energy-efficient public transportation, account for only 66 per cent of the national average energy consumption. Those living in the suburbs of New York used three times as much fuel as those who live within the city. It seems clear that some changes are necessary.

Planned urban development is an expansion of the cluster concept of subdivision. Its goal is to convert a parcel of land into an integrated complex of living units that will assure maximum privacy and occupancy while preserving natural landmarks. It provides for all types of housing, open spaces, car storage, pedestrian and automobile traffic, necessary utilities, and some social amenities. If planned densities comply with those set by the minimum property standards of the U.S. Department of Housing and Urban Development, government assistance is made available.

New Towns

New towns are an attempt to redirect growth by decentralizing population. Although usually located within 20 or 30 miles of a metropoli-

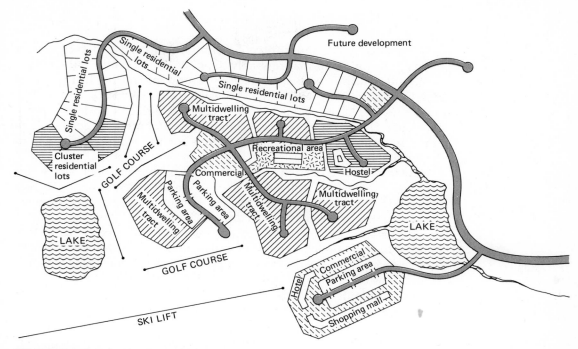

FIGURE 5-6 A planned unit development.

tan center, they are designed for independent operation. The definition of a new town is based on population and acreage: about 6,000 acres and 10–60,000 people. The town integrates industry and all types of dwelling units, so that people of all ages, economic strata, education, race, and religion have an opportunity for gainful employment.

This is not a new concept. Aristotle saw the same need in 332 B.C. The modern version of the new town was originated by an Englishman, Sir Ebenezer Howard, and the European community has led the way. Britain enacted enabling legislation as early as 1946; the Soviet Union has built more than 800 such communities, many of which have grown and prospered.

In the United States, a relatively free market has successfully integrated desirable living conditions at reasonable cost. The new towns established during the settlement of the West decreased the population of the larger metropolitan centers, delaying perception of the need for "new town" policies. A "new town" policy was not suggested until the 1920s and was not seriously considered until the early 1960s. A major problem has been financing; only corporations with substantial long-term capital can withstand the financial burden. Another problem is that Americans tend to believe land ownership is a civil right and that any regulation of land use reduces individual freedom.

Municipal and local governments resent any interference with their policies.

In the early 1970s about fifteen communities could be labeled "new towns": Reston, Virginia (probably the oldest); Columbia and Croften, Maryland; North Palm Beach and Port Charlotte, Florida; Irvine Ranch and California City, California; Forest Park, Ohio; Park Forest, Illinois; and Sun City and Lake Havasu City, Arizona. (Among these only Lake Havasu City is a free-standing community; several, such as Sun City and Port Charlotte, were built for the elderly and cater to designated constituencies.)

New towns have been most successful in preserving open space and providing recreation facilities and programs. Participation in recreation tends to be higher in new towns than in cities, perhaps because the residents are closer to the facilities. The schools, however, are criticized by parents, professional educators, and developers, and the low number of retail outlets causes dissatisfaction among shoppers. Health care services are no better or worse than those in other subdivisions. Transportation, although limited, is considered satisfactory, probably because residents live close to most facilities, but distances from work are not reduced unless the new town is a free-standing community.

What seems essential is the approval and support of local governments. Public acquisition of land reduces the tax base until the new development is operational, thus creating an unfavorable situation for governmental services. A better approach might be to restrict free-standing shopping centers, strip highway commerce, isolated offices, and schools. Much could be accomplished by requiring an analysis of environmental impact prior to the development of either new industry or new residences. A detailed description of the proposed development, an analysis of its direct and indirect effects (both positive and negative) on the environment, and an assessment of feasible alternatives might prevent the irreversible commitment of resources. If approval of the proposal depended on the assurance that education, health services, and shopping facilities would be provided, much discontent might be avoided.

SUMMARY

Human beings enjoy social interaction. A rural environment appeals to many because it offers the opportunity for a close association with nature. Others prefer the cultural and educational advantages of the city and its suburbs. Both rural and urban development require regulation if the greatest good for the majority is to be obtained.

Some of the attempts to obtain these positive benefits have included housing codes, building codes, and zoning regulations. Unfortunately, people resist such regulation, but burgeoning population and the desire for improved environment have created a need for more flexible codes and longer-range planning.

Housing Heritage
and Style

THE styles of houses reflect the needs, aspirations, and tastes of their occupants. As Mumford states,

> . . . [architecture] sums up the civilization it enshrines, and the mass of our buildings can never be better or worse than institutions that have shaped them.[1]

Housing in America began with nature, not man, in control. The settler's first shelter was a burrow in a hillside, a lean-to of poles covered with matted brush and earth, a sod dwelling, or a tent made from the hides of animals or the sails of the vessel that brought him to this continent. Early forts and homesteads reflected the European influence: thatched roofs and exposed struts with fillers of lath and plaster, brick or stone. The log cabin, which was to become the symbol of early America, was introduced in 1638 by Swedes who settled in Delaware, and variations were introduced later by German, Scottish, Irish, and Russian immigrants. Most cabins were one-room structures with timbers notched together at the corners and chinked along the joints. As the immigrants became more prosperous and built new houses, the log cabins were left for the use of newcomers, converted into storage places or slave or servant quarters, or simply left to decay.

Each succeeding advance on the frontier followed the same pattern. First a temporary primitive shelter was made from the materials at hand. This was replaced by a more permanent structure, which was, in turn, replaced by a sophisticated replica of the houses left behind in Europe or in the cities along the eastern seaboard. Periods of extensive building preceded the War of Independence and followed the Civil War, World War I, and World War II. Each period encompassed a

[1] Lewis Mumford, *Sticks and Stones* (New York: W. W. Norton & Company, Inc., 1924), p. 238

range of styles that varied according to the income and status of the intended owner. The result is an architectural heritage richer and more varied than that possessed by any other nation.

COLONIAL HOUSES

In the Colonial Period (1600–1800), houses tended to be square or rectangular, with a fireplace for warmth and cooking. Windows were few and small. Glass was an imported luxury, so glazed windows were removed and stored when not needed; oiled paper and animal skin were frequent substitutes for glass, and shutters protected the opening during inclement weather. Beds were usually attached to one of the walls or placed in an alcove. During the day, or for privacy and warmth, they were covered with curtains. Minor differences occurred in window and door design, the use of balconies and porches, and decorative motifs.

English Influence

In the original thirteen colonies, especially along the coast and in New England, the English influence prevailed. The English cottage was reflected in New England by sturdy construction, a plain clapboard exterior and small windows. The manor house became popular in the South, a rural society with no urban center of consequence, where slaves worked the land and the master dwelt in patriarchal magnificence.

Cape Cod Colonial. Typical of the cold climate of New England is the small, compact home designed to conserve as much heat as possible. Chimneys were located in the center of the building so that a fireplace could be installed in each room. Small diamond-paned windows permitted the passage of some light and air, and were often protected with shutters. Bedrooms were usually located on the first floor, but the steep, gabled roof made room for a sleeping loft if the first-floor ceiling was low enough. The Cape Cod Colonial has adapted well to modernization and remains popular today because of its economical size and shape.

Southern Colonial. The typical Southern plantation home was a Cape Cod cottage modified to suit a warmer climate. Although some were built of brick or stone, the majority were of wood, with a roof extended over a porch to shade the windows on the sunny side of the house. Since the roof shaded all the windows, regardless of the number of stories, it was supported by a series of columns. To dissipate the heat from cooking, fireplaces were placed at the outer ends. Eventually food preparation was moved to a separate building.

A. Cape Cod Cottage

B. Salt box Colonial

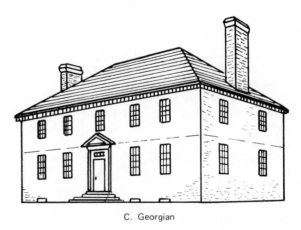

C. Georgian

FIGURE 6-1 The English influence.

As wealth increased, houses became larger and subsidiary structures needed for farm operation flanked the owner's living quarters.
An entrance hall large enough to be another room, usually featured a
graceful stairway that led to the upper floors.

Salt-Box Colonial.   The salt-box Colonial, which also evolved from the English cottage, began as a one-and-a-half- or two-story structure with a steep pitched roof. When changing family circumstances required more room, a lean-to was added to the rear, giving the dwelling an appearance similar to that of the boxes used to store salt.

Georgian.   By the beginning of the eighteenth century, there was much trade between the Colonies and the mother country. Williamsburg, Virginia, a cultural and political center, followed the English fashion in architecture. Plans and designs based on those developed during the reign of the Georges were imported. The simple exteriors had little ornamentation and conveyed an impression of spaciousness, dignity, and elegance. Most were two- or three-story rectangular brick structures topped with a slate or copper hip roof. Double-hung windows had small, square panes of glass. Chimneys were placed at each end and at the rear of the house. An interesting variation introduced in New England was the Captain's Walk: a flat-center roof enclosed with a hand rail (and sometimes equipped with a cupola) from which the wife of the fishing fleet captain might watch for his return.

Interiors were sophisticated. Walls were finished with plaster or wood paneling, and sometimes with wall paper. Ceilings were high, and separate rooms were designated for sleeping, eating, and leisure, with food preparation usually relegated to the back of the house.

Dutch Influence

Along the Hudson, houses built by Dutch settlers expressed domesticity, friendliness, cleanliness, and comfort. Usually built of stone with plank floors and tiled hearth and walls, most of these homes had a single story. The unique feature was the gambrel roof, which had a

FIGURE 6-2 The Dutch influence.

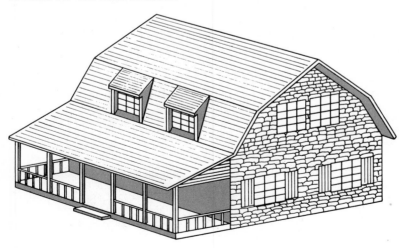

built-in step gable at the front (to aid the chimney sweep). At first this space was reserved for storage; growing families were accommodated by the addition of wings. When the thrifty Dutch recognized the saving that could be obtained by storing food elsewhere and using the space beneath the roof for living, small windows were added at floor level to light and ventilate the upper rooms. The roof was extended at the front to cover a small porch where people could sit and chat. Eventually the roof was extended on both sides and the gable smoothed to a gentle curve.

A distinctive minor feature was the door, which was divided horizontally: the upper half could be opened to admit light and air while the lower half remained closed to prevent the entrance of stray poultry or the exit of straying children. Shutters with decorative cutouts added to the *décor* and special cupboards provided efficient storage of food and utensils in the kitchen.

Spanish Influence

The Spanish left a deep impression on the architecture of the South and West, expecially Florida and the states adjoining Mexico. The typical hacienda, which adapted the adobe building material of the Indian and the designs of Spain, had three wings around a patio or open court. The roof, supported by wooded posts, extended over a corridor or veranda that faced the patio. Tiles manufactured at the local mission became the standard roofing material. Windows were barred, not glazed. Walls were plastered and whitewashed, their starkness sometimes relieved by accents of brilliant color on painted wooden doors or in the tiles of the floor.

French Influence

The plantation house of the Louisiana Territory was patterned after the French villas of the West Indies. The main floor was raised to avoid malarial dampness and the one at ground level was used for cooking and for servants quarters. The building, with a hipped roof, was symmetrical in design: outer stairs led to upper floors, and each

FIGURE 6-3 The Spanish influence.

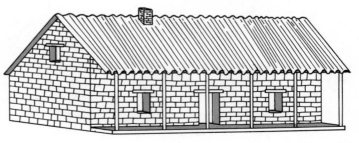

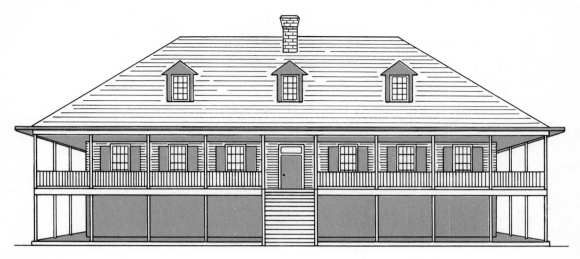

FIGURE 6-4 The French influence.

floor had a surrounding porch or *galerie* to give access to the rooms. Slender turned posts and simple railings or delicate, almost lacy, grill-work guarded the porch. Floor-length windows with louvered shutters provided ventilation and privacy.

NINETEENTH CENTURY

The nineteenth century was characterized by the growth of cities and the accumulation of vast fortunes from industry and commerce. The members of the money aristocracy brought new standards of convenience, comfort, and privacy to their houses, and these were copied by the less affluent. Many new styles were introduced, reflecting rapidly changing tastes and making the period one of architectural revivals, extremes, and extravagance.

The Classic Revivals

The revival of Greek and Roman designs lasted longest, and underwent several stages.

Federal.   The transition from Colonial to Classical was called the Federal style. More Roman than Greek, it emphasized oval and octagonal rooms, and curved exterior projections. Two- or three-story houses had columns around the entrance, and a variety of roof styles (sometimes on a single structure) to complement the unusually shaped rooms. Stairs to upper stories were moved from the center hall, and a service stair was added. In urban areas, a typical design was a tall, square, flat-roofed three-story house, windows symmetrically ar-

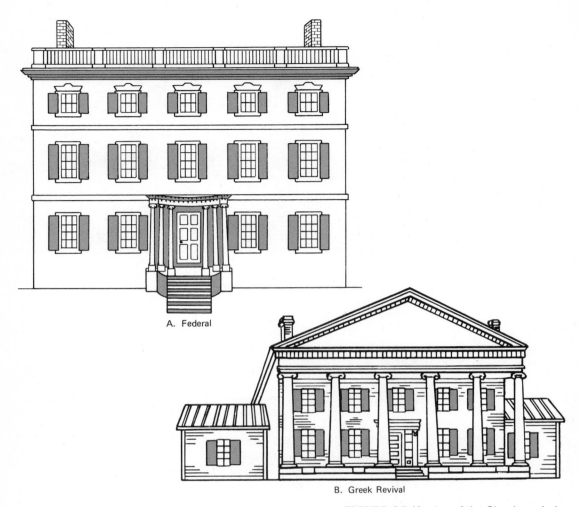

A. Federal

B. Greek Revival

FIGURE 6-5 Houses of the Classic period.

ranged on each side of the entrance to give the structure formal balance.

Greek Revival.   The Greek temple plan ended the Classic Revival. It provided a dignified framework for the formal life style of the 1840s. Used for all types of houses, the design featured flattened roofs and cornices carved with Greek motifs. Many of the earlier Georgian houses were updated by the addition of Greek columns and porticos. The style rapidly spread from the East to the Midwest and the South, where it proved particularly suitable for the climate. Southern planters required a large structure to house business, family, and guests. Halls were large, and the rooms were arranged so that doors could be opened to make several rooms into one. To facilitate large-scale entertainment, there was usually a parlor, a library, and a study on the

DORIC   IONIC CORINTHIAN

C. Details of Greek motifs

main floor. Sometimes there was a downstairs bedroom, but usually the sleeping quarters were on another floor. As Hamlin states,

> these later houses are enormous in scale, ceiling height and room size; lavish in interior trim, at times to the point of lush decadence; palatial rather than domestic. . . .[2]

Victorian Age

The Victorian Period was marked by romantic nostalgia for the past. Architectural features from various historical periods were fused together—towers, porches, balconies, bay windows, steep gables and dormers—resulting in structures with informal balance, broken lines, and irregular masses. High ceilings, tall narrow windows, and high chimneys all emphasized the vertical, in the manner of European Gothic.

[2] T. Hamlin, *Greek Revival Architecture in America* (New York: Oxford University Press, Inc., 1944), p. 208.

A. Gothic Revival

B. Romanesque

FIGURE 6-6 Houses of the Victorian Era.

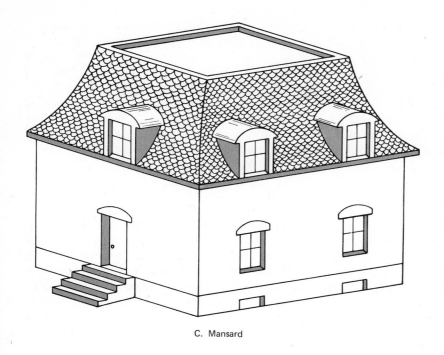

C. Mansard

This was a time of technological change. During the latter half of the century the development of central heating, plumbing, electric lighting, and elevators marked the need for new building methods. With the invention of the scroll and band saws, ornament became as important as structure. Ornate doors and windows became the fad, along with wood filigree and lacy trim. For this reason the latter half of the nineteenth century was often referred to as the Gingerbread Age.

Gothic Revival. The European Revival began around 1830, reappeared in slightly altered forms after the Civil War and again at the turn of the century. The style is identified by pointed-arch windows and steeply sloping roofs. In its early phases, houses were one color and material; later, the design became increasingly elaborate. Houses built in this style after 1880 (also referred to as Queen Anne), were picturesque, their irregular shape emphasized by a variety of surface textures, materials, colors, and window designs. Often there was a projecting upper story or turret or a cutaway corner with windows.

Romanesque. Very popular in the early 1800s, the Romanesque style was used extensively for public buildings. Frequently built of stone, these structure were large, often massive in appearance, with round or semicircular arched openings and pyramidal roofs and dominated by one or more dome-topped towers, making them an appropriate symbol of the owner's new-found wealth and status.

Mansard or French Second Empire. This style came from France, where it was popular during the Second Napoleonic Empire (1852–70). Its four-sided two-sloped roof was designed by François Mansard in the 1600s. The steeper of the two roofs was often covered with half-round slates that accented round or arched dormer windows; the second roof slope was sometimes so slight as not to be visible from the street. Other features associated with French houses were usually incorporated, including double doors of small-paned glass that opened outward onto deep porches framed with decorative ironwork.

CONTEMPORARY HOUSING DESIGNS

The end of the nineteenth century brought a reaction against the ostentatious designs of the Victorian era. This movement, led by Frank Lloyd Wright, who labeled the new style "organic," argued for honesty in architecture: form was to follow function; houses were to be designed to satisfy the physical and psychological needs of the inhabitants, and to harmonize with the environment. The result was a scattering of low, wide houses with flattened roofs extending beyond walls dotted with rather small casement windows. The Green Brothers translated this design to the "bungalow" for the middle class. The name, adapted from a Bengalese word meaning a low-roofed house, described a compact, one-story home, usually of wood, with windows set rather high so that furniture could be placed under them. A common feature was a covered front porch with pillars made of heavy brick or stone. This emphasized the low, solid, somewhat rustic character of the structure.

During the prosperous period that followed World War I, however, the well-to-do preferred the palatial elegance of houses modeled upon those of the European Renaissance. The less affluent tried to capture the charm of the picturesque European cottage. Exteriors were faithfully copied, but the interiors had to accommodate automobiles, plumbing, wiring, and central heating systems—which had not been provided for in the original design.

Economic and social changes put an end to the building of large town houses. Servants were lured to the factory, the electric light

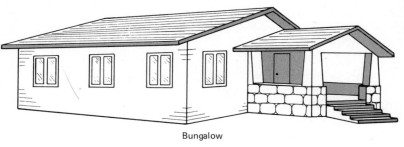

Bungalow

FIGURE 6-7 The forerunner of houses of the modern era—the Bungalow.

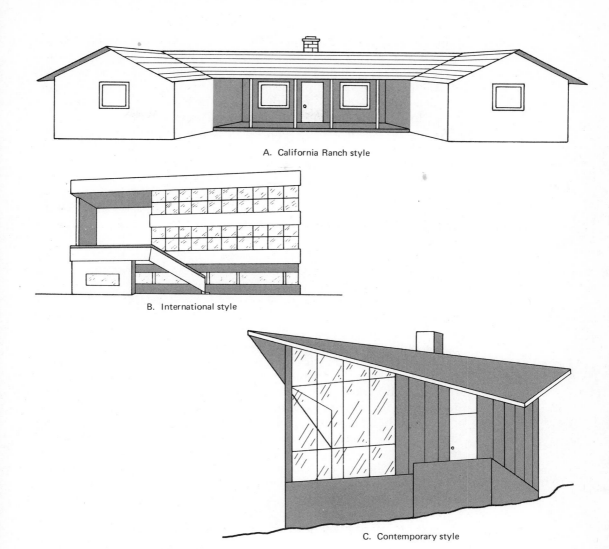

A. California Ranch style

B. International style

C. Contemporary style

FIGURE 6-8 Houses of the Modern Era.

shortened night and the telephone compressed time and distance, while the auto beckoned to the out-of-doors. Houses were now built in the suburbs where large country estates with broad lawns and winding shaded streets became the new symbols of prosperity. Commercial towers and city monuments replaced the town houses of the captains of industry.

The stock market crash of 1929 put an end to prosperity and curtailed building. Large homes were converted into multiple units, and upper stories were made accessible by the addition of outside stairways or fire excapes. Kitchens became kitchenettes; eating areas, dinettes. Styles that offered the most space for the money were preferred.

In California, the informal life style and favorable climate invited the integration of work and leisure space as well as a closer association between interiors and exteriors. This trend resulted in larger windows with outdoor views and rooms arranged around patios, making all the house as important as the facade. This style derived from trends developing in Europe, especially those of the German Bauhaus.

As World War II approached, European proponents of the International style emigrated to America, taking their designs with them. This style was based on the idea that the house was a machine for living: living space should promote health by admitting more sun and air, and economy by providing convertible, flexible space. Early designs featured flat roofs, smooth wall surfaces, and windows (especially at the corners) that were part of the wall rather than openings in it.

The post-World War II period added a new dimension to housing design. Consumer magazines featuring home and decorating sections became increasingly influential. New designs introduced in one section of the country were rapidly adoped across the land. Facilitated by advances in technology, these trends presaged the end to regionalism and the beginning of modernism.

The building boom that followed World War II brought with it a unique problem. The individual homeowner, the first to accept the modern styles, found his needs neglected by the architects, whose services were diverted to designing social housing or beautiful, dignified domiciles for leaders of commerce and industry. The construction of individual houses was left to the speculator, who built for an unknown market, and for whom any deviation from standard design represented additional expense. The new houses are horizontal rather than vertical, with little ornamentation; exposed rafters are reminiscent of the bungalow, but new materials are used; doorways are nontraditional; and a large glass window marks the principal room, with other windows of either casement or awning type. All the new houses suggest an informal life style and economical use of space.

SUMMARY

Some architectural historians believe housing styles repeat themselves every thirty years. Others feel that new forms evolve with new needs, new materials, and new techniques. There is some truth to both views.

The Colonists' urgent need for protection from the elements made sod houses, tents, and even hillside caves—as primitive as the structures of the American Indian—appropriate places to live. As settlers grew more prosperous, they built houses that were adaptations of those they had left behind. Early designs include the Cape Cod, the Salt-box, and the Georgian designs of the eastern seaboard; the Dutch gambrel roofs of New York; the French villas of the Louisiana Territory; and the Spanish haciendas of the South and West.

As life styles became more formal and more elaborate, the new wealth and stability were reflected in the Classical Revival and later in the Gothic and Renaissance Revivals.

Modernism, launched in the early 1900s by Frank Lloyd Wright as a revolt against Victorian ornateness, grew with the desire to create something uniquely American. Modernism flourished after World War II, resulting in houses designed to fit land contours and to integrate indoor and outdoor spaces.

7

Housing Types and Design

THERE are basically two types of residential structures: those which house a single family of four or five, and multifamily structures which serve several families. There are advantages and disadvantages to both.

SINGLE-FAMILY DETACHED UNITS

Land ownership has been synonomous with wealth and status. The desire to own land gave impetus to the westward movement in the United States. Land was cheap, plentiful, and available. Under these conditions, it is not surprising that the most popular form of housing in the United States became the free-standing, single-family structure surrounded by land.

A single-family living unit is defined in the U.S. Census as a detached structure designed for occupancy by one family. Its acquisition is one of the goals of the average wage-earner, who views private ownership as evidence of personal accomplishment. A survey in 1968 of 32 metropolitan areas in the United States showed 70 per cent of the respondents lived in a single-family dwelling, 85 per cent preferred to live in one, and two thirds of those living in multifamily units wanted to live in a private house. The 1970 Census reported a total of 46.8 million single-family units, 72 per cent of the national total of all housing units, an increase of approximately 6 per cent since 1960. Ninety-three per cent of those considering the purchase of a new home prefer this type of housing.[1]

[1] "Professional Builder's National Consumer Builder Survey on Housing," *Professional Builder*, January 1975, pp. 81–97.

In general, a single-family detached living unit has more flexibility, more freedom and privacy, more sunlight and air, more space for children's play, and fewer risks from off-property hazards. The single-family unit has some deficiencies. It costs more to build than do multiple-unit structures and it is less economical of land.[2] In fact, a 1974 study conducted for the U.S. Department of Housing and Urban Development found single-family dwellings to be a major cause of undesirable environmental impact, land sprawl, traffic congestion, and air and water pollution. The environmental issues and continued population growth of the 1970s may force reconsideration of the way in which land is used. Zoning codes may prevail over traditional rights of ownership. Most important, the rising cost of land, building materials, and labor may make the ownership of a single detached house a fading dream.

FIGURE 7-1 The two-story house.

[2] W. Michelson, "Most People Don't Want What Architects Want," *Transaction*, July–August 1968, pp. 37–43.

Two-Story Houses. From pre-Revolutionary days to about 1920, the two-story house dominated the landscape. Some residential neighborhoods even had restrictions on the construction of single-story buildings.

Two-story houses are economical to build (the ratio of foundation and roof to living space is lower than that of a single-story house) and to heat. They facilitate the planning of leisure, work and private zones within the total space and the inclusion of more separate activity centers. Some people believe that upper-floor sleeping areas are more private and safe.

The principal objection to the two-story house is the necessity of climbing stairs to move from one level to another. Children, the elderly, and the handicapped often find stairs difficult, if not impossible. If possible, therefore, a bedroom and bath should be located on the main floor. Besides the difficulty they may pose, stairs and halls waste space. Also, upper-floor rooms do not have access to the outside. Finally, the exterior design of two-story houses is limited as well as being difficult to enlarge and to maintain.

FIGURE 7-2 The one and a half story house.

Story-and-a-Half Houses. From the 1930s to the 1960s, the story-and-a-half house enjoyed wide popularity. Usually the roof is steep enough to provide additional living space or extra storage space. This is a relatively inexpensive way to add living space because additional foundations, roofs, or exterior walls are not required.

Second-floor rooms in such houses, however, are often small and cramped, particularly if the house is narrow and the roof steeply sloped. Attempts to expand the half-story may lead to unforeseen problems in heating, ventilation, and plumbing. Lack of insulation under the roof can make the new room difficult to heat. Lack of roughed-in plumbing can make it difficult or impossible to add sanitary facilities, and missing ducts may mean a second heating system must be added—and the furnace may be too small to heat the extra space.

One-Story Houses. One-story houses are increasingly more common, appealing to young couples with small children as well as to the elderly and the handicapped. Porches, patios, terraces, and planters help to blend indoor and outdoor living. The exterior is easy to maintain because the roof can be reached from the ground or by using a short ladder. This is especially helpful for changing screens and storm windows, for painting, for fixing the roof, or for cleaning gutters. A one-story house, however, requires a relatively larger lot: the ratio of walls, slab, basement or crawl area, foundation, and roof to total living space is high, making construction costly.

Multilevel Houses. Multilevel houses were originally adaptations to hillside lots, dwellings designed to conform to the contour of the land. They have since become popular on level lots as well: the basement raised several feet above the ground makes possible the entry between

FIGURE 7-3 The one story house.

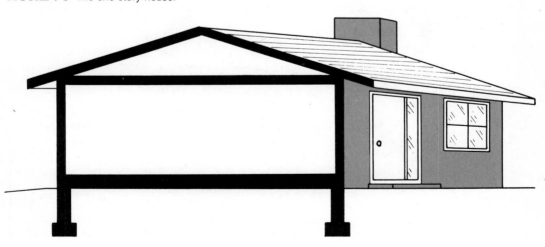

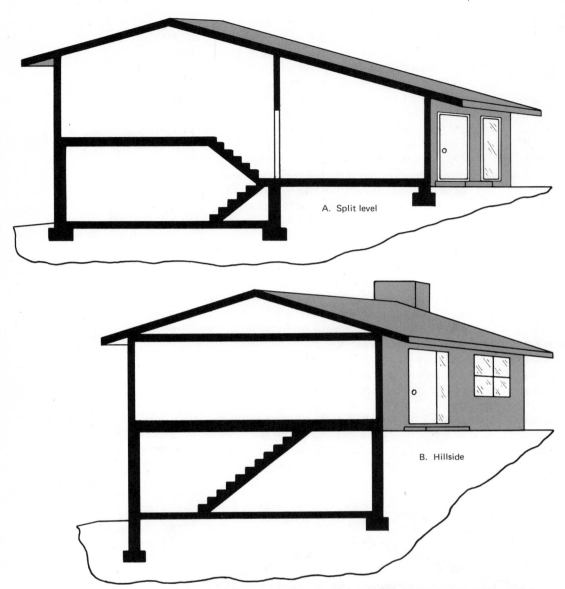

A. Split level

B. Hillside

FIGURE 7-4 The multilevel house.

floors at ground level and larger basement windows, thereby producing additional daylight and a more pleasant atmosphere for the lower level.

Multilevel designs provide more usuable and accessible space than do two-story houses of the same total area; they define and separate the various zones of the dwelling unit more effectively than do one-story houses of the same area. Because the lower level need not be finished until needed, initial costs can be relatively low. Split-level

108

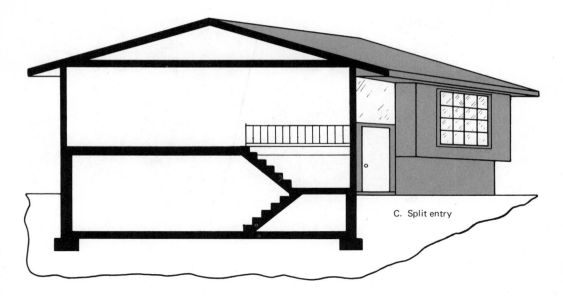

C. Split entry

houses offer the economies of multistory houses, since they require less lot space than do one-story basementless houses.

Multilevel houses, however, do have stairs, which may pose a problem to the elderly or the handicapped. Construction tends to be more complicated for the multilevel house than for either a one- or two-story house because of the interconnecting levels.

Mobile Homes.   The mobile home, which evolved from the camping trailer, is a transportable structure designed for use as a dwelling. Mobile homes dominate the under-$20,000 housing market, constituting 94 per cent of the houses in that price range and 40 per cent of all new homes built for sale. A single-section mobile home is 12–14 feet wide and 30–70 feet long. Two or three single sections can be joined and other features expanded or telescoped.

Mobile homes are not very mobile. They are shipped or towed from the factory to a sales lot; from there they are sent either to a mobile-home park or to an individual lot. If the mobile home is to be used for year-round living, the wheels and axles can be removed and stored or sold. Skirting, steps, handrails, and landscaping help make the mobile home more attractive. Other features of the site-built house—pitched roof, horizontal siding, gutters and awnings, carports, patios and storage sheds—can also be added.

Where zoning regulations permit, mobile homes, usually a double wide, can be placed on permanent foundations on individual lots. Thus they offer an economically sound solution for residents in rural areas, where other alternatives may be limited. (In fact, 10 per cent of the buyers of mobile homes in 1970 were farmers.) More frequently, however, the buyer rents space (with gas, water, and sewer connections) in a housing-oriented or service-oriented mobile home park. Housing-

FIGURE 7-5 The Mobile home, Courtesy Bendix Home Systems, Inc.

oriented parks emphasize residential atmosphere; service parks (found primarily in warmer climates and attracting retired persons) supply recreation facilities and organized social activities, with rental fees often including charges for these activities as well.

Mobile-home parks offer a way to structure and maintain neighborhoods. The park owner can select tenants and control the behavior of those accepted. Such selection and control tend to create a homogeneous group the members of which choose a level of social interaction, mutual aid, and social control. Conversely, an invasion of personal freedom can occur when some mobile-home park operators designate rules of behavior to which residents must adhere. Nevertheless, surveys show that 60–75 per cent of the mobile-home owners are satisfied with this type of housing because it is economical and because they prefer to own rather than to rent.

A major advantage of the mobile home is economy: purchase price and initial costs are substantially lower than similar costs for other dwellings. The average mobile unit sells for less than $20,000 (with 10 per cent down) compared to $35,000 (with 25 per cent down) for the conventional house. Financing is easier to arrange, and furniture, appliances and draperies are often included in the purchase price.

Little upkeep is required for the mobile home itself. Mobile homes are usually less expensive to heat and to maintain than are many site-built houses. But their value, like that of new cars, depreciates rapidly: they lose about half their original value in five years. Also, there is a potential danger from fire because of the density of furniture, the flammable paneling of "kindling thickness" on interior walls, and more fuel per square foot of space. The fire hazard associated with mobile homes makes insurance costly. Another financial disadvantage posed by mobile homes is the higher interest rate for loans (12 per cent for mobile homes, 8.5 per cent for conventional loans), and since most loans for mobile homes are financed as installment contracts, there is less protection against foreclosure. In addition to the financing costs there is the monthly rental fee, and the cost of skirting and foundations. Some of these disadvantages will be ameliorated if the trend toward improved building/zoning codes and state statute and financing continues.

MULTIFAMILY UNITS

During the latter half of the twentieth century, population growth increased costs of construction and of land, and changes in value converged to cause a need for higher-density housing (structures with less than ten units are labeled according to the number of units, whereas those with ten or more units are usually referred to as apartment houses). High-rise structures provide the individual with no territory on the ground, and their appearance violates the traditional image of what a home should be. Still, certain segments of the population—singles, the newly married, the elderly, and the urban rich— prefer this type of housing (the urban rich, because they have houses elsewhere; the others, because they have other priorities).

A large increase in the number of multifamily living units, mostly in the metropolitan areas, was reported in the 1970 U.S. Census. Nearly 28 per cent of all housing in 1970 (as compared to 24 per cent in 1960) was comprised of multifamily structures (see Table 7-1).

TABLE 7-1   Increase in Single-Family and Multifamily Unit Buildings 1960–70

Structure	Region	1970	1960 (Millions)	Increase
Single	NE	8.8	8.7	.1
	NC	13.4	12.9	.5
	S	16.2	14.7	1.5
	W	8.3	7.4	.9
Multifamily	NE	7.2	6.0	1.2
	NC	4.7	3.6	1.1
	S	3.8	2.3	1.5
	W	3.1	1.9	1.2

Adapted from *We Americans, Our Homes*. U.S. Department Commerce Social and Economic Statistics Administration, Bureau of the Census. (Washington, D.C.: U.S. Government Printing Office) October 1972.

Many people erroneously associate multifamily housing with public housing for low-income families. Although evidence suggests that the economically deprived gravitate to such structures because rent and maintenance costs tend to be low, many multifamily dwellings are designed for high- and middle-income groups.

Some fear that multifamily housing forces people to conform to similar living patterns. Remodeling of interiors by tenants is seldom approved and little individuality is permitted on the exterior. Storage space within the individual unit is often insufficient. Small bedrooms limit the inclusion of furniture to relieve the storage problem. Storage areas—if they are available—tend to be inconveniently located, and parking space is often limited or lacking, making it difficult for both tenant and guests.

One of the greatest disadvantages of the apartment complex is the lack of privacy. Units built before 1930 had little or no sound control. New materials and new technqies have improved sound control in post-World War II units. Still needed is an innovative design that affords privacy while accommodating large numbers of people.

The Duplex.　A duplex, or double, is a single structure initially designed and built to contain two living units. The duplex developed in response to the needs of the low-income family that could not afford the luxury of a single detached house. It may be rented or owned through a cooperative or condominium arrangement. A buyer may choose to live in one unit and rent the other, thus reducing housing costs.

Some styles are characteristic of various sections of the country. Some doubles consist of one living unit on each of two levels. Units so arranged often lack individual entrances, and a poorly designed stairway can magnify sounds. Outside space is often ill defined: since the land surrounds the downstairs apartment, its use by the upstairs occupant may be limited or impossible.

In another duplex design, the two units are set side by side, separated by a party wall. This arrangement is more conducive to privacy, since it usually involves separate entrances. Each unit has sun and air on three sides, and outside space is available to both.

Town Houses.　Town houses are attached single-family dwellings: a row of three or more single units separated by party walls. Usually, each has a private entrance and a small yard at front and rear. During the 1800s New York town houses faced with chocolate-colored sandstone (brownstone) were very fashionable, and they are still popular because of their desirable location. In the West, especially in the San Francisco area, each unit had an individualized design such as a bay window or highly decorated exterior.

Early town houses eventually became identified with low-cost housing, so that the term *row house* acquired a negative connotation. But town houses now are the fastest growing segment of the housing market, accounting for 40 per cent of the expected market in 1975. Rarely found in town despite their name, they are typically located in the suburbs and beyond. They are especially popular for resort developments or as communities for the elderly. Landscaping, a park, a lake, or a strip of woods help to prevent a hemmed-in feeling. Privacy can be increased by enclosing courtyards and keeping recreation areas far from the sleeping centers of any individual unit.

FIGURE 7-6 Townhouses at Big Sky of Montana, Courtesy Gallatin Canyon Study, Montana State University, National Science Foundation.

Town houses provide an opportunity to build equity and require relatively little maintenance. Town houses are often offered in condominium purchase, but they may also be rented, leased, or purchased on a fee simple or cooperative arrangement. Their purchase price tends to be comparatively low (owing to more concentrated land use, shorter utility lines, and party walls), but this may be offset by the inclusion of parks, playgrounds, or clubhouses. Privacy may be sacrificed in poorly planned units, or in units with a high concentration of pets and children.

Apartment Complexes

No one description suffices for the many types of apartment complexes. A complex may be part of predominantly single-family structures or it may be a community in its own right. An apartment can be advantageous for the resident who no longer wants to worry about repairing the roof or maintaining the exterior; a complex can be a lucrative investment for the builder who wishes to economize on labor and materials.

The living unit may vary from a one-room efficiency to as many rooms as the average single-family detached dwelling. Most apartments are located on a single level although there are some two-level designs. An efficiency apartment has one room for all living activities

A. A high rise luxury tower, Courtesy of Portland Cement Association.

B. Student housing, Courtesy of Montana State University.

FIGURE 7-7 Apartment buildings.

except personal hygiene. Sometimes a meal-preparation area is hidden behind folding doors or separated from the living area by cupboards. Laundry and storage facilities are generally located in a central area for all the building occupants. Other common facilities that may be included as part of the complex are playgrounds, sunrooms, roof gardens, swimming pools, recreation rooms, shops of various kinds, restaurants, and garages.

The number of floors determines whether or not elevator service is required. Three floors are the usual maximum for walk-ups in the United States but up to five flights are common in the older cities along the eastern seaboard. The older the building the less likely is elevator service to be available. Buildings of more than five floors must supply elevator service as well as exit stairs. Tower buildings permit high occupation densities. Marina City, overlooking the Chicago river near downtown Chicago, is a good example. In addition to 896 apartments, the 60-floor complex includes a recreational center, a health spa, shops, a restaurant, a marina, and a theater. "Garden" apartments, like town houses, coordinate a natural setting with the living unit, emphasizing grass, trees, flowers, and playgrounds. The penthouse, like the house at the top of the hill, implies status, privacy, and quiet.

Large apartment buildings tend to offer little opportunity for outdoor leisure and recreation. A balcony permits an adult to sit in the sun, but is a dangerous location for children's play. Interior corridors or courtyards may serve as play areas but lack the personal quality of a backyard. Apartment dwellers indicate that a greater degree of supervision for children's play is necessary when the neighborhood street traffic is heavy.

Laundry is another problem for the apartment dweller. Modern washers and driers do not demand constant tending and the efficient launderer can accomplish other tasks while the clothes are being washed. In many multifamily structures, laundry equipment is not permitted in the individual units. A central laundry area makes coordination of activities difficult and its atmosphere is not conducive to tasks requiring concentration.

HOUSING DESIGN

Architectural design influences the lives of the inhabitants as well as the market value of the building and of the neighborhood. It is important to recognize and evaluate both the aesthetic and the functional effects of a house.

Design is often confused with taste, or with fashion. Actually, "good design" is something more permanent and fundamental.

Concepts of Design

Point is the smallest concept of building design. Theoretically, it has no size or shape and is represented on a buiding by a doorknob or small decoration.

Line is often referred to as a path of motion recorded by graphic means, guiding the eye to help establish planes, forms, and spaces in the mind. Its direction gives meaning—horizontals are restful, quiet, earthbound; verticals suggest effort, alertness, dignity; diagonals denote excitement; zig-zags, disaster; curves either happiness or sorrow depending on whether they rise or fall.

The planes of the house are those parts that have length and width, such as floors, walls, and ceilings. The addition of a third dimension gives depth to planes defining forms and space.

The most common of man-made forms is the rectangle. Long thin rectangles placed horizontally evoke the same feelings as horizontal lines; placed vertically, they suggest height. Most houses are composed of one or more rectangles topped with one or more triangles.

FIGURE 7-8 Common forms used in housing design.

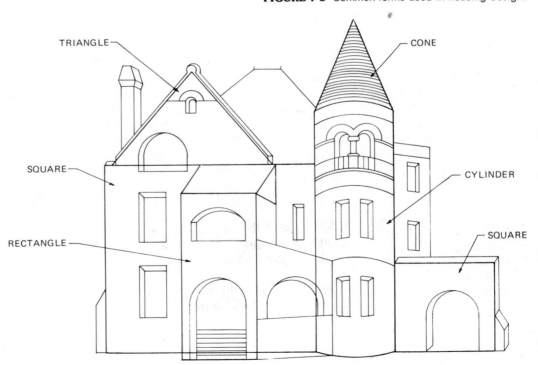

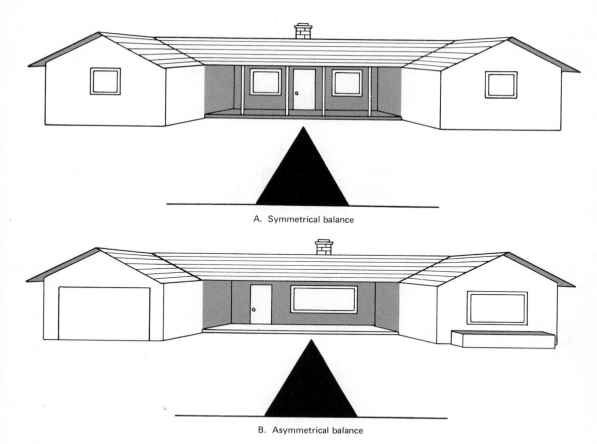

A. Symmetrical balance

B. Asymmetrical balance

FIGURE 7-9 Balance in housing design.

Aspects of Design

Symmetry or balance gives the structure equilibrium, repose, stateliness. Asymmetry, more difficult to achieve pleasingly, suggests casualness and informality.

Continuity holds together the elements in the design while helping to avoid monotony. One method of achieving continuity is by repeating a decorative motif or structural element such as a window to establish a rhythm the eye will follow. Another is to gradate the elements in a series.

Emphasis calls attention to the design, and is achieved through size, intensity, or contrast.

Proportion is concerned with the relationship of one part of the building to another—the ratio of width to height, or the ratio of a part of the building to the entire structure. The classic Greek proportion approximates a ratio of 5:8 when comparing height to width of the building or feature and is considered most pleasing. In contrast, the use of a 1 : 1 ratio is monotonous and should be kept to a minimum.

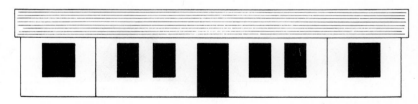

FIGURE 7-10 Rhythm created by architectural elements in the housing design.

Scale is that aspect of proportion that relates the size or apparent size of the house to the person. Each residence establishes its own relationship through the use of details. The height of the various levels can be ascertained by window placement and then can be easily compared to the human size. When the house appears very large, it projects social importance, regimentation, or authority because it minimizes the individual's stature. People are more comfortable when length, coziness, intimacy, and informality are communicated.

Texture is primarily a characteristic of surface. It can be simulated through the process of light reflection and absorption.

Color is strongly suggestive. Bright colors are associated with ad-

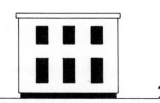

FIGURE 7-11 Housing facades establish scale by architectural detail.

venture, passion, violence, or arrogance while muted tones suggest subtlety, refinement, and peace. Earth-toned exteriors help to fit the building into its natural surroundings.

Light, filtered through tree leaves and branches or through an architectural device such as a shutter, creates illusions and fanciful effects. Shadows created by wide overhanging roofs or cantilevers suggest coolness, while intense direct rays playing over the house suggest heat.

SUMMARY

Housing type and design complement one another. Housing type is determined by land or occupancy densities and correlates with a family's financial ability. Design, an artistic expression, communicates the building's function.

Types of living units range from a single-detached house for an individual family to a multifamily structure for hundreds. The single-family unit is most popular. Of its many variations, the mobile home is most economical, and the multilevel house fits best with contour of the land. Town houses increase density but retain some semblance of the single-family dwelling, while apartment complexes are viewed as being most satisfactory in metropolitan areas.

The vocabulary of design aids in understanding function. The elements of design are point, line, plane, form, and space. Color, texture, line, balance, continuity, emphasis, and proportion are the main aspects of design that can make a structure more or less appealing.

PART THREE

the influence of the micro-environment: the interior

We require from buildings, as from men, two kinds of goodness: first, the doing their practical duty well: then that they be graceful and pleasing in doing it. . . .

John Ruskin
The Stones of Venice

The Space for Living

THE interior environment of buildings is influenced by law, by the occupant, and (to some extent) by the builder. Building codes are concerned with health and safety; the occupant, with efficiency and beauty; the builder, with a profitable return for his investment. When compromises are necessary, they usually involve efficiency, attractiveness, or cost.

Very few individuals can afford to live in custom-built houses. Most are limited to merchant-built tract houses, mass-produced manufactured houses, or government-regulated projects. Each type of housing is designed for people within specific economic categories or with certain types of needs.

Most individual living units are designed to adhere to legal standards for space and occupancy: the number of people expected to dwell in a given area, and the provision of minimum conditions of safety and sanitation. Specifications formulated by government agencies or health associations emphasize safe, palatable water, sanitary storage and efficient removal of trash, disposal of sewage, and adequate heat, hot water, and light. Space is often determined by a total number of square feet per occupant (see Table 8-1). The greater the expected number of occupants in a unit, the more space is likely to be added in areas for personal activities or leisure; work areas tend to remain relatively stable in size because normally the number of workers in a household remains constant.

Merchant-built housing is designed to meet consumer preferences. If the builder hopes to obtain financial help through a government-insured loan, the living units must conform to the minimum property standards of the U.S. Department of Housing and Urban Development; these stipulate a safe and healthful environment, attractive and adequate facilities, ease of circulation and housekeeping, privacy, and

TABLE 8-1   Space Requirements for Public Housing

Persons	Minimum Space/ Living Unit (Sq. Ft.)	Space/Person (Sq. Ft.)
1	400	400
2	800	400
3	1,000	333
4	1,200	300
5	1,450	290
6	1,550	258

Adapted from C. E. A. Winslow, *Provisions for Housing Codes in Various American Cities*, Housing and Home Financing Agency, Urban Renewal Bulletin, No. 3. (Washington, D.C.: U.S. Government Printing Office), p. 125.

economy of maintenance, economical use of space, accessory services, and sanitation facilities. These specifications (incorporated in many local building laws), however, do not guarantee a good floor plan: rooms may be poorly located or the wrong size or shape for the intended purpose, or they may require inefficient arrangement of furniture and fail to provide sufficient storage space.

CONSUMER PREFERENCES

What constitutes the perfect living environment is influenced by many variables—the roles and values of the occupants, their ages and length of residence, the value of the house, and the general economy, to name a few. A major source of discontent stems from the space within the dwelling. It is usually deemed too little (occasionally, too much), and poorly designed or lacking in provision for storage.

Space

Government agencies and consumers place great emphasis on the floor plan of the living unit; yet consumer dissatisfaction centers on this very feature. People are conditioned to think of interior environment in terms of the number and size of rooms. This attitude goes back about two hundred years, when space was designated according to the type of furniture placed in a room: or the main activities taking place in it (e.g., bedroom, living room).

Actually, there are three major types of interior space: space for personal activities, space for the household work, and space for leisure or recreation. Because each person has similar needs, the amount of space should increase with the number of people to be housed. An ideal measure of total space would take into account the total floor area, the number of rooms, the number of sleeping areas, the number

TABLE 8-2   Per Cent of Crowded Homes in the U.S.

Region	1960	1970	Difference
Northeast	8.1	6.5	−1.6
North Central	10.1	7.3	−2.8
South	16.2	10.3	−5.9
West	11.3	8.4	−2.9

Adapted from *We Americans: Our Homes*, U.S. Department of Commerce, Social and Economic Statistics Administration, Bureau of the Census (Washington, D.C.: USGPO), October 1972.

of occupants as well as their ages, sex, and relationship, the way in which leisure time is spent. In reality, measure is limited to total floor space computed in number of square feet. This measure does not mean that all the major types of space are provided or that even minimum conditions of privacy are met.

The U.S. Census indicates that the number of uncrowded homes had increased from 46.9 million in 1960 to 58.2 million in 1970 (see Table 8-2). The greatest increase was in the South. The data suggest that the chief obstacle to achieving adequate living space is not the supply of housing, but the distribution of space.

Families as Reimer notes, satisfy needs in order of priority:

> Size and number of rooms may not be high on the scale of preference as long as the family does not have a bathtub. Once tolerable occupancy standards have been achieved, the housewife will begin to consider the adequacy of storage facilities. . . . Needs appear, are satisfied and fade out, only to make place for new needs.[1]

Once the need for adequate space is met, the need for larger rooms arises. What appears to be a statistically adequate number of rooms can actually be overcrowded, because the rooms may not be large enough.

Shifts in population and in values may be responsible for changes in the size of house desired. The general population increased from 1950 to 1970, while the average household size decreased, yet the overwhelming preference for six-room houses in the early 1950s, was replaced by a preference for nine-room houses in 1970. The change may stem from the growing belief that no more than two persons may share a bedroom—and only if they are married, are children of the same sex (or of opposite sexes under six years of age), or are an adult and a very young child. In the 1970 U.S. Census, 48 per cent of the dwellings had more than three bedrooms (see Table 8-3).

The living and working areas of the dwelling may be more important than bedrooms for the consumer. Reimer's 1945 study suggested that households with densities of more than one person per room

[1] S. Reimer, "Architecture for Family Living," *Journal of Social Issues,* January–February 1951, p. 148.

	Bathrooms					Bedrooms
	More Than 1	1½	2	2½	3	More Than 3
United States	27.3	11.4	11.2	2.6	1.9	48.0
Region						
NE	25.3	12.6	7.4	3.3	1.9	49.9
NC	25.4	14.1	7.6	2.4	1.2	50.3
S	26.5	8.8	13.3	2.2	2.1	47.0
W	17.6	10.1	2.2	2.6	2.5	43.3
Population						
Rural	20.9					54.4
Farm	18.8					66.9
Nonfarm	21.4					51.7
Urban	29.5					45.7
In SMSA	30.4					46.9
CC	23.3					37.9
NCC	37.3					55.5
Outside SMSA	20.6					50.2

Adapted from the U.S. Bureau of the Census. Census of Housing 1970, Vol. 1, *Housing Characteristics for States, Cities and Counties*, Part I. U.S. Summary. Washington, D.C.: U.S. Government Printing Office.

rated as the most unsatisfactory aspects of their homes the space allotted for leisure, for cooking, and for eating (in that order).[2] A 1970 study showed that the areas for sleeping, television viewing, personal care, and eating were those used most frequently by most respondents.[3]

Arrangement

There is little argument over the fact that certain activities should occur in a specified area—cooking should take place in the kitchen, sleeping in the bedroom—but one may dine at a kitchen breakfast bar or at a table in a formal dining room. In the 1930s only low-income families used space allotted to eating for other activities. By 1959 kitchen-dining rooms were reported as acceptable[4] and in 1962 nine out of ten meals were reported to be eaten in the kitchen.[5] Even when a separate dining room was available, approximately 64 per cent of the

[2] S. Reimer, "Maladjustments to the Family Home," *American Sociological Review*, October 1945, pp. 646–48.
[3] P. S. Kimura, Family Activity Patterns as a Basis for House Design. Master's Thesis, Purdue University, Purdue, Ind., 1970, pp. 32–34.
[4] R. A. Linke, "Development of Housing and Family Needs," *Forecast for Home Economists*, October 1959, p. 34.
[5] A. E. Murdock, *Satisfaction of New Homemakers with the Livability of Their Homes.* Master's Thesis, University of Mississippi, Oxford, Miss., 1962, pp. 24–25.

meals were eaten in the kitchen. More dissatisfaction seems to occur if only one dining area is provided, especially when the space provided is a "dining L." Most satisfaction seemed to accrue from the provision of two dining areas—one in the kitchen, and another where formal meals could be served for the family and its guests.

Highly rated by families with children are those kitchens that have a window overlooking an outdoor play area and a view of other rooms in the house. If a family member prepares the meals, an arrangement that does not isolate him or her from the rest of the family is also deemed desirable, even though that arrangement allows kitchen noises and odors to permeate the house.

Most homemakers seem to prefer a separate laundry.[6] For economy's sake, laundry facilities have usually been located in the basement, but the best arrangement seems to be one on ground level.

Plumbing contributes to good health in that it supplies hot and cold water to operate flush toilets and bathtubs or showers and facilitates the preparation of food. In 1970, seven per cent of all living units in the United States still lacked basic plumbing (see Table 8-4), whereas 27.3 per cent had more than one bath (see Table 8-3). (If only one bathroom is available it should be centrally located; minimum property standards require that the main bath be near the sleeping area.) Beyer reported that two thirds of the people surveyed disliked having others around while they were dressing.[7] Women, especially, do not like to share bathroom facilities, which initiates a desire for a second facility.

TABLE 8-4   Per Cent of Homes in the United States Lacking Basic Plumbing

Region	1960	1970	Difference
Northeast	10	4	− 6
North Central	16	6	−10
South	28	12	−16
West	8	3	− 5

Adapted from *We Americans: Our Homes*, U.S. Department of Commerce Social and Economic Statistics Administration, Bureau of the Census (Washington, D.C.: USGPO, October 1972).

Dissatisfaction with leisure areas arises when people do not have privacy. This seems more important to renters than to owners. For television viewing, a quiet area, free from interruption, has a high priority. Leisure rooms that are passageways are objectionable, particularly when they are located between the entry and the kitchen. Im-

[6] Kimura, *Family Activity Patterns as a Basis for House Design*, op. cit., p. 65.
[7] G. H. Beyer et al., *Houses Are for People: A Study of Home Buyer Motivations* (Ithaca, N.Y.: Cornell University Housing Research Center, 1955), p. 25.

properly located windows also cause concern because passersby can see in, or the occupants are unable to take proper advantage of the sun, or are obliged to place furniture awkwardly.

THE HUMAN FACTOR

The human body establishes the base for specifications of the living environment. The first step in planning space is to understand the room the body needs to perform various activities (see Figure 8-2). Ideally, personally designed environments would be matched to each individual's size, but the human being is adaptable, so the design of interior space is usually based upon average measurements.

Modifications

Some people—the handicapped, the elderly, the very young—cannot adjust to standard specifications. The physical environment must be designed so as to promote security, comfort, and convenience for them as well.

FIGURE 8-1 The Measure of Man.

$$a : \Sigma = \Sigma : (a - \Sigma)$$

$$\Sigma = \frac{\sqrt{5} - 1}{2} a$$

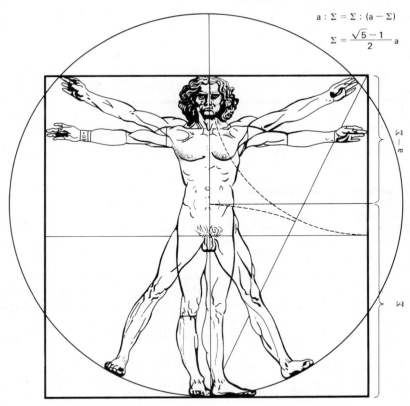

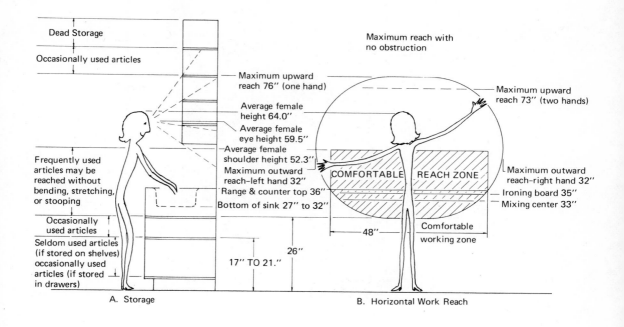

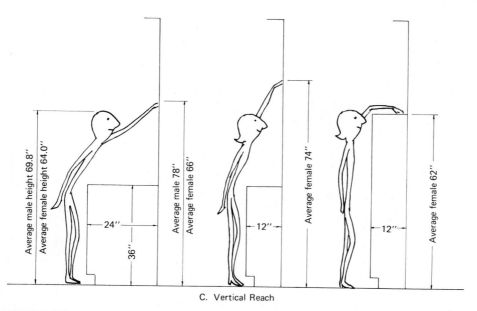

FIGURE 8-2 Measurements of the human body important in planning space.

The Handicapped. Major modifications are necessary to provide comfortable housing for the chronically disabled—those who are blind or deaf or who require the assistance of a cane, crutches, or a wheelchair. The standard wheelchair, for example, reduces the user's height

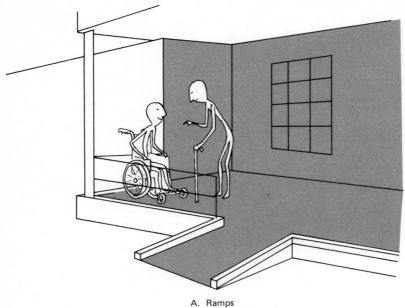

A. Ramps

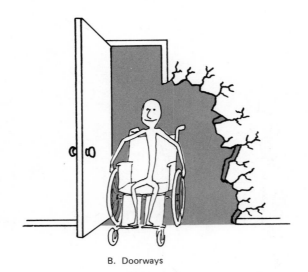

B. Doorways

FIGURE 8-3 Modifications required for wheelchair users.

and doubles the width of space required so that a 36-inch path and a 54-inch turn space are essential; an individual on crutches requires only about a 32-inch path. Halls and doorways should be widened correspondingly. The reach of the average adult from a wheelchair is 13 inches less vertically and 2 inches less horizontally than that of the normal adult; this limitation would affect the placement of electrical outlets, water faucets, medicine cabinets, mirrors and/or counter tops, and storage areas. Stairs pose great difficulty for the handicapped.

Ramps, a moving chair, or an elevator should be installed. Other helpful modifications for the handicapped include single-level living space, nonskid floors, toilet rooms with extra space and grab bars, elimination of doorsills, entries with sliding doors of a pressure control to open them outward, an intercom between the personal living space of the handicapped and other areas of the living unit, an oversized garage or carport to accommodate the passage of a wheelchair.

The Elderly.   Most modifications intended for the elderly are meant to compensate for any diminished physical ability. Often the older person cannot stoop readily or maintain his balance easily, and has less strength than a younger person. In living units designed for the elderly, the most important activity area should be centrally located and related activity areas placed together; storage areas for all items needed for the activity should be within easy reach and surfaces should be large enough to accommodate all equipment needed, and within easy reach. Visual effort, especially for those who must wear bifocal lenses, can be reduced by storing items where they can be seen easily. Because bending may be difficult for the elderly, undercounter storage is not desirable, and minimum property standards forbid the installation of undercounter refrigerators, winding stairs, or stairs with open risers. Minimum property standards stipulate too that bathtubs and showers be provided with seats, that there be ready access to the main entrance, and that interior doors and halls be wider than average.

Children.   Adjustments for children in the living environment are temporary because as the children grow they become able to cope with standardized designs. Hooks, rods, and shelves for storage of clothing should be lowered to their height, and attachments can modify the size of sinks and lavatories. Work surfaces may be protected by a washable, wear-resistant finish so that maintenance is as effortless as

FIGURE 8-4 Energy expenditure required to store items at various levels.

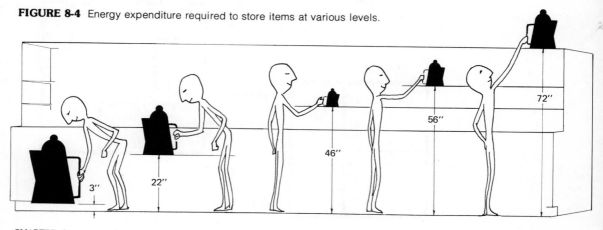

possible. As children grow older, closet fittings can be raised and special attachments discarded until gradually all signs of the childhood period disappear from the surroundings.

SPATIAL DIVISION

The floor plan of the typical contemporary house in the United States can be very individualistic. There are two general types of floor plans related to the degree of privacy desired: the open plan and the closed plan.

Closed Floor Plans

A closed floor plan designates space as rooms for specific use, enclosing each with walls and doors that restrict movement to other areas. This arrangement makes possible individual room heating and greater

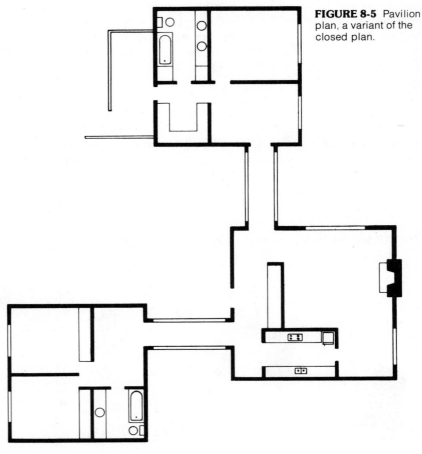

FIGURE 8-5 Pavilion plan, a variant of the closed plan.

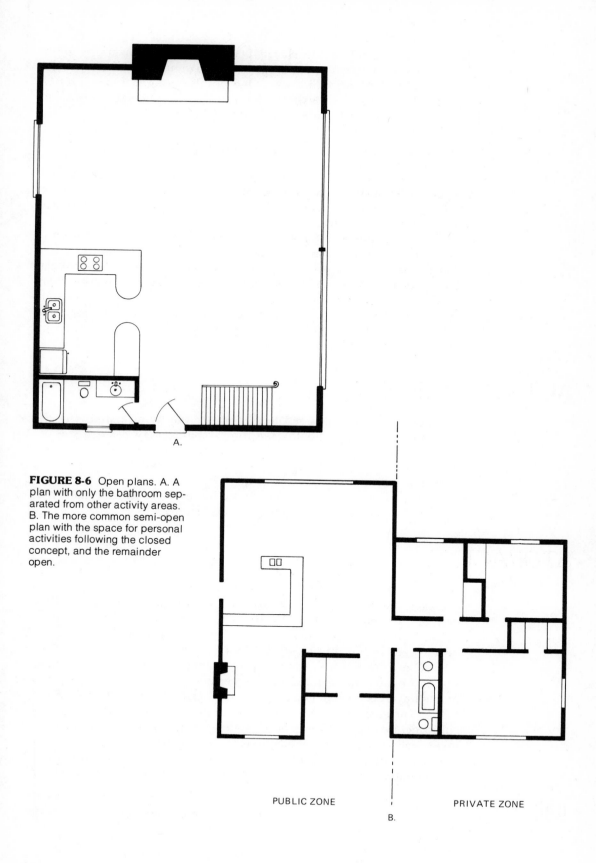

FIGURE 8-6 Open plans. A. A plan with only the bathroom separated from other activity areas. B. The more common semi-open plan with the space for personal activities following the closed concept, and the remainder open.

A.

PUBLIC ZONE   PRIVATE ZONE

B.

privacy. A variant of the closed plan is the pavilion arrangement, which provides separate buildings linked together by galleries, roofed passageways, or enclosed decks. One building might house a retreat for adults, another be designed for younger members of the family, and yet another for laundry, workshop, or studio.

Open Floor Plans

Open floor plans seem to fit the informal servantless life style typical of today. Because one space flows into another, the view of other activity areas is unimpeded and the space for various activities appears larger. Privacy, however, may be impaired.

More acceptable to the majority of consumers is the combination of an open plan in the leisure and work areas of the house, and a closed plan for areas where privacy is desirable. This provides free circulation in those areas set aside for entertaining, eating, and work, where screens, storage partitions, or sliding panels may be used to separate functions. The private areas can be provided with balconies, glass walls that open onto a patio or garden, or clerestory windows through which the sky and trees may be seen.

ACTIVITY AREAS

Interiors should be designed to conform to the living patterns of the occupants. A design should take into account every facet of the occupants' life style and activities, their relationships, and their requirements for space and storage. This kind of listing will make it possible to evaluate each area.

Design specifications for various activities have been established and will be discussed in the chapters that follow.

STORAGE

While the possessions of the average family increase, storage spaces decrease: the cavernous attic, the roomy basement, the convenient barn are no longer available for items too important to discard but no longer in daily use. As housing grows more expensive, less space can be allowed for furniture designed for storage.

Some architects believe that approximately 25 per cent of the house should or must be devoted to storage, and minimum space requirements have been established by the U.S. Department of Housing and Urban Development. One study suggested that a minimum of 284 cubic feet be reserved for general storage, hobby and recreation equipment, collections, unfinished projects, out-of-season possessions and outdoor equipment. The U.S. Department of Housing and Urban Development designates 200 cubic feet for this purpose, with a suggested reduction of 50 cubic feet if exterior maintenance is done by someone other than the occupants.

Storage requirements are greatest during the earliest and latest stages of the family cycle. The greatest need at present is storage space for articles used by children out of doors, and for trailers and camping equipment. Items should be stored close to the area in which they will be used. One study revealed, for example, that lawnmowers were stored in as many as six different locations, none of which was especially expedient. Storage space may be open (in order to display special items) or closed (in order to conceal clutter); the storage unit may be temporary and free-standing, screwed to the wall, or permanently built-in. (Closets, especially walk-in closets, may have one third less storage potential than a storage wall of equal square footage.) The current preference is for freestanding storage components that can be taken along in case of a move.

SUMMARY

The interior environment, the space for daily activities, is influenced by the consumer, the builder, and the government. The amount and allocation of space should be determined by a systems analysis. Proper use of space increases efficiency, economy, and comfort.

Space for Personal Activities

THE personal activities of the individual help to establish a sense of identity and personal worth, and usually require a degree of privacy. The facilities provided depend largely upon the size of the family, its socioeconomic status and values, and its attitudes toward sex and human physiological functions. As society has become more sophisticated, the manner in which the individual's needs are satisfied has become increasingly complex.

SLEEPING AND RESTING

Sleep and rest are essential to well-being. A feeling of security induces the relaxation that, in turn, induces sleep. Too large a sleep area may cause insecurity, while too small an area may initiate fear. As Blum and Candee note

> Discomfort in small spaces may be related to mild forms of claustrophobia. It is possible that bedroom design must allow for a somewhat larger space than is actually necessary in order to overcome this fear.[1]

People usually rest and sleep in a prone position. The average caveman improvised a bed with leaves or straw whereas the more fortunate might have had a sleeping mat of furs or hide. In early civilizations, sleeping couches (sleeping mats on legs) varied from simple wood frames with straw ticking to elaborate canopied frames of choice wood, precious metal, or ivory supplied with down-filled mattresses.

The size of the bed is important in space planning. Beds may range from cradle to king-sized (see Table 9-1). Reclining chairs and couches

[1] M. Blum and B. Candee, *Family Behavior, Attitudes, and Possession* (New York: John B. Pierce Foundation, 1944), p. 50.

TABLE 9-1   Standard Mattress Sizes

Type	Size (Inches)
Cradle	18×36
Bassinet	20×38
Crib	27×40 to 32×65 average: 30×54
Youth	36×68
Single/Studio	30×75
Twin	39×75
Twin Long	39×80
Twin/Bunk	39×75
¾	48×75
Double/Full	54×75
Queen	60×80
King	75×80

Adapted from *Bedroom Planning,* Small Homes Circular #C5.6, Univ. Ill. Bull. Vol. 71, No. 144, Univ. Ill. Office of Publication, Urbana, Ill., July 1974.

Mattress sizes provided by *Montgomery Ward Catalogue,* Winter 1975, pp. 559, 562, 1139, and 1141.

also are attractive resting places and require less space than the average bed, but it is important to provide sufficient space both in front and behind the chair or couch.

Too small a space requires more energy for making the bed or clean-

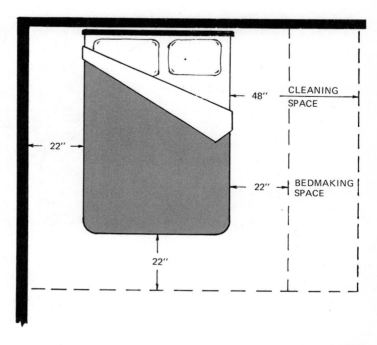

FIGURE 9-1 Space required for making and cleaning under the bed.

ing under it. If during either process the bed must be moved, even more energy is required. The best location for a bed is one that provides access to both sides and to the foot.

Physical comfort in the sleeping area can be increased by low-intensity lighting and fresh air. Because natural air and light are so important, the U.S. Department of Housing and Urban Development requires that window size be equal to at least 10 per cent (with the ventible portion equal to 5 per cent) of the floor area in the room. If there is no exterior door in the room, one window must be large enough to provide an emergency exit. Window placement should encourage air circulation yet prevent drafts. Insufficient humidity, air movement, or natural light can be supplemented by mechanical aids. Bed coverings are usually necessary. The number required for warmth has decreased significantly owing to improved fabrics and central heating, but there remains the problem of storing blankets that are not in use. Enough space must be supplied to store (without wrinkling) linens, blankets, or comforters. A space 24 inches wide fitted with adjustible shelving will accommodate folded bed linen and blankets effectively.

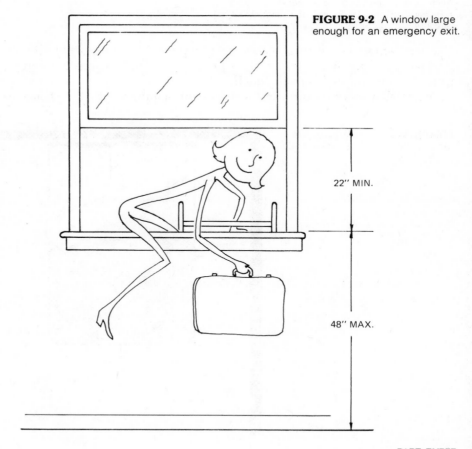

FIGURE 9-2 A window large enough for an emergency exit.

22" MIN.

48" MAX.

The space needed for dressing and undressing varies with the individual. One authority suggests that the average adult requires a space 7 feet in diameter and 8 feet high; others have suggested that 42 square inches in front of the major storage area are sufficient.

The lack of storage space for clothes is one of the universal complaints about modern housing. Some people want a storage space in which clothing is not only readily accessible but also ready to wear as it is removed. A person with a limited wardrobe needs a minimum of approximately 9 square feet for the hanging of clothes.

Most house plans conform to the minimum storage requirements established by the U.S. Department of Housing and Urban Development: 3 to 5 feet of rod and open shelving in a bedroom closet, 2 feet of rod in an entry closet. (The number of people to occupy the bedroom will determine the specific minimum. See Table 9-2). There are no specifications for built-in storage, though some authorities contend that needs can be more fully met, rooms can be more easily arranged and cleaned, and furniture costs can be reduced if built-in storage is planned.

TABLE 9-2   Minimum Sizes of Bedroom Furniture and Closets

| Item | Bedroom Occupancy | | | Coats and Outerwear |
	Primary	Double	Single	
		Inches		Inches
Dresser	18×52	18×42	18×42	
Closet	24×60	24×60	24×36	24×24
Chair	18×18	18×18	18×18	

Adapted from *Minimum Property Standards for One- and Two-Family Dwellings*, Vol. 1 (Washington, D.C.: U.S. Department of Housing and Urban Development, 1973), p. 4–4.

All clothing should be stored in the same space—hats with coats, trousers with jackets, blouses with slacks—to facilitate maximum usability. Hanging garments should be grouped by length so that space under the shorter garments may be used more effectively. Hooks reduce the amount of space needed. Ideally, frequently used small items or accessories such as jewelry, gloves or scarves should be stored so as to be accessible and visible. They are best located between 2 and 4 feet from the floor. Clear plastic drawers or containers also increase visibility. Out-of-season garments should be protected from moths. Garments should be cleaned prior to storage in sealed plastic bags, a steel wardrobe sealed with masking tape, or a cedar closet.

A full-length mirror is helpful, and can be placed on a closet door or on the entrance door to the dressing area. The height at which it should be placed must be related to the height of those who will be using it.

PERSONAL HYGIENE

Cleanliness is essential to good health. The space reserved for personal hygiene should allow for convenience, comfort, and frequency of use. Many public health authorities in the United States blame the lack of proper facilities on poor housing, which, in turn, is associated with poor health. The correlation is unmistakable: when facilities for personal care are improved, contagious diseases—especially those of the skin—are consistently reduced.

Cleansing

The major purpose of cleaning the body is to rid it of contaminants, dirt, and odor. Cleanliness, however, is also associated with social, religious, or moral values. Cleansing is ritualized in many religions, and related to moral or spiritual purification. Words constantly relate cleanliness to other values: a young man, for example, is more appealing if he is "clean cut"; an obscene book is "dirty"; a criminal is asked to "come clean"; the rejection of cleanliness by some young people is an obvious revolt against authority. In the United States cleanliness is important to social acceptability, and dirt and odor are considered "offensive." Body cleansing can also serve as a relaxant, a refreshant, a stimulant, or even a therapy.

Bathing

Bathing in a tub is generally considered more relaxing and more luxurious than other forms of cleansing. Attitudes toward bathing vary with different cultures. The Romans, for example, erected elaborate bathhouses, while early American settlers considered bathing injurious to health, conducive to promiscuity and (if the water were hot) the loss of one's "magnetism." The first tub in the United States was imported by Benjamin Franklin in 1790. Until the late 1800s tubs were portable and were brought into the kitchen or bedroom to be placed before the fire. As America became more bath-conscious, a room for bathing became an integral part of the home.

Bathing requires a container large enough to hold the body and sufficient water to cover it. Warmth is necessary, achieved by an auxiliary heater or a heating system design that can supply extra warmth if the body becomes chilled. Around the bathing area it is helpful to use materials that are impervious to moisture. Electrical switches and equipment should be grounded and well out of reach of the bath, shower, or lavatory. It is important that there be supports near the tub so that the bather can maintain his balance while entering, and exiting from, the tub. The tub should be long enough for the bather to sit with his legs extended, and one end of the tub should be contoured so that the bather may comfortably recline. The tub should be deep enough to prevent splashing, and wide enough to permit movement by the bather. The recommended width, approximately 25.5 inches, can be reduced if a seat is incorporated into the tub design.

Bathtub models range from walled-one-piece units to double-width tubs set on or in the floor. The sunken bathtub, though elegant, can be hazardous, and difficult to clean. Bathtubs vary from 3 to more than 7 feet in length. Generally they are 34 inches wide, but space must be allowed on one side of the tub for the bather to get in and out.

Tubs should not be located below windows because excessive moisture from condensing steam may cause the window frame to deteriorate, whereas cold drafts from the window may cause discomfort to the bather.

Fiberglass or acrylic tubs are easy to clean and to maintain because they are both waterproof and mold-resistant. Many offer a slip-resistant surface as a safety measure, but effective substitutes include a grab bar, decorative adhesives, or a rubber bath mat placed on the bottom of the tub. Another safety feature is the placement of tub controls higher than the average person's reach, on the entry side of the tub. It is convenient to have within reach towels and a washcloth, as well as cosmetic items—soap, softener, shampoo, bath oil, and talcum

FIGURE 9-3 Space required to use personal hygiene equipment.

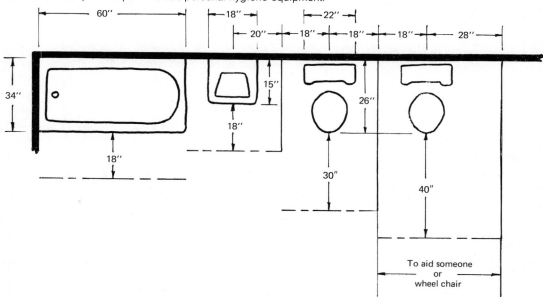

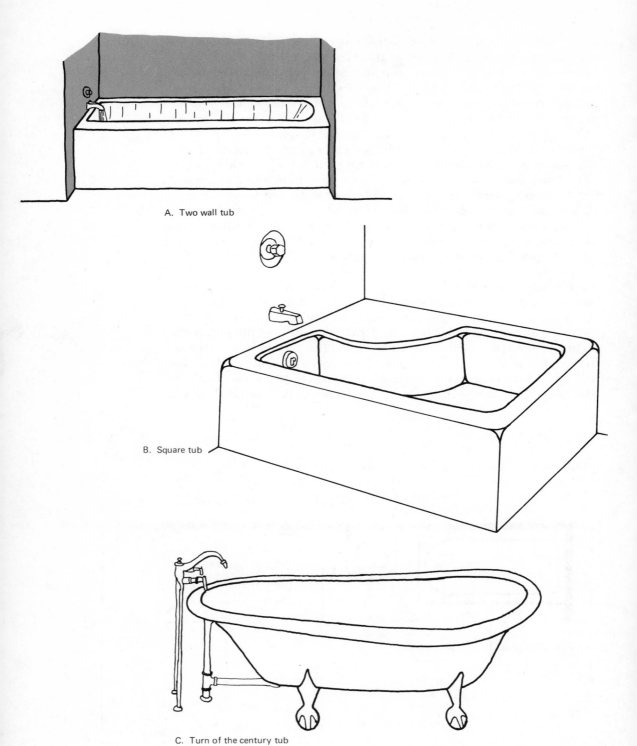

A. Two wall tub

B. Square tub

C. Turn of the century tub

FIGURE 9-4 Common bathtub models.

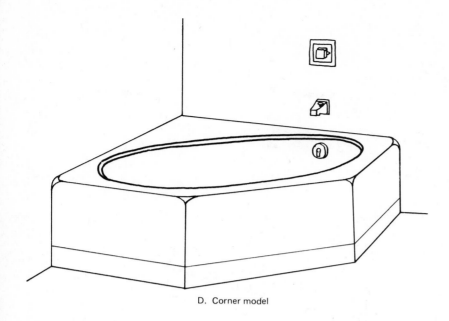

D. Corner model

powder. Decorative flowers or plants profit from the humid atmosphere.

The greatest objection to tub bathing is that it inhibits proper rinsing. A flexible shower or faucet will help but a tub-shower arrangement is often preferred—it costs little to install, requires no additional space, and permits proper rinsing.

A shower bath is refreshing, inherently more hygenic, and overwhelmingly preferred by adults. Shower space ranges from 42 by 30 inches to as little as 30 square inches. Those made of fiberglass or prefabricated steel are easy to install, clean, and seamless. An alternative is a floor pan with a nonskid surface walled with moisture-resistant material. Shower controls should not be located under the shower head nor in any place difficult to reach from outside the shower area. To prevent splashing and to provide privacy, a curtain or a door should be added.

Special bathing arrangements must be made for the very young, the elderly, and the handicapped. For babies and small children, a portable tub can be placed within the bathroom. The lavatory sink or kitchen sink can be used to bathe infants. Special apparatus is available for anyone who has difficulty maneuvering in a standard tub; showers used by the elderly should have a stool and additional support bars.

Until the turn of the twentieth century, a pitcher and bowl were standard equipment in every dressing area. With modern plumbing, the washing basin was permanently fixed near the source of the water supply. The largest basin built into the largest countertop is the most convenient. This will provide space along the sides of the basin for

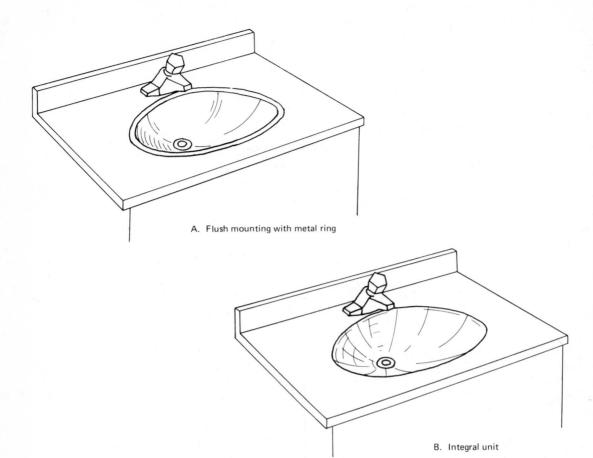

A. Flush mounting with metal ring

B. Integral unit

beauty aids, shaving equipment, and other items. Space under the counter can be used for storage of linens or other bathroom accessories. Sinks suspended from the wall and placed on legs often lack such storage space.

The most popular inexpensive basin model attaches to the counter with a metal ring, but the self-rimmed lavatory is easier to clean. A one-piece basin and counter top are probably easiest to clean. Enamel, cast iron or steel, acrylics, and fiberglass are the materials most commonly used, but only acrylics and fiberglass can be molded into an integral basin and counter.

A rectangle as small as 15 by 18 inches or a corner with only 16 inches on each side suffices for a wash basin, but another 18 inches must be allowed in front of the basin for the user. If another fixture is located across from the basin, 24 inches should separate them. Faucets and drains should be easily reached, so that they can be cleaned and properly maintained, and faucets should premix hot and cold water.

A mirror is essential in any lavatory. It should be approximately 30 inches square, and placed approximately 66 inches from the floor. A

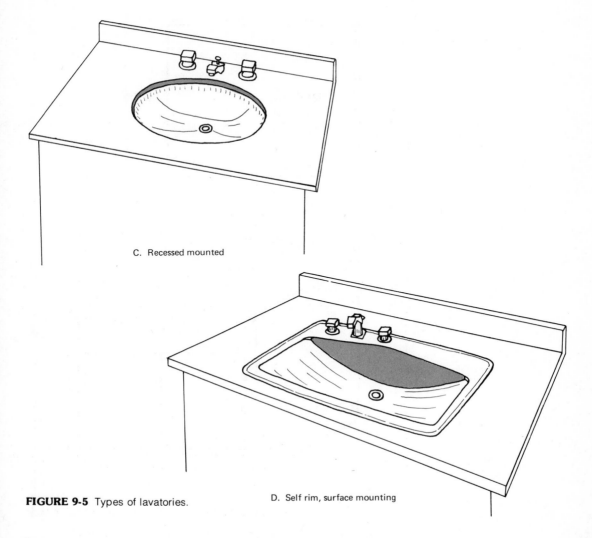

C. Recessed mounted

D. Self rim, surface mounting

FIGURE 9-5 Types of lavatories.

larger mirror can be decorative, and make the area seem more spacious and bright.

Good lighting is also important. A ceiling fixture is seldom adequate. Fixtures on each side of the mirror evenly distribute light and are more effective than a single light over the mirror.

Storage space in the lavatory needs to be versatile because some items are used only occasionally, others need be stored only briefly, and still others can be decorative. Medicines are usually stored behind the mirror, out of reach of small children. The cabinet under the basin may be used to store extra linens, large items, or a tip-out clothes hamper, towel racks to store linens, or as emergency grab bars for the handicapped. A 24-inch rack is sufficient for a bath towel and wash cloth. A convenient height is between 36 and 42 inches above the floor. Towel rings and hooks are helpful for supplemental supplies.

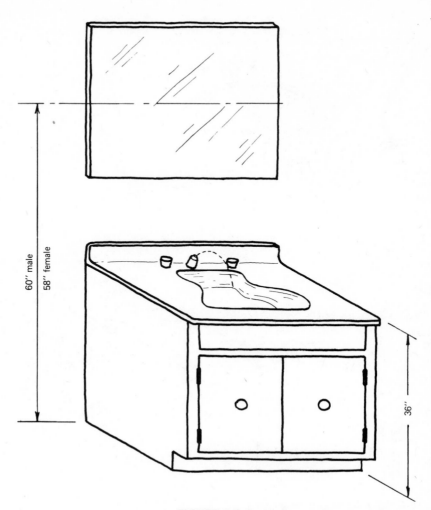

60" male
58" female
36"

FIGURE 9-6 Positioning a mirror over a lavatory.

Elimination of Body Waste

The treatment and disposal of human waste are important in maintaining an odor-free environment and preventing the incubation of disease-spreading bacteria. The watercloset or flush toilet performs the function of carrying away human waste. Before the invention of the water closet, a chamber pot was stored under the bed or in a commode. Even when the outhouse became common, the chamber pot was retained. The modern watercloset disposes of waste more effectively. Newer models require little maintenance and are simple to clean. But according to Kira, much improvement is needed if waterclosets are to conform to human anatomy.[2] Ideally, a watercloset

[2] A. Kira, *The Bathroom* (New York: The Viking Press, Inc., 1976), p. 129.

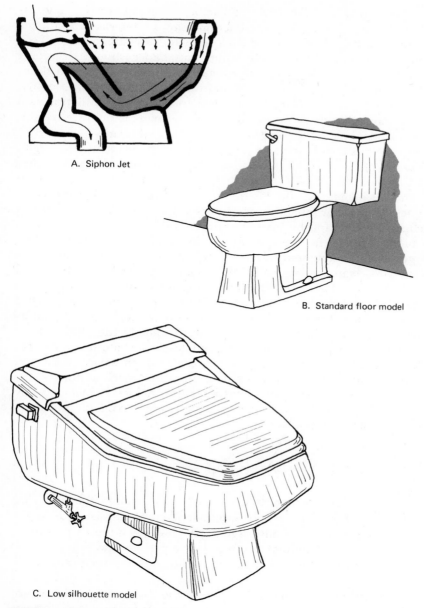

A. Siphon Jet

B. Standard floor model

C. Low silhouette model

FIGURE 9-7 Types of waterclosets.

should rinse, flush, and refill quickly and quietly. Of the types available, the siphon jet is most efficient, quiet, sanitary, and expensive. A large water surface makes the appliance less subject to fouling, staining, and contamination. Wall-hung waterclosets require wall brackets—installation is expensive but maintenance is easier. The reverse-trap watercloset is the most often installed variety because of its self-cleaning features and satisfactory flushing action. The efficiency of the flushing and refill action may be determined and the noise factor established if the watercloset is flushed after a piece of tissue has been placed in it: the water and paper should disappear quickly, surely, and quietly. Seats should be sturdy and easy to clean. Plastic ones are long-lasting, while painted wooden seats chip easily. Seats with a split front are less subject to decay. If ventilation is a problem, toilets with self-venting exhaust systems should be considered, or a separate ventilating fan can be installed nearby.

The watercloset will usually range from 19 to 29 inches in height, with a tank 20 to 24 inches wide that extends approximately 26 inches from the wall. At least 18 inches of space should be allowed on each side and 30 inches in front. Extra space around the sides and front may be required for a handicapped person in a wheelchair. A special attachment will adapt the seat for children.

A bidet is useful for both males and females. A standard fixture in Europe, it is not commonly used in the United States. Its water jet is designed to clean the perineal area of one who has used the toilet. Some bidets also have a drying jet. A pop-up stopper holds water in the basin during the washing process, and a spray rinses and flushes the bowl surface after use. Most bidets feature a douche for vaginal irrigation. The most popular model is approximately the same size as the watercloset and is installed adjacent to it. An alternate arrangement is a seat attached to the watercloset, which saves space and money but adds to the storage problem. In most American houses, the bidet is not a consideration; instead a paper holder is installed low and to the right of the watercloset, with sanitary napkins and extra toilet tissue stored within reach.

COURTSHIP AND LOVEMAKING

Courtship and lovemaking, integral parts of a healthy life, must be considered in housing design. Adolescent courtship is undeniably enhanced by the romantic atmosphere provided by a fireplace, a pool, a beautiful view, or subdued lighting. When privacy and proper atmosphere are not available at home, the adolescent may seek them elsewhere.

Mumford points out that every part of the dwelling should be arranged with an eye to sexual privacy.[3] In most societies, sexual partners have a private space for their most intimate moments. In some African tribes, each woman has a sleeping hut. The Moslem potentate has his separate quarters. In other societies, screened alcoves or curtained beds provide privacy. In American society, the master bedroom performs that function. Privacy can be assured by the in-

[3] Lewis Mumford, *Culture of Cities* (New York: Harcourt Brace Jovanovich, Inc., 1938), p. 432.

stallation of a good night latch on the door, and soundproof partitions will help isolate the area acoustically.

Comfortable, beautiful surroundings enhance intimacy. Many adults prefer low-intensity lighting, which complements nudity, to total darkness, which hides it.

Though contraceptives have traditionally been stored with other personal hygiene products, many marriage counselors consider this inappropriate in that their retrieval may interrupt sexual activity. Storage for contraceptives should be provided in various parts of the house.

People in many cultures bathe before and/or after intercourse. In addition, lovemaking sometimes induces thirst and the need to urinate. The positive cleansing needed after coitus may take the form of a partial or complete bath, a shower, or a vaginal irrigation. Good planning makes it possible for lovers to reach these facilities without undue difficulty.

SUMMARY

Privacy for personal activities and physiological functions must be provided for all the occupants of a dwelling.

Sleep and rest are essential to health. The sleep area must be neither too large nor too small, with enough space for the bed to be comfortably made. Temperature control, low-intensity lighting, and sufficient storage space are important aspects of the dressing area.

There have been few changes in the last half-century in the design of bathroom fixtures though lavatories are too low and too small, showers too cramped, and waterclosets poorly fitted to the human anatomy. The proximity of plumbing equipment, sinks and waterclosets, makes their installation more efficient and less expensive. It is customary for manufacturers to coordinate their style and color of lavatories, waterclosets, bathtubs, showers, and bidets.

Intimate moments are enhanced by special design considerations that emphasize comfort and atmosphere. Color and lighting should complement personal coloring. Access to cleansing facilities is also essential.

10

Space for the Work of the Household

THE care of the household entails physical and mental effort. Passages describing woman's labors can be found in the Book of Proverbs.

> She worketh willingly with her hands . . .
> she bringeth food from afar . . .
> she riseth also while it is yet night and
>   giveth meat to her household . . .
> she layeth her hands to the spindle . . .
> she looketh well to the ways of her household.
> Prov. 31:13–15, 19, 27

Large household retinues were once common. There were slaves to do the work in early Rome, serfs during the Middle Ages, and servants during the Victorian Age. During the Colonial Period in the United States, there was no lack of work to be done—spinning, weaving, sewing, preparation and cooking of food, cultivation of herbs for medicinal purposes—and all of it fell to the lot of the woman of the household. In the contemporary United States, many of these tasks have been taken over by professionals, but a member of the household must still prepare meals, purchase personal and household items, maintain the house, and care for the children and the sick.

MEAL PREPARATION

Fifty per cent of the work in the home involves the preparation of meals. Not including the time used for preparing refreshments for

150

guests or for holiday meals, at least 1,638 hours a year, or from 2 to 4½ hours a day, are spent preparing food in the average household.

Work Centers

The daily activities of meal management begin with preparation and end with cleaning up after the meal is eaten. Each cook has an individual style that affects the selection of food and equipment and the size and arrangement of the work area. Some cooks like to experiment in the kitchen but others prefer to spend as little time in it as possible. When the meal is over, waste food must be disposed of, leftovers stored, dinnerware cleaned and put away.

Weekly or monthly activities include the planning of meals, and the purchase and storage of foods. The planning process may vary, but for

TABLE 10-1   Requirements for Meal Preparation Centers, Appliances and Standard Cabinets

	SERVE	COOK	COOK AND SERVE	PREPARATION	SINK	MIX	PREPARATION AND MIX	REFRIGERATOR	RANGE COMMON SIZE
AMPLE SPACE									
Liberal supplies									
Wall	27"	21"	30"	_15"_	36"	30"	36"	35"	
Base	_30"_	18"	48"	78"		_36"_	114"		
Limited supplies									
Wall	21"	15"	24"	15"	30"	24"	30"	32"	
Base	_24"_	15"	39"	60"		_33"_	93"		
MINIMUM SPACE									
Liberal supplies									
Wall	21"	15"	24"	15"	30"	24"	30"	32"	
Base	_24"_	15"	39"	66"		27"	93"		30"
Limited supplies									
Wall	15"	_15"_	18"	_15"_	24"	18"	24"	28"	
Base	_18"_	15"	33"	_48"_		21"	69"		
MINIMUM PROPERTY STANDARDS Two bedroom house family of four									
Base	15"	21"		42"	24"	36"	36"		

— SOME UNUSED SPACE BECAUSE STANDARD SIZES WERE USED

Adapted from *Cabinet Space for the Kitchen,* Small Homes Circular No. C5.31, Univ. Ill. Bull. Vol. 46, No. 43. Univ. Ill., Office of Publication, Urbana, Ill., February 1949, pp. 6–7.

Minimum Property Standards for One- and Two-Family Dwellings, Vol. 1, U.S. Department of Housing and Urban Development (Washington, D.C.: U.S.G.P.O.) 1973, p. 4–8.

the average cook, a few cookbooks and recipe files or cards, and paper and pencil suffice. Food can be ordered by telephone from a local market that has a delivery service; but it is far more common for one family member to do the shopping and store the supplies.

An annual activity (usually in the fall) is food preservation. The family with a garden or with a successful hunter in the household has need for extra space to process the crop or preserve the game. Work centers, flexibly grouped, must be planned to accommodate both daily and periodic activities. Each work center should reflect the number of family possessions and the emphasis the cook places on the activity (see Table 10-1).

Storage/Refrigerator Center.   The purpose of the refrigeration center is to provide storage for food that may require further processing, to prevent spoilage, and to keep leftovers as fresh as possible. The refrigerator should be so located that it does not block movement from one activity to another. Refrigerators are made with either a right-hand or left-hand opening, but most storage areas are planned to accommodate one with a right-hand opening. To the left of the refrigerator should be a cabinet with a work surface of at least 15 square inches. This provides space for placing groceries from the market or items removed from the refrigerator. Unopened canned and bottled foods are sometimes stored in the refrigerator but wall cabinets can accommodate more such items at less cost.

Preparation–Clean-up Center.   The tasks performed in the preparation–clean-up center range from the peeling of potatoes to the scraping of pots and pans. Its central appliance, the kitchen sink, provides the water for cleaning food and the drainage for waste. Some cooks prefer that the sink be located under a window in order that they may, while working, supervise children playing outdoors. The window also provides the pleasure of a view, or serves as a place for plants and flowers. Some find, however, that a window above the sink creates glare and adds to the installation expense.

After-meal clean-up may employ more than one person so it is best to have from 9 to 15 square inches of counter at each side of the sink. New sink design has made drainboards unnecessary because dishes can be drained in one of the sink bowls or in a dishwasher.

Storage cabinets should allow for space for paper towels, soaps, detergents, dry storage for fresh vegetables, linens, small storage containers, and sometimes even dinnerware. A cabinet under the sink as small as 48 inches wide and a wall cabinet 15 inches wide will accommodate everything but dinnerware. When a dishwasher is to be included, another 24 inches along the wall is needed. If efficiency in after-meal clean-up is important, dinnerware should be stored in the sink center. For family-style service, serving bowls and platters can be stored in the range center; glasses and pitchers, next to the refriger-

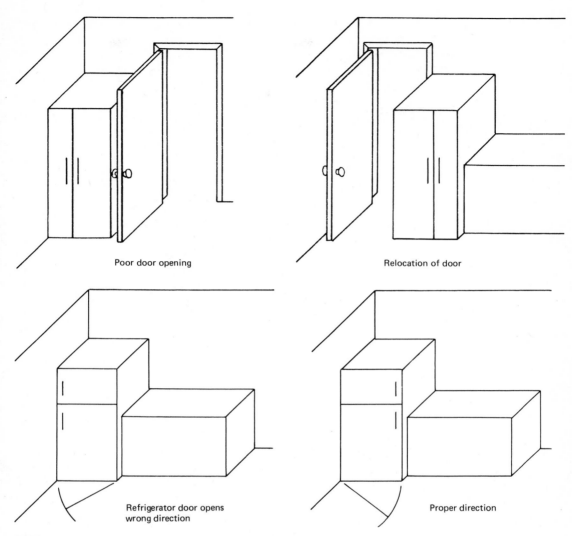

Poor door opening

Relocation of door

Refrigerator door opens
wrong direction

Proper direction

FIGURE 10-1 Providing adequate work space for refrigerator centers.

ator; the dinnerware, next to the dining area. A serving cart helps to transport the various pieces from one place to another.

Cook—Range center.   The traditional symbol of the kitchen is the range. Cooking appliances come in different styles: the one-piece free-standing range, various types of built-in units, and even small appliances. A one-piece range concentrates the heat in one section of the meal-preparation area. A free-standing range with auxilliary appliances can be moved from one place to another. A two-piece range makes it possible to plan a separate area for baking, and thus dissi-

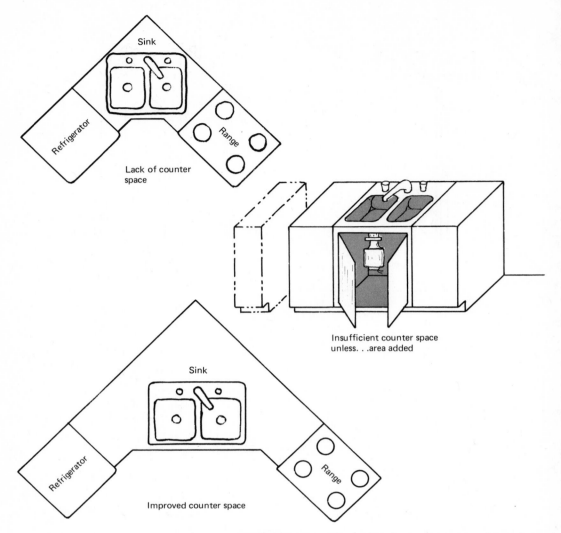

FIGURE 10-2 Providing adequate work space for sink centers.

pates the heat (an advantage in cold, dry climates). Ranges should not be located beneath windows because curtains can catch fire or grease may spatter on the panes.

Storage requirements are relatively modest. Space is needed for cooking utensils, seasonings, hot pads, and such items as stirring spoons, testing implements, ladles, and turners. Some space is often incorporated in the range design, especially the one-piece free-standing models. A 15-inch base cabinet with heat-resistant surface supplies a resting place for hot foods.

Mix Center.   The activities in the mix center involve the assembling and mixing of ingredients. If baking is an important activity, it should

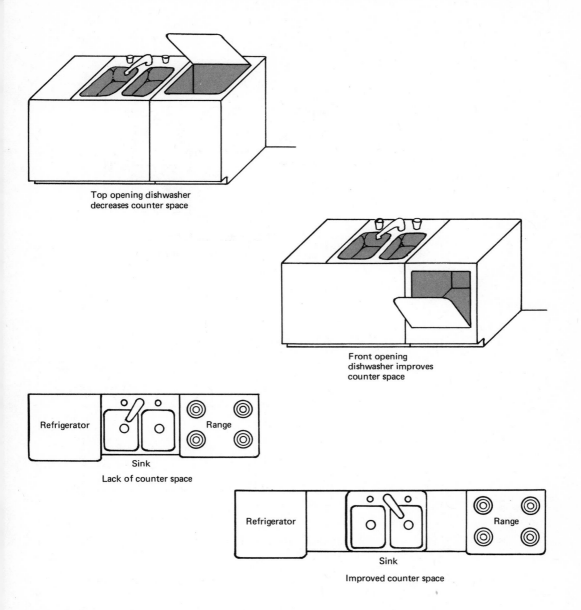

Top opening dishwasher
decreases counter space

Front opening
dishwasher improves
counter space

Refrigerator

Sink

Range

Lack of counter space

Refrigerator

Sink

Range

Improved counter space

occupy a separate center that includes a built-in oven. If baking is not important, the mix center can be combined with another work area. Many authorities incorporate it with the sink center because both involve the preparation of food; others prefer to add it to the storage/ refrigerator center because the storage requirements for staples and spices are similar to those for baking and mixing utensils and equipment; most recommend that a mix center be adjacent to the range center, particularly if a built-in oven is not provided in the mix center.

Counter space with electrical outlets allow for the placement and operation of small appliances that facilitate the mixing process. Ap-

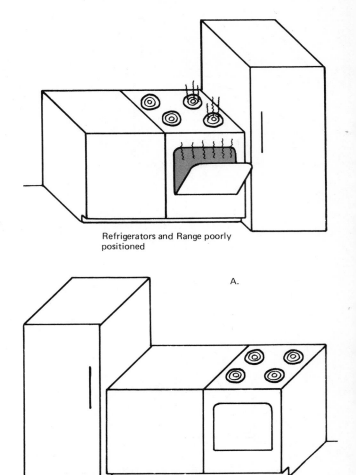

Refrigerators and Range poorly
positioned

A.

More efficient positioning of
refrigerator and range

FIGURE 10-3 Providing adequate work space for range centers.

proximately 16 inches of clear space above the blender and mixer will permit the addition of ingredients to a mixture. If these appliances cannot be placed on lower than standard stock cabinets, the wall cabinets may have to be raised above the average woman's comfort zone. Work surfaces should be lowered to reduce the fatigue factor. A sturdy pull-out shelf, a lower counter height that can substitute as an alternate eating place, or a pull-out pop-up shelf to which the appliance can be attached can be useful.

Many space savers have been designed for items stored in the mix center. Revolving shelves for corner cabinets, step shelves, and door storage help make items more visible and accessible. Vertical storage files for trays and cookie sheets increase accessibility and decrease

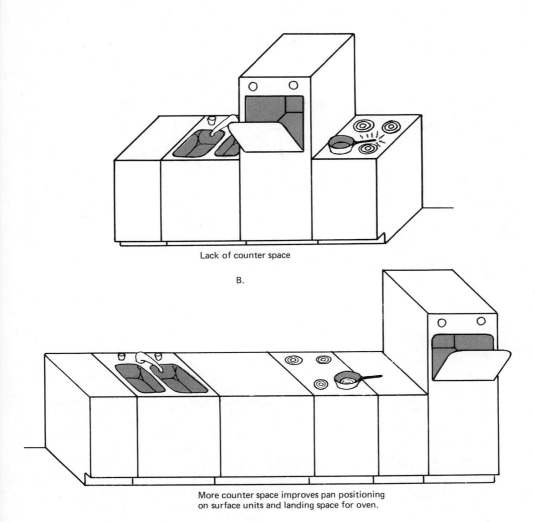

Lack of counter space

B.

More counter space improves pan positioning
on surface units and landing space for oven.

space requirements. Pull-out, pop-up shelves and drawers as well as sliding shelves make items more visible but are seldom a part of standard cabinet design. Custom-built cabinets, adaptive hardware, or separate devices are good investments because they can be removed and taken to another house.

Serve Center.   Foods prepared at the range are made ready for consumption in the serve center, where the more formal, valuable utensils are stored. Several appliances used at the table—toaster, waffle iron, or warming tray—may be located here.

The serve center is often combined with the range or refrigerator center. Most commonly ready-to-eat foods (jellies, pickles, crackers, cakes) are stored here. Some prefer to store serving dishes in this area to expedite the transport of food from the range to the table.

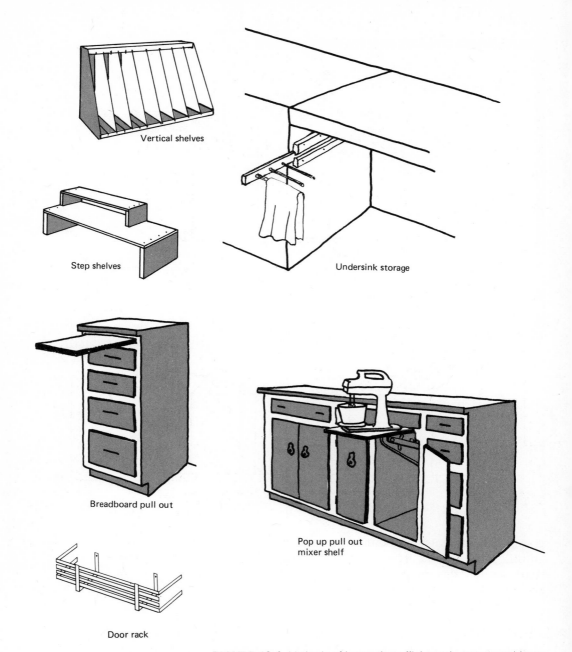

Vertical shelves

Step shelves

Undersink storage

Breadboard pull out

Door rack

Pop up pull out mixer shelf

FIGURE 10-4 Methods of increasing efficiency in storage cabinets.

Arrangement of Work Centers

An efficient kitchen requires at least three work centers. The chosen centers should be so located that a minimum of walking is required among them. The path between refrigerator, range, and sink should not exceed 22 feet.

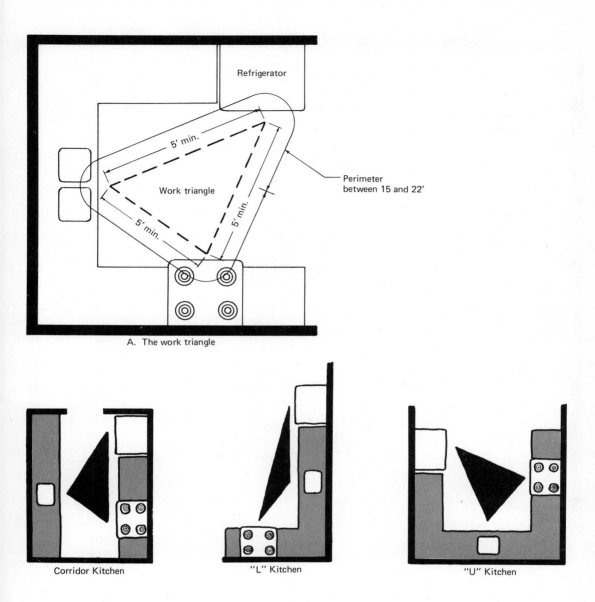

A. The work triangle

Refrigerator

5' min.

Work triangle

5' min.

5' min.

Perimeter
between 15 and 22'

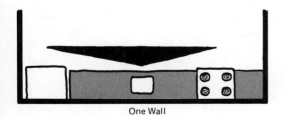

Corridor Kitchen

"L" Kitchen

"U" Kitchen

One Wall

B. Arrangements of centers

FIGURE 10-5 Arranging the work centers in the meal preparation area.

159

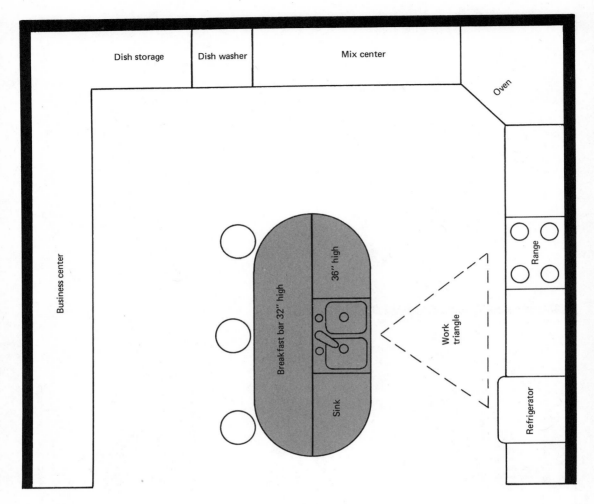

Dish storage   Dish washer   Mix center   Oven

Business center

Range

Breakfast bar 32" high   36" high

Work triangle

Sink   Refrigerator

A. Island kitchen

FIGURE 10-6 Alternate methods for attaining good relationship between work centers.

The location of the sink should be considered first. Since this center is used more frequently than any other, it should form the shortest leg of the work triangle. The range should be considered next, and the best place for it is usually near the serve or eating area. A mix center, if there is one, should be located between the range and sink. The refrigerator/storage center should be located near the point of entry or exit, with the sink to the right and the range to the left. Related centers should be no farther than the average woman's horizontal reach (approximately 48 inches), and efficiency can be gained if they are at right angles to each other.

Kitchen planners recommend one of four types of arrangement: the single wall, the *L*, the corridor, or the *U*. The one-wall cooking area is

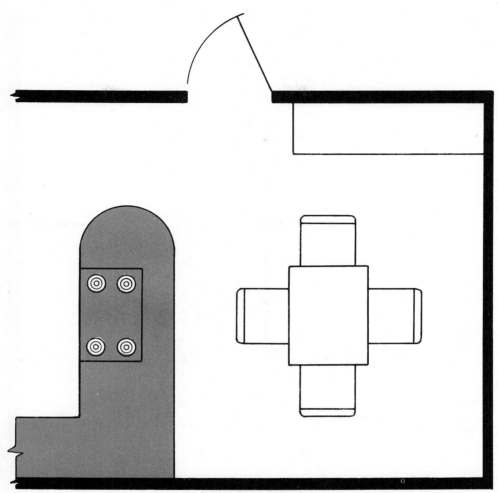

B. Peninsula kitchen

a good plan for an apartment, small house, or vacation home. The *U*-shaped meal-preparation area has three sides along which to distribute the centers, with the sink center at the base of the *U*. This is considered the ideal arrangement, offering continuous work space and preventing through traffic in the work area. The *L*-shaped kitchen rates second in efficiency, facilitating uninterrupted work by providing an area that can successfully accommodate more than one cook. If the two walls of the *L* are continuous, the area is kept free of traffic. The corridor or two-wall kitchen is the least preferred. Two-wall kitchens often become passageways and people walk through while work is in progress. If a window is placed at one end, the corridor kitchen can attain the best features of a compact work triangle and eliminate the dead-end corners of the *U* and *L*. Peninsula or island

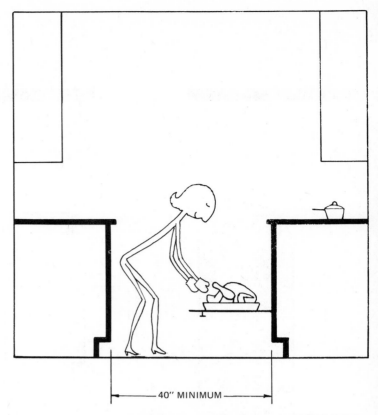

FIGURE 10-7 Space required between cabinets.

counters may be a creative way to add space to each center and establish a good working relationship between them.

Crucial to the successful arrangement of the work centers is the planning of space between cabinets and the location of doors and windows. In a *U* or corridor kitchen 48 to 60 inches is needed in order for people to pass each other freely. The U.S. Department of Housing and Urban Development stipulates a minimum passage space of 40 inches. Cabinets at right angles require 30 to 38 inches of space between them in order for doors to be opened. The effectiveness of work areas is reduced when doors are placed at the corners or where they open against cabinet doors or against each other. A sliding or folding door or even an arch may be better. Windows should be so located that wall cabinets are not sacrificed. Most inadequacies in the meal-preparation area can be blamed on insufficient cabinets; absence of a work counter beside the refrigerator, the range, or the sink; poorly placed doors or windows; traffic through the work areas.

Special adaptations in the meal-preparation center are required for the handicapped and for the elderly. Persons in wheelchairs need knee space under major work surfaces, and lower counter heights, sinks,

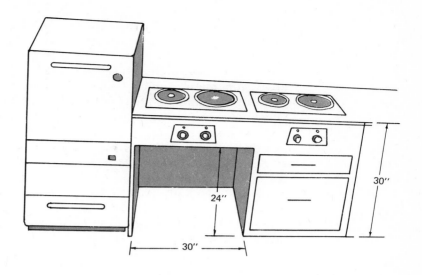

FIGURE 10-8 Space modification required for a wheel chair.

surface units, and shelves in wall cabinets. Metal edging along the openings of the base cabinets protects the cabinets from damage by the wheelchair. Pull-out units will make needed equipment easier to reach and will lower work surfaces for the person sitting in the wheelchair without deviating from standard counter height for the rest of the family. A pull-out unit with a recessed space in it can hold a mixing bowl, which is helpful for the one-handed worker. Shelves should be slanted or have lips on them so items will not fall off when the door is opened.

Distances that food must be carried should be as short as possible. Although an under-counter refrigerator is an advantage to the wheelchair occupant, it should not be placed in the living units of the elderly.

Meal-Preparation Equipment

The placement of equipment is crucial to efficient planning. Although individual height may vary as much as 12.5 inches, comfortable working height varies less than 2 inches. Standardized equipment causes no significant increase in worker fatigue.

Cabinets.   Mass-produced cabinets are less expensive than those that are custom made. Typical base cabinets that conform to the minimum property standards of the U.S. Department of Housing and Urban Development are 36 inches high, with a 24-inch counter over a drawer and two fixed shelves, and come in 3-inch increments from 9 to 42 inches. Pull-out and revolving shelves make items more visible and accessible. The standard 24-inch counter is 8 inches deeper than the reach of the average worker. Common practice is to use this space for storage of frequently used items—cookie jars, can-openers, canisters—though people object to the "messy" appearance that results.

A typical wall cupboard is 30 inches high, 12 inches deep, and has three shelves. (Adjustable shelving is more desirable but more expensive.) The third shelf should be no higher than the vertical reach of the average woman—72 inches above the floor. Wall cabinets can also be designed for placement over a sink, a range, a refrigerator, or a built-in oven. Because they are not easily accessible, the space they provide is excluded from the required shelf area for wall cabinets in the mini-

FIGURE 10-9 Typical cabinet dimensions.

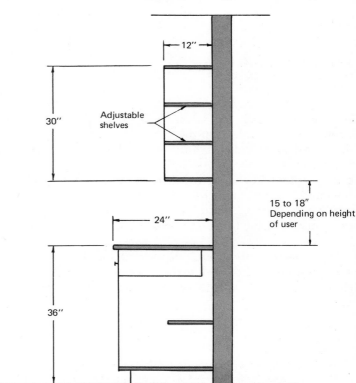

mum property standards of the U.S. Department of Housing and Urban Development.

Cabinets can be constructed of metal or wood. Cabinet fronts may be made of enamel or plastic laminates that come in many colors, patterns, and textures. Plain wooden cabinets usually cost less than the others. Desirable features include magnetic door catches, smooth rollers on pull drawers or shelves, and a revolving shelf for a corner base cabinet.

Sinks.   The most commonly used sink is designed with a double bowl but it is possible to have only one bowl or as many as three. The one-bowl sink and at least one bowl of a multiple-bowl sink should be large enough for the typical broil pan. A multiple-bowl sink should have a shallow bowl for cleaning vegetables, and for the installation of a garbage grinder. One-bowl sinks are recommended only when a dishwasher is part of the sink center. Shallow-sink bowls with drains at the back provide knee space and prevent burns from hot pipes for those in wheelchairs.

Waste Disposal.   Food waste may be placed in a container in the sink or in a container with replaceable liner on the door of the cabinet below the sink. A garbage grinder will eliminate the mess of food waste and reduce odor problems.

A waste compactor may be beneficial, inasmuch as it can reduce paper, cans, and bottles to one fourth their normal size. Its addition to the sink center requires an additional 15 inches of wall space.

Other Equipment.   The space required for the range and refrigerator varies according to make and model. The U.S. Department of Housing and Urban Development minimum property standards require a refrigerator space of 33 inches and a door that opens within its own width. A minimum range or built-in surface unit requires 24 inches; a built-in oven, another 24 inches; and a deluxe model range may be as wide as 40 inches. The one sold most often is the 30-inch free-standing model and this conforms to the space required for a range under minimum property standards.

Technical Aspects

The meal-preparation area can be more satisfying if it is pleasant as well as efficient. There should be adequate light and ventilation, and the area as a whole should be easy to keep clean.

Light.   Windows provide both light and ventilation. The U.S. Department of Housing and Urban Development minimum property standards require a ventible window area equivalent to 5 per cent of the floor area. Natural daylight fluctuates in intensity: in winter the light

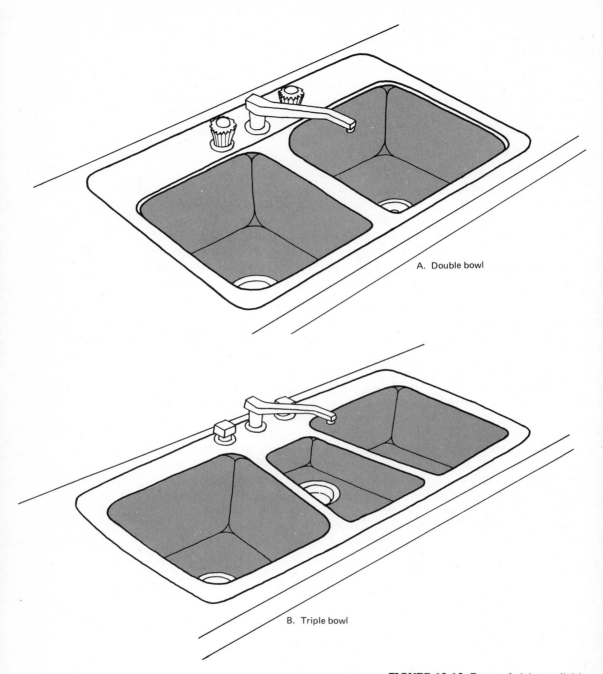

A. Double bowl

B. Triple bowl

FIGURE 10-10 Types of sinks available.

may be insufficient; in summer the glare may be distracting. The meal-preparation area should face the east.

Glare can be reduced if the windows are protected by trees, overhangs, heat-resistant glass, or blinds. Artificial light can compen-

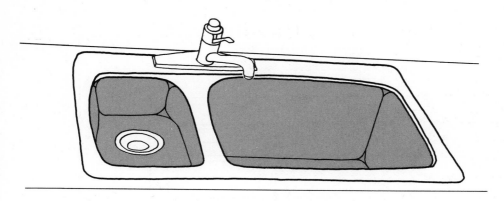

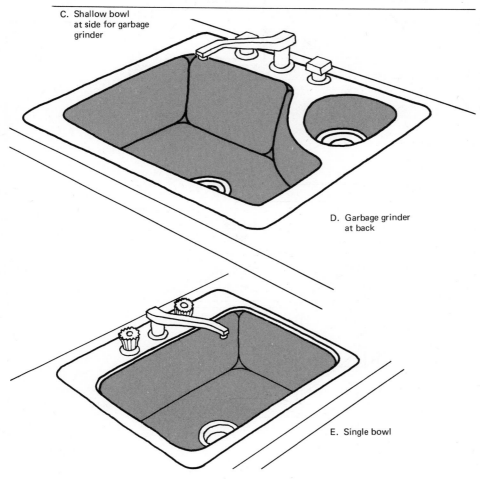

C. Shallow bowl
at side for garbage
grinder

D. Garbage grinder
at back

E. Single bowl

sate for insufficient natural light. Balanced, glareless, and well-diffused artificial light reduces the risk of accidents and relieves visual strain. A central fixture for general illumination is the least expensive and most common solution. Light may be more evenly diffused by

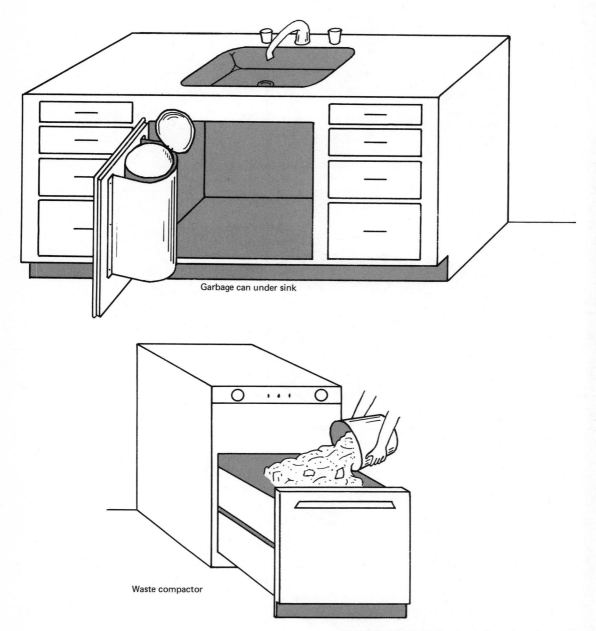

Garbage can under sink

Waste compactor

FIGURE 10-11 Methods of disposing of waste.

ceiling or perimeter fixtures. Shadows can be reduced by small tubes or lights concealed under cabinets. (This is one of the most requested improvements for the meal-preparation area.) Fluorescent light is ideal because the tube takes little space and the light is cool. Care should be taken that the type of light chosen does not adversely affect the color of the food. Whether light is warm or cool is a matter of individual preference, but decorative lighting can help make a room more cheerful.

Ventilation. Proper air circulation makes the kitchen a comfortable place to work. In cold and inclement weather, when windows or doors must be closed, excess heat, smoke, moisture, and odor tend to accumulate. A range hood with a blower or exhaust fan installed in a wall or in the ceiling near the greatest source of most of the heat, the range, is helpful.

Acoustics. The cooking area generates a great deal of noise: the rattle of pots and pans, the clatter of dishes, and the whir of motors. Sound becomes annoying when it reaches 50 decibels (or just above the normal volume of television); many appliances, blenders, mixers, disposals, and even fans exceed that level. The location, shape, and size of the room can be planned in such a way as to reduce noise. Another problem is that hard surfaces, which are necessary to insure sanitation, amplify sound. Sound-absorbent ceilings, resilient flooring, and curtains will help to muffle sound.

Plumbing. Federal, state and local codes regulate the installation of water and drain pipes. Because hot water should be 114–120°F. (46–49°C.) for sanitary purposes, a mixer valve should be installed. Garbage grinders require a good flow of cold water to congeal grease and increase its flow down the drain while preventing stoppage and cooling the motor. A vent pipe helps to deflect objectionable odor from the disposal system.

Finishes. In the meal-preparation area, finish for walls, floors, and counter tops should be easy to clean, nonabsorbent and water- and grease-resistant. Plain surfaces and dark colors show dirt more readily than light-colored patterned surfaces. Counters near the range should be heat-resistant; those near the sink should be impervious to knife cuts.

Plastic laminates are currently popular, and properly installed produce moisture-proof contoured tops with no moldings or edging under which dirt might collect. A new material simulates marble, resists heat and stain, yet is as easy to cut and shape as wood. Laminated hardwood, although it is not heat proof, is a good choice for a carving or kneading board. Ceramic glass provides the heat resistance and the smooth surface ideal for cooling candy and slicing hot meat or bread.

Washable paint is the most common wall finish but ceramic or plastic tile, plastic laminates, and plastic wallpaper have also proved suitable. Floorings may be hard, resilient, or soft. Once only smooth, hard surfaces were recommended for floors, but though such surfaces have been improved by a foam backing and/or a no-wax finish, other materials are gaining acceptance. Kitchen carpeting, available in interesting textures, reduces noise. If installed in tile form, each square can be replaced if stained or burned. Hard materials—wood, flagstone, terrazzo, brick, or marble—are durable, and new sealers increase their resistance to water and stains, but they may be uncomfortable to stand on for long periods.

FOOD PRESERVATION

Food is preserved in a number of ways. Common preservation methods used at home today include canning, freezing, and the making of jellies and wines.

Storage space is necessary for processed food and for the equipment used for processing. Most experts agree that a standard under-the-counter cupboard 28 inches wide will take care of the pressure cookers and containers for scalding. Smaller supplies like freezer wrap, marking pencils, jar lids, and special preservatives will fit into a standard wall cabinet 3 feet long.

Frozen food can be stored in the frozen food compartment of the refrigerator. If space is not available or is inconveniently located, addition of either an upright or a chest freezer may be necessary.

FIGURE 10-12 Canned food storage.

Shelf space must be provided for empty and filled jars. One-row storage is highly recommended and a shelf 5 inches deep is sufficient to hold jars ranging from pints to half-gallons. An efficient arrangement is a floor-to-ceiling cupboard 18 inches wide and 18 inches deep. Adjustable shelving can accommodate different jar heights more efficiently. Enclosed shelves keep out dirt and provide a neater appearance.

MEAL SERVICE AND DINING

The manner in which food is served and the space allotted for dining are significant. Throughout history, those with wealth and status established dining customs to set themselves apart and to display their refinement and culture. In English manor houses the lord, his family, and his honored guests sat at a table on a raised platform while less important guests and retainers were seated at another table on a lower level. Salt was placed in the middle of each table and inferiors were seated "below the salt." The Victorian "groaning board" owed much

FIGURE 10-13 Space required for serving and dining.

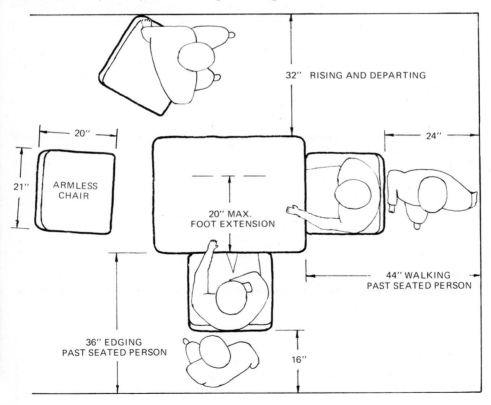

to the availability of servants, who cared for the many dining accouterments and prepared and served the splendid meals. The dining room was also the family social center—a place to exchange stories, play games, crack nuts, and drink wine after the meal was finished. The 1920s brought an end to household help. So there would be less work for the lady of the house, the size of the eating area was reduced and meal service simplified. Eventually the dining room disappeared from many homes, a victim of economy and rising building costs.

The design of the eating area must be in accord with the number of persons to be served and the time of day they are to be served and the atmosphere desired for the main meal. If most meals are to be formal, a separate dining room is necessary. On the other hand, for informal meals a variety of eating areas may suit.

Ideally, size requirements for an eating area should be determined by the number of persons to be seated and served. Two can be seated in an area 6 feet 10 inches square. The minimum space for a family of four depends more on the seating arrangement: if a person is seated at each side of the table, the minimum space must be 10 feet 6 inches square; when people are seated on only two sides of the table, the areas must be longer but can be narrower. Similarly, a dining counter in a kitchen will increase the length of the eating space and decrease its width.

The U.S. Department of Housing and Urban Development bases the size of eating areas on the number of sleeping areas in each living unit. Because the assumption is that no more than two persons sleep in a single room, an efficiency apartment and a one-bedroom house would have the same eating space (see Table 10-2).

TABLE 10-2   Minimum Dining-Area Space

Number of Bedrooms	Number of People	Table Size	Separate Room (Sq. Ft.)	Combined Space (Sq. Ft.)			
				LR/DA	LR/DA/SL	LR/K/DA	K/DA
0–1	2	2'6×2'6	NA	NA	250	NA	100
1	2	2'6×2'6	100	210	NA	270	100
2	4	2'6×3'2	100	210	NA	270	120
3	6	3'4×4'0	100	230	NA	300	140
4	8	3'4×6'	120	250	NA	330	160
Least Dimension*		NA	8'4"	19'4"	27'4"	—	—

Abbreviations: LR—Living room
                     DA—Dining area
                     K—Kitchen
                     SL—Sleeping area
                     NA—Not applicable
* The minimum measurement for either length or width of the room.

Adapted from *Minimum Property Standards for One and Two Family Dwellings*, Vol. 1 (Washington, D.C.: U.S. Department of Housing and Urban Development, 1973), p. 4–6.

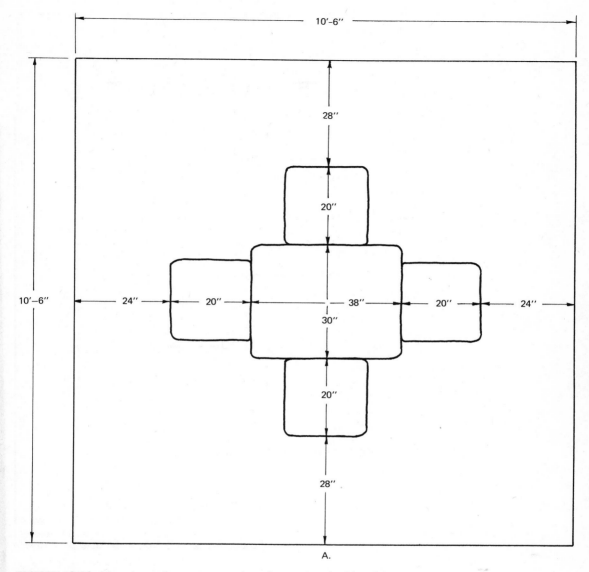

FIGURE 10-14 Alternate seating arrangements and space required for dining.

An atmosphere that promotes relaxation and sociability adds to dining pleasure. A good view and space for flowers or plants help to enhance the atmosphere. Natural light and ventilation should adhere to the minimum property standards established by the U.S. Department of Housing and Urban Development. If natural light is not available, a central light fixture with a dimmer switch is desirable. If the meal-preparation area is properly planned, there should be no problem of cooking odors invading the eating area. Acoustical control may be achieved by using sound-absorbent techniques and materials.

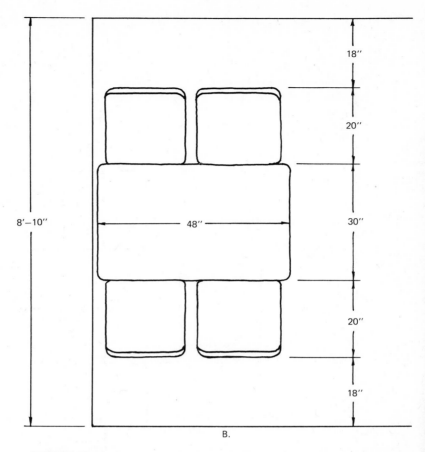

FIGURE 10-14 Alternate seating arrangements and space required for dining.

TABLE 10-3 Wall Cabinet Storage Requirements for Dinnerware Using Standard Cabinets

Service for (Persons)	Wall Cabinet Width in Inches	
	Minimum	*Ample*
4	21	24
6	30	36
8	42	48
12	60	72

Adapted from *Cabinet Space for the Kitchen,* Small Homes Circular No. C5.31, Univ. Ill. Bull. Vol. 46, No. 43 (Univ. Ill., Office of Publication, Urbana, Ill., February 1949), p. 6.

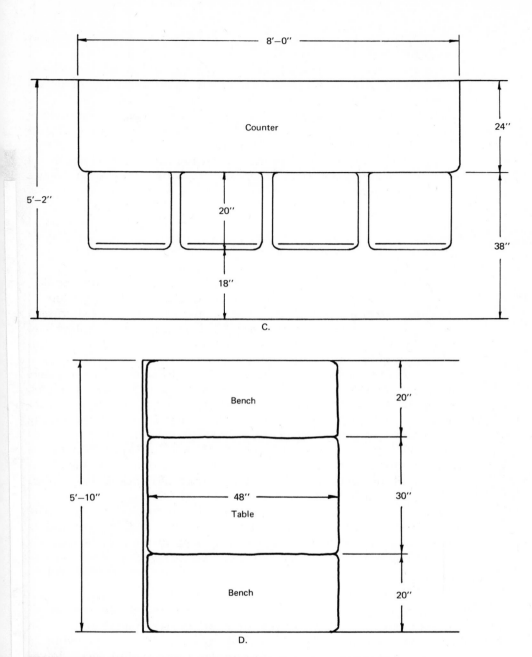

FIGURE 10-14 Alternate seating arrangements and space required for dining.

Storage space for china, glassware, flatware, serving dishes, and linens may be located in the dining area or in the food-preparation area. The amount of storage space is determined by the number to be served (see Table 10-3). With few exceptions, a shelf 12 inches wide

CHAPTER 10
SPACE FOR THE WORK OF THE HOUSEHOLD

175

for single-row storage is most desirable. Adjustable shelves make "nesting" of dishes unnecessary.

Compartmented drawers lined with pacific cloth are recommended for flatware. Service for eight can be stored in a drawer 14 inches wide, 21 inches long, and 4.5 inches deep. If serving utensils are added, a wider area is required. A storage wall between the cooking and eating areas, accessible to both, can reduce the amount of dinnerware necessary and increase efficiency.

Linens should be stored so as to be ready for use. A cupboard 24 inches wide, 16 inches deep, and 24 inches long with sliding shelves or bars will hold enough linens for the average family.

LAUNDRY

Clean clothes and linens are vital to sanitation, comfort, and beauty. The ancient Egyptians loosened dirt by beating clothes with paddles, sticks, and stones and flushed the dirt away in the flowing water of the Nile. Laundering is described in Homer's *Odyssey* and discussed in the texts of ancient Rome. Early Christians related cleanliness to vanity and the practice of cleaning clothes did not again become important until the nineteenth century.

During the 1800s, two thousand patents for mechanical washers were issued. Mechanical and chemical aids—scrub boards, wringers, soap, starch—and moving the laundry process to an indoor "washhouse" also helped. But it was not until a reliable method of obtaining water and disposing of it was developed that a laundry room was incorporated into the average home. At the end of World War II, the mass production of automatic home laundry equipment and the development of improved fabrics eliminated much of the drudgery, dampness, and disorder of the weekly laundry.

Cleaning methods are as varied as the number of cleaners. The washing process begins with the collection of soiled items and ends when they are ready for use again. Each step in the process requires certain equipment, supplies, and space (see Table 10-4).

Collection

Soiled items can be collected from the various rooms, but a more efficient method is to have a clothes hamper or bag in a central location where soiled items can be deposited. In a multiple-level dwelling, a laundry chute eliminates the necessity of carrying soiled items downstairs.

Preparation

The laundry process begins with the inspection and sorting of soiled clothing, the pretreatment of stains, and the determination of the size of each laundry load. A flat surface or several bins, water for pretreatment, and various chemical agents should all be available. The floor

TABLE 10-4   Laundry Space*

Equipment	Maximum Width in Inches	Maximum Depth in Inches
Automatic Washer		
Top-opening	30	30
Front-opening	31	30
Dryer (standard)	32	30
Combination (washer and dryer)	36	30
Stacked—Washer and Dryer	31	30
Sink and Sorting Counter	48	24
Nonautomatic Washer		
Single-tub	31	31
Twin-tub	44	24
Laundry Cart or Basket	16	28
Laundry Tub		
Single	24	24
Double	48	24
Sorting Center	60	24
Ironing Board	54	15
Clothes Rack		
Floor-type	24	22
Hanging-type	22	20
Pull-out	18	24

* Adapted from *Laundry Areas*, Small Homes Council Circular Series, Bulletin C5.4, University of Illinois, Urbana, Ill., pp. 4–5.

can suffice as a sorting area, but a higher work surface, such as a counter top or a table, reduces fatigue and can also serve as a place to fold and stack clean dry clothes. The best location is next to the sink or the laundry tub.

Supplies should be stored in an enclosed cabinet above the sink to keep soap from dampness and poisonous chemicals beyond the reach of small children. Since many of these solutions also cause stains, shelves and counter tops should be made of materials that are impervious to both moisture and chemicals.

Washing

Automatic washers are found in many living units, but some items need to be washed by hand. The need for space to carry out hand-washing cannot be underestimated. If automatic equipment is used, space for the equipment plus 4 feet in front of it is needed. Nonautomatic equipment requires more space because tubs as well as work space must be added. An island arrangement is usually recommended so that people can walk around the equipment.

Drying

Automatic clothes dryers have been available for over thirty years but many homemakers still prefer to use an outdoor line on warm bright

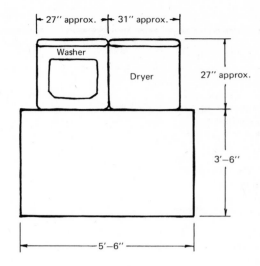

Automatic equipment

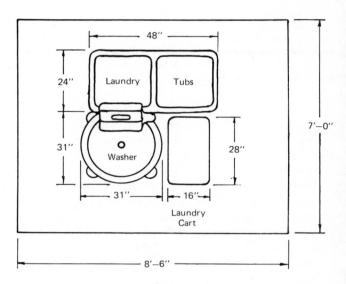

Nonautomatic equipment

FIGURE 10-15 Space for laundry equipment.

days, either to save energy or to display a clean white wash to neighbors.

Space for a dryer or 20 feet of line per person (or both) should be provided. Multiple lines should be 8 inches apart. Some fabrics must be drip dried. This is not a problem outdoors, but a drain should be located under the place they are hung indoors. A pull-out wall rod

PART THREE
THE INFLUENCE OF THE MICRO-ENVIRONMENT: THE INTERIOR

over a sink or tub, or a hanging closet, can be used. If limited space makes one of these impossible, wall hooks or a clothes rack in the bathtub or shower can substitute.

Finishing

Many items, if properly dried, need not be ironed. New fabrics have all but eliminated ironing. For other fabrics, only pressing is required. Starch can be applied during ironing. Drying can be timed so that no sprinkling is necessary. Sprinkling, if needed, can be done on the same surface used for sorting.

A space of 5 feet 10 inches by 3 feet is recommended for an ironing table. This includes space for a chair and basket or a cart to hold items ready to be ironed. A clothes rack should be available for ironed garments. There are wall models as well as free-standing models from which to choose. The ironing table can be efficiently stored in a hanging closet, or in a storage unit with a vertical slot 65 inches high.

An ideal laundry has a full complement of equipment—washer, dryer, sorting bins, ironing table, iron, laundry cart, clothes rack, a small sink, adequate counter space, a hanging closet for drip-dry items, storage space for the ironing table and other laundry aids. This much space may often be difficult to justify.

FIGURE 10-16 Space for the finishing process.

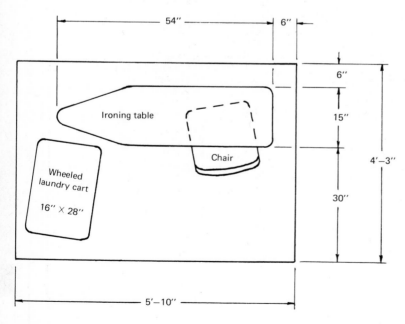

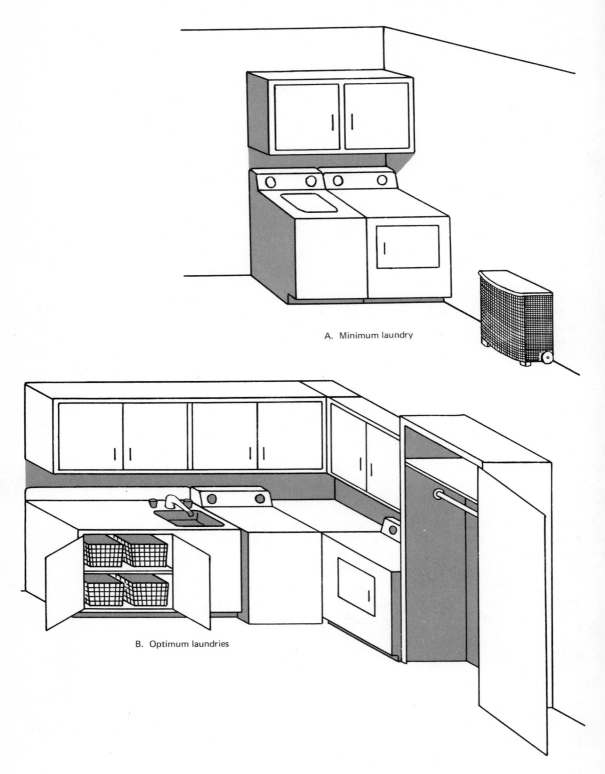

A. Minimum laundry

B. Optimum laundries

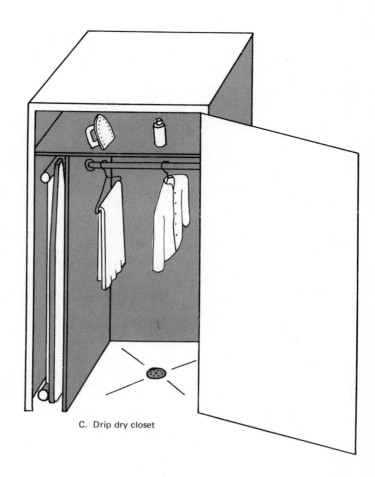

FIGURE 10-17 Arrangement of laundry equipment.

C. Drip dry closet

Arrangement of Laundry Centers

The laundry task can be simplified by having all work operations flow toward the place where the clothes are dried. Because the work for a right-handed person flows from right to left, the process will be facilitated if the dryer is placed to the left of the washer.

Most dryers require outdoor venting; without it, they will be inefficient and may add too much moisture to the atmosphere. The dryer should be located on or near an outside wall, because a vent longer than 25 feet retards drying action. Plumbing should be flush with the wall, and the floor covering beneath the appliances should be waterproof and stain-resistant.

Mending and Repair

Another important aspect of the laundry routine is repair and mending. A drawer or container for thread, needles, and other sewing supplies is all that is required. Since the amount of space needed is minimal, it is possible to have sewing supplies in several locations without significant increase in cost.

BUSINESS CENTER

The keeping of family records is an important activity. Important documents may be given to the bank for safekeeping and some are recorded in government offices. But receipts must be kept by family members, as well as invoices for purchases, addresses of friends, medical records, and tax forms and records. Even household hints and recipes and general household inventories require safekeeping. More important are documents that date and record such family events as births, deaths, and marriages. Legal papers—deeds, wills, insurance policies, and contracts—should be safely stored.

The business center in which these documents can be stored can be called a den, a study, or an office. In the 1920s, a "comfort corner" in or near the kitchen provided a place for someone to take a brief rest,

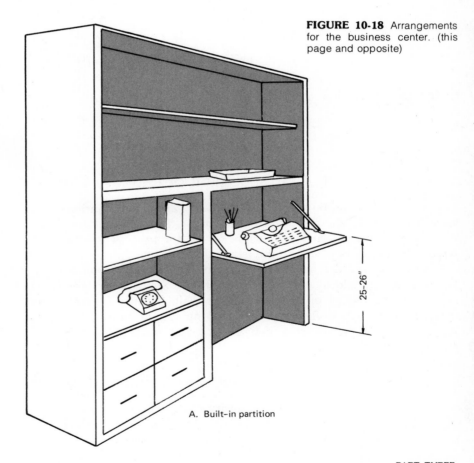

FIGURE 10-18 Arrangements for the business center. (this page and opposite)

25-26"

A. Built-in partition

182

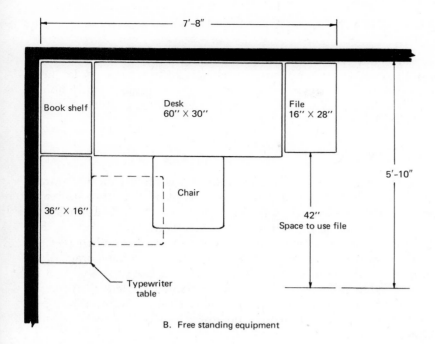

B. Free standing equipment

hold a telephone conversation, keep household accounts, file bills, and store recipe books. Fifty years later the family center has taken on increased importance. If it is to be efficient, it must be an area not only for maintaining records but also for communication.

A business center should include space for a desk and chair, storage for writing supplies, a telephone, a bulletin board, and necessary reference and record books. A space 32 inches wide and 16–36 inches deep will allow room enough for writing. For most adolescents and many adults, the most comfortable writing height is 28 inches from the floor, two inches lower than the standard desk. On the other hand, a desk offers the advantage of drawer storage. When a typewriter is added to the business center and is frequently used, an additional work surface 18 inches deep, 24 inches wide, and 26 inches high should be provided. Built-in units provide maximum storage though they increase housing cost and decrease flexibility. Bookcases and files for reference materials may be other needs to be considered. A wall telephone is helpful when space is limited.

More elaborate arrangements may be necessary if the business center is used as a place of employment. Any need to confer with clients makes a conversation area necessary and direct access from the outside desirable. For greater privacy, an out-of-the-way location is preferable, but if that is not possible, acoustical control can screen out household sounds. The desk should have a light nonglossy surface to prevent glare. Artificial light should be planned so there are no shadows in the work area, and high-intensity lamps should be positioned where reading or writing takes place.

HOUSE CARE AND MAINTENANCE

Care and maintenance activities have changed significantly since the turn of the century. It is no longer necessary to trim wicks or lay fires, and improved tools and cleaning agents have facilitated many household tasks. But there is a need to make beds, to put rooms in order, and to keep the grass cut.

House Care

For effective maintenance, well-fitted and conveniently located storage units are essential. The usual practice is to place a utility cabinet for cleaning tools and supplies in the kitchen, but tools and supplies used in cleaning should be located in each zone of the living unit. A shelf within a closet may suffice, but its height should be within reach of the average person yet not so low as to interfere with the storage of tall equipment. Storage racks on the closet door increase capacity. A closet 16 inches wide and 45 inches high will accommodate a minimum supply of cleaning equipment. Since many cleaning supplies are poisonous, it is important that they be stored out of the reach of small children.

Yard Care

Yard maintenance requires storage space for lawnmower, hose, ladders, and tools. Simply stacking them in a corner of a basement or garage can result in confusion. Peg boards or storage shelves close to

FIGURE 10-19 Storage for cleaning equipment.

the exit will increase order and improve appearance. If a storage shed is built for large equipment, it should be weatherproof, set on a raised foundation, and designed to blend into the surroundings. Sheds should be fitted with drawers and bins for small tools.

Maintenance and Repairs

Repair work is often relegated to the garage or basement. For someone involved in only minimum repair work, a drawer or shelf in a central location or near the rest of the cleaning supplies is all that is needed.

A larger workshop may be desirable for larger tools. A panel fitted with racks for each individual tool is very efficient. A sturdy workbench in a well-lighted area also facilitates maintenance tasks. The

FIGURE 10-20 Tool storage.

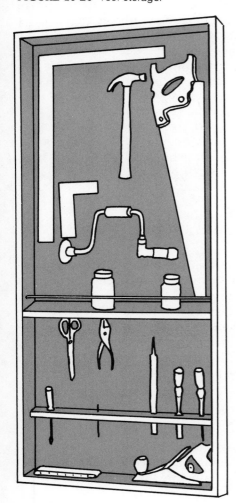

workshop should have a tight-fitting door to help control dust and noise. Additional outlets and circuits should be provided to assure sufficient current for power tools and hand equipment. The area should be dry and well ventilated so that equipment will not rust or lumber warp.

CHILD CARE

Although children are encouraged to be self-reliant, they still require supervision. At first, the infant's waking hours can be confined to a bassinette or carriage. As the child becomes more active, a playpen helps insure the child's safety and that of adult possessions. It is more convenient if the playpen can be rolled around inside the house and pushed outdoors without being folded. Wide doorways between rooms facilitate movement of the playpen.

As the child grows, storage for dolls, stuffed animals, mechanical toys, blocks, books, and games should be provided at a central location accessible to the child. Bookshelves 12 inches deep will accommodate most of these items, but should be low enough to be within the child's reach. Those who dislike the messy appearance of toy shelves can enclose them with doors or substitute a toy chest or bin.

For school-age children, a study area is important. The study area needs good lighting, a flat surface for writing, compartments for writing supplies, a comfortable chair, and a quiet location. For children who do not work well in isolation, or who need to consult with parents, a study area near an adult work or leisure area should be provided.

CARE OF THE SICK

The accessibility of professional medical care seems to have reduced the duties related to the care of the sick in the home. Unless constant bed care for a family member is required, the homemaker's chores may not increase significantly as a result of illness in the family.

A cheerful atmosphere, important in any sickroom can be encouraged by a sunny location that has a pleasant window view. It is more convenient if medicines and such paraphernalia as heating pads and thermometers are located at the patient's bedside.

SUMMARY

The work of the household includes those activities required to sustain the health and happiness of the family. Space must be provided for preparing and serving meals, for laundry, for keeping household records, for repairs.

A meal-preparation area should be designed to establish efficient work patterns and to provide maximum storage space. The dining area should be well lighted, well ventilated, and protected from kitchen noise and odor.

The laundry area should accommodate appliances and provide space to sort soiled laundry, to hang drip-dry garments, and to press clean garments.

Every dwelling should have a place to store records. More elaborate business centers may be desired when the dwelling is also a place of employment.

Adequate storage for tools, equipment, and supplies is important to efficient household maintenance and repairs. The amount of space required depends upon the interest and involvement of the occupants.

11

Space for Leisure Activities

L **EISURE** provides an opportunity to refresh both mind and body. Statistics show that about one third of a person's time is devoted to leisure.

CHARACTERISTICS OF LEISURE ACTIVITIES

Many activities qualify as leisure activities—sports, games, even daydreaming. They vary with the family life cycle, the ages of the family members, and the economic status of the family.

Leisure Activities of Children

Since the very young do not have the strength or muscle coordination of either adolescents or young adults, their activities may need to be separated from those of the family group. Very young children, who do not like complete isolation, cannot be expected to be enthusiastic about a separate playroom with windows above their eye level. Supervision of children is more convenient if their play space is close to, or within, adult work centers. A hedge or fence can protect outdoor play areas, giving adults a respite from continual supervision.

Healthy children engage in active play. On rainy or cold days, children's noise may interfere with adult activities, so that a separate location for indoor play may be desirable. As children grow older, their need for supervision is replaced by the desire for privacy. A basement, an attic, or a porch provided with adequate light, heat, and ventilation, may meet the needs of adolescents for a place in which they can be alone, free from adult interference.

Recreation for Adults

The reduction of the work week—with the consequent increase in leisure time—increases the need for space to accommodate adult leisure activities. Many leisure activities are pursued outside the home; yet there remains a need for daily relaxation, for a quiet place within where one can escape everyday problems and "get away from it all."

Entertainment of friends and relatives is another leisure activity. Space for entertainment must take into account the type of activities that the adults of the household enjoy, the numbers to be invited, and the possibility of converting other areas to accommodate entertainment needs.

A third type of leisure activity includes hobbies, gardening, and creative pursuits. Often these can be coordinated with the normal work activities of the home but require storage or work space.

Recreation for the Elderly

The elderly do not often share the need for amusements important to the young, preferring instead to raise flowers and vegetables, to engage in charitable activities, and to entertain friends of their own generation. Hearing loss may cause the elderly to talk in louder tones or to play electronic equipment at higher levels. Because the opportunity to be a part of the family while continuing to do things in their own way is important to the elderly, acoustical control that prevents intrusion of disruptive noise but does not cause isolation is recommended.

PASSIVE LEISURE ACTIVITIES

Passive or quiet leisure is characterized by the enjoyment of books, music, pictures, television, conversation, furnishings, or the natural environment. An enhancing atmosphere for quiet leisure requires an architecturally neutral background, sufficient space, appropriate furnishings, and efficient storage.

Individual Activities

Reading, listening to music, and daydreaming require a comfortable seat and segregation from unwanted sounds. Beautiful surroundings— a fire, flowers, pictures, the view from a window—help set the stage. As natural light is undependable, some type of artificial light is necessary.

Storage needs for the booklover may be minimal if there is a library close by. For those with a large number of books, magazines, and newspapers, a special collection center can be created. Shelves may be enclosed or mounted on wall brackets.

Music must be projected from the source to the listener but should not interfere with activities in other parts of the living environment. Interference is reduced when the area is surrounded by sound-deadening materials. Storage for sound equipment includes a place for radios, phonographs, tape decks, and speakers. A sound center can be arranged on a bookshelf, or speakers can be placed in several locations. Connections should be planned prior to construction so that wires can be hidden and more direct routes between control center and speakers devised. If the living environment cannot be altered, it is possible to run minimal-current wire under carpeting (provided the wire does not cross main traffic patterns). Wall-to-wall carpeting may make it necessary to run wires along the baseboard.

If television, home movies, slides, or the outdoors are to be viewed comfortably, chairs should be placed in relation to the object to be observed. The smaller the object, the closer the viewer must be. Special lighting effects help reduce eye strain and make viewing more pleasurable. Low-key lighting with no sharp contrasts, most often achieved by small lamps, enhances television viewing. Home movies and slides may require more complete darkening, and a control switch for several outlets or a dimmer switch for general lighting is helpful. Highlighting paintings hung on walls increases the viewer's appreciation. Care should be taken so that light from a small window or lamp does not reflect from the glass covering of some art work. Dry, ventilated storage is needed for water colors, oils, or photographs. A place to keep projectors, screens, cameras, and other supplies is a necessity for the photography buff.

Smoking often accompanies leisure activities. Most smokers carry their own supplies of tobacco but ashtrays are usually needed. The pipe smoker needs storage space for tobacco, pipe cleaners, humidor, and extra pipes. Good ventilation is particularly desirable in smoking areas.

FIGURE 11-1 Storage for sound systems.

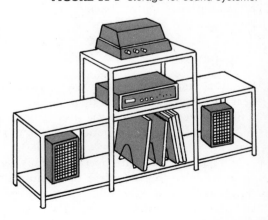

Hobbies. Creative activities are a form of self-expression, and the home must be organized to accommodate them. Ideally, once a project is under way, it should be left undisturbed until finished. If possible, a place should be set aside for creative work where the various supplies and equipment in use do not interfere with the standard operating procedures of the household.

Arts and crafts have a high priority in many families. For beginners or children, the simplest conditions suffice; for the more serious, a special table or work area must be supplied. If running water is needed, a nonabsorbent flooring should be installed in the work area; if flame or chemicals are used, counters and flooring should be resistant to fire and corrosion and the room should be particularly well ventilated. Natural north or east light is preferred by artists because it produces the least color distortion, and white walls provide the best background for their work. Ample storage space is essential: roll-about or drop-down units can be arranged to hold a large assortment of items.

People who sew prefer the sewing space as compact and attractive as possible so that it can be used for other purposes. The sewing aids and equipment usually needed include a level, smooth cutting surface about 38 inches wide, 72 inches long, and 32 inches high; a sewing machine (either portable or standard), a chair, and storage for scissors, measuring tape, thread, zippers, buttons, patterns, and fabrics; a dress form and a hanging space for unfinished garments; pressing equipment; and a mirror for fitting garments.

Natural light is best but artificial direct light that comes from the left and about 6 inches behind the chair is also satisfactory. For prolonged sewing, both general and source lighting must be supplied.

Music—instrumental or vocal—can provide much pleasure both for the performer and the listener. Space is needed for the chosen instrument (whether a harmonica or a pipe organ), room for a bench and accommodation for all participants. The size of the area must depend on the individual instrument to be used: for instance, a harp takes up 12 square feet, whereas a standard grand piano requires 50 square feet. Pianos are the most popular household instrument because they provide not only solo music but accompaniment for singers or for other instrumentalists.

Sound must have just the right resonance within the room yet not be disturbing to the neighbors. High-pitched sounds are more difficult to control and to tolerate. Practice rooms are best located in the basement or separated from the house.

Most people are collectors. Some like to display their collections in cabinets with glass doors and interior lighting. Others prefer to show their collections only on special occasions, keeping them in locked storage units at other times.

An increasingly popular hobby is the cultivation of plants and flowers. The fragrance, blossoms, and greenery make a solarium or garden room one of the most attractive rooms in the house, providing

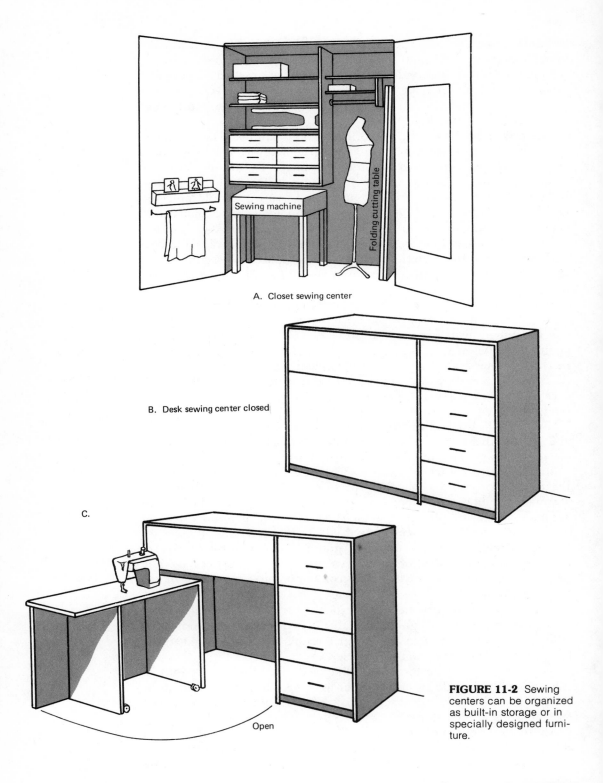

A. Closet sewing center

B. Desk sewing center closed

C.

Open

FIGURE 11-2 Sewing centers can be organized as built-in storage or in specially designed furniture.

a pleasant transition from the outdoors. Each window is a potential greenhouse, but the avid plant grower will require a room for seedbeds, for transplanting, and for special lighting to aid plant growth.

Group Activities

Some leisure activities require group participation—whether of the family or of friends and relatives. If the purpose of the activity is to bring the family together, a centrally located room is best.

Conversation.   Although many claim conversation to be a lost art, it is still a medium for the exchange of ideas and a means of entertainment. For extended conversation, comfortable places to sit—chairs, sofa, love seats—become a necessity. If the space between speakers is too large, voices must be raised and intimacy is lost. If the space is too small, the feeling of crowding may be an inhibiting factor. The maximum distance the human voice can be heard without strain is 8 to 10

TABLE 11-1   Dimensions for Basic Furniture Used and
                                  Clearance Required for Conversation Centers

| Furniture/Activity | Approximate Size in Feet | | | |
	Depth	Length	Diameter	Distance Between
Sofa	2½–3½	6–7		
Love Seat	2½	3½–4½		
Chairs				
Club	2¾	3½		
Wing	2½	2¾		
Bridge	1½	1½		
Tables, Rectangular				
End	1¼	1–1½		
Coffee	2	3		
Bridge	2½	2½		
Console	1½	3		
Tables, Circular				
Lamp			2	
Coffee, Drum, Piecrust			3	
Passage				
Major Traffic				3
Minor Traffic				2
Major Furniture				5
Minor Furniture				1½–2
In Front of Furniture				
Straight Chair				1½
Lounge Chair				2–2½

Adapted from J. Panero, *Anatomy for Interior Designers* (New York: Whitney Library of Design, 1962) pp. 20–21.

Minimum Acceptable Practices for Minimum Property Standards, Vol. 4. U.S. Department of Housing and Urban Development (Washington, D.C.: U.S.G.P.O. 1973), pp. 401–403.

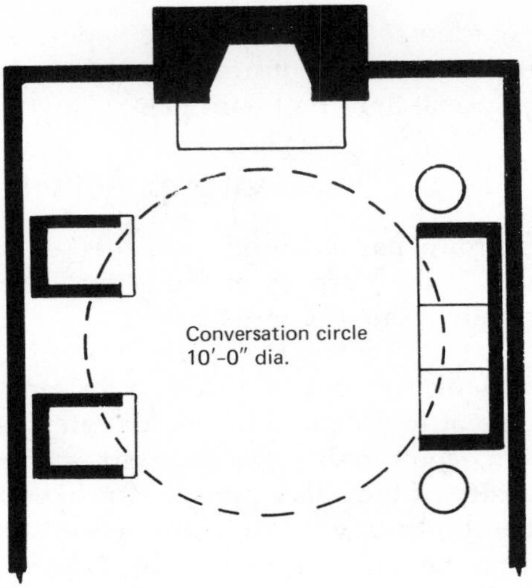

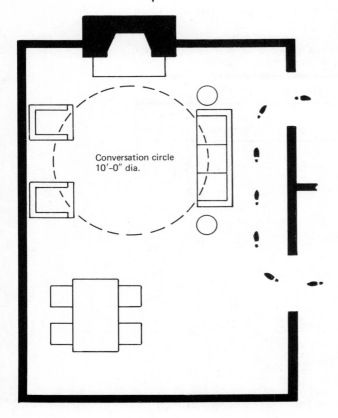

FIGURE 11-3 Dimensions required for a conversation area.

Conversation circle
10'-0" dia.

FIGURE 11-4 Traffic lanes should not interfere with a conversation area.

Conversation circle
10'-0" dia.

feet. People usually see body language, gestures, and facial expressions within a 10-foot diameter. This proximity provides the basis for a conversational group.

Conversation occurs more freely in an intimate, private atmosphere.

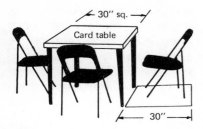

FIGURE 11-5 Space for table games.

Soft lighting fosters intimacy. A dead-end room or one with a single major entrance assures freedom from interruptions, traffic, and noise. The below-level, built-in conversation well gives the effect of uninterrupted space, but it prevents people from entering or leaving inconspicuously.

Telephoning.   An alternative to conversation in person is conversation by telephone. If considerable telephone time is needed, a second phone or a phone jack that permits a change in location for the instrument should be considered. If only one phone is economically feasible, it may be better to place the phone in a quiet location near the business center, supply a comfortable chair, and space for writing materials. A long cord is sometimes helpful.

Table Games.   Children and adults enjoy cards, games, and jigsaw puzzles. The dining area is often suggested as the proper area for such play. A leisure area for card tables and chairs may be more desirable. Storage space for card tables must also be provided.

ACTIVE LEISURE ACTIVITIES

Active leisure activities usually produce noise and involve several people. The size of the household group is a good basis upon which to begin planning. Of prime importance is consideration of an easily accessible location for both family and visitors. The activity area should be designed to discourage transmission of sound; another possibility is to seal other rooms so that noise from activity areas does not penetrate them. Active leisure activities that take place outdoors cause less stress on those within the house. Because public facilities offer alternative means for active leisure, including such leisure space in the living environment may not be deemed economically justifiable.

Games and Exercise

Many families enjoy regular exercise. For children, exercise is a way to get rid of extra energy and to develop strength and coordination. For the adult exercise is a way to maintain or reduce weight, and to keep in good physical condition. Exercise may be an independent or a group activity. Some sound insulation is essential. Equipment for indoor exercise may include an exercise bar in a doorway or a punching bag in the garage. Dancing may be a part of a child's training or a social activity; in either case, a large free area with hard smooth floor is desirable.

Entertainment

Guests can be both a blessing and a problem. Visitors must be made to feel welcome whether they remain a few hours or for longer periods. When travel was difficult, visits might last for months. Modern highways and time limitations make this type of visit improbable. There are occasions when relatives and friends do come to stay. Some people are able to have a guest room waiting at all times. Others find sleeping mats or convertible furniture a wiser solution. Provisions for eating and sleeping must be made, as well as for storage areas for clothing brought by guests and for linens needed by them. A visitor

FIGURE 11-6 Storage space for luggage.

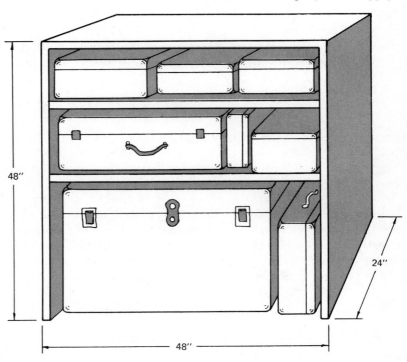

may bring only a small case with a few items, or several large bags, depending on the length of his stay and method of transportation.

Between trips, a place to store the family's own luggage is mandatory. Storage space must keep luggage dry, clean, and ready for use. If space is used economically, a storage unit 48 inches wide, 24 inches deep, and 48 inches high can hold even a large dress trunk. Space for guests' luggage can be found in an attic or garage, but that is inconvenient. Some airplane luggage can be stored on a closet shelf near the secondary entrance or in a bedroom.

TABLE 11-2	Luggage Sizes
Item	Approximate Size (Inches)
Dress Trunk	36×20×24
Foot Locker	30×15×12
Garment Bag	44×24×5
Pullman Case	30×23×8
Weekend Case	21×15×6
Tote Bag	15×14×6
Cosmetic Case	14×9×9

Festivals and Celebrations.   In most homes, guests are invited for holidays and such family occasions as weddings or anniversaries. The environment plays an important part in the celebration and the memories of it. Christmas, for example, takes on great significance in evaluations of space: decorations and lights must be stored, and a fireplace is found by many to be desirable. Birthday celebrations often involve food and games, so that space for additional people in an eating area is important.

Teas and Cocktail Parties.   Tea parties and cocktail parties are popular forms of adult entertainment. Dramatic use of light can create a more festive atmosphere. Space for small tables to hold glasses and dishes must be available in conversation centers. Decorative serving containers should be stored in the leisure center.

Romantic Cooking.   Involving guests in the cooking process is a good way of providing both entertainment and refreshments. Toasting marshmallows, mulling wine, popping corn, and broiling meat over an open fire stimulate fellowship, but require cooking facilities not normally found in the meal-preparation area, that is, a fireplace or barbecue pit. Decks, porches, patios, and gardens are appropriate for these, and an easily cleaned flooring is essential. Storage space for cooking forks, special pans, and grills should be located nearby.

SUMMARY

When young children are a part of the household, space should be provided for their more exuberant activities. Adult leisure activities are more quiet, and often productive as well: conversation, reading, listening to music, hobbies. The hobbyist and the collector may need special facilities. Storage space helps reduce clutter, making the area efficient when in use and more attractive when it is not. Entertaining friends and relatives is important, especially for the elderly.

12

Organization of Space

AN environment for living can foster cooperation among occupants and provide security and comfort for each individual. To insure sociability, provisions must be made for all the activities in which the occupants desire to participate.

Activities should be classified into a uniform, consistent plan. If a family is large or desires little privacy, or if there is little space available, several activities may take place simultaneously. Those that are compatible should be grouped; those that are not should be separated. Personal needs and preferences, the amount of money available, and the number of people involved inevitably influence these decisions.

ZONING

A living unit can be "zoned" for compatible activities. The functions desired should be listed, then grouped according to the degree of privacy or sociability required for each. Three possible groupings or zones are (1) public, living, or social; (2) operative, work, utility, or service; and (3) private, sleep, or rest. These groupings almost parallel the space for personal activities for work and for leisure. Two transitional zones are sometimes added to provide separation between the public and operative activities, and to differentiate between operative and private areas.

The Public Zone

The public zone provides a buffer between the world and the occupant and facilitates socialization. It should be easily located by strangers and have optimum natural light, the best view, and the most space.

199

Entrances. A good entrance makes it easy for strangers, friends, and family to approach. Strangers who want only to make a delivery—mail, newspaper, or parcel—need a convenient visible receptacle where the item may be deposited. For others a convenient, well-marked path to the door is necessary. The entrance should be compatible with the design of the structure and with the economic level of the neighborhood. A form of identification that is visible in dark and in daylight distinguishes the dwelling from those of the neighbors. In most urban areas, street numbers provide such identification, although some individuals have other indicators, such as a monogram on the chimney, or a title over the door. The mailbox placed at the end of a drive serves this purpose in rural areas.

A low, wide entrance suggests spaciousness; efficient parking, adequate space to maneuver, and temporary space for service or delivery vehicles suggests generosity and shelter. A concrete walk to the entrance provides protection underfoot. If steps are necessary, they should have nonskid surfaces to prevent falls, and should slope to one side to keep free of water and ice. Bushes should be far enough to the sides of the path so that branches do not brush against anyone walking on it.

The minimum property standards of the U.S. Department of Housing and Urban Development require a main entrance to have an exterior platform not less than 3½ feet square. Sheltered, it protects guests and occupants from rain or snow while they wait for the door to be opened. A seat suggests that the guests' comfort has been anticipated. Bell buttons should be at the same height and side as the doorknob. A knocker between the exterior door and the screen or storm door is not easily visible, but a knocker on an apartment door *is* visible and adds a touch of individuality.

The width of the exterior door should be at least half the height. A door wide enough to permit passage of two persons also permits large furniture to be moved into the house. Glass doors are inviting; heavy doors tend to seem forbidding.

The visitor frequently has a psychological advantage at the door whereas the occupant is often taken by surprise. A peephole, or a window that overlooks the entrance, can provide a view of arrivals.

In bad weather, muddy boots or shoes, wet garments or umbrellas pose a problem. A mat outside the door, or a built-in mat with sunken drain inside the door, encourages people to clean their shoes. The flooring in the entry should be one that does not show dirt, is easy to clean, and does not stain when wet. Tile, flagstone, and synthetic materials are all good choices.

Locks help prevent forcible entry. The U.S. Department of Housing and Urban Development requires that all exterior doors (except sliding doors) have an interlocking vertical bolt and striker, a minimum half-inch throwbolt, or a half-inch throw self-lock dead latch. A chain and lock should be added.

A main entry should lead guests to the leisure centers, service per-

FIGURE 12-1 Methods of identifying property.

A. Rural road sign

B. Urban house numbers (below)

C. Mail
boxes in the
suburbs
(below)

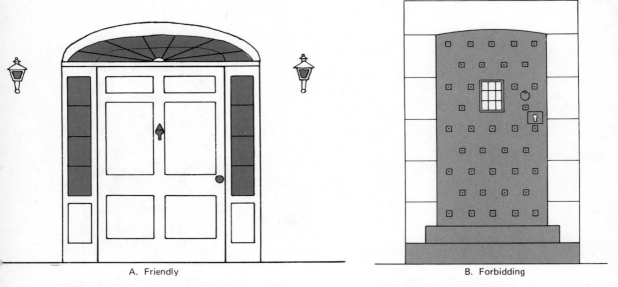

A. Friendly

B. Forbidding

FIGURE 12-2 Impressions received at the entrance.

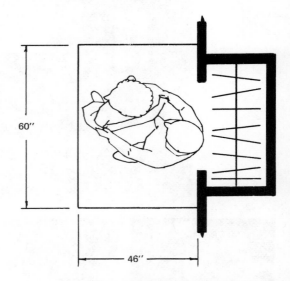

60"

46"

FIGURE 12-3 Space for entries.

sonnel to the work centers, and occupants to the private zones of the living unit. Ample space is needed to accommodate the donning and removal of outer garments. A seat is needed for adults to remove boots or overshoes. A mirror enables people to reassure themselves of a satisfactory appearance. Also useful is a table or shelf on which a guest

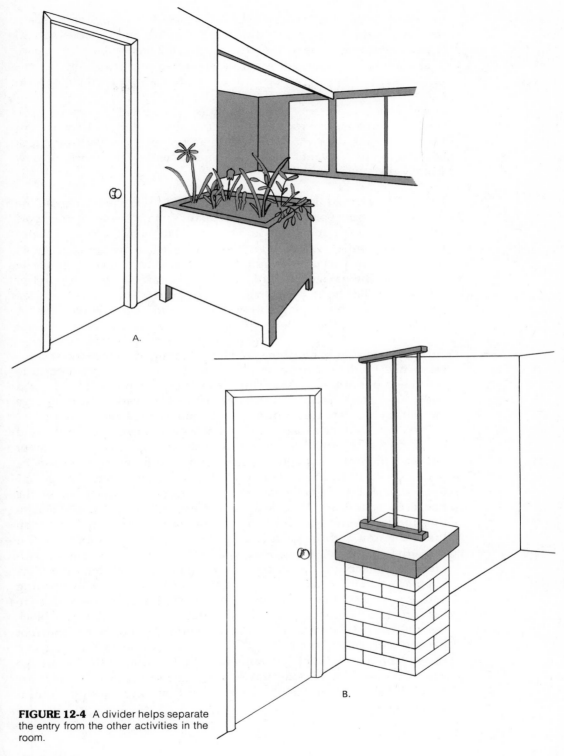

FIGURE 12-4 A divider helps separate the entry from the other activities in the room.

CHAPTER 12
ORGANIZATION OF SPACE

can leave things that he does not need during the visit. Storage space for outer garments is essential: the U.S. Department of Housing and Urban Development specifies a closet at least 2 feet wide. When space is at a minimum, main entries are designed as part of the leisure center; in such instances, a bookcase or planter can be used for separation.

A secondary entrance often provides convenient access to work areas and an alternate escape route. Once designated the "service entrance," it was used primarily by domestic help and led from work centers to the servants' quarters. The secondary entrance is now usually the favored family entrance.

Exits. Exits provide access to the public street. Exits should be planned to correspond with the occupant's main mode of transportation. The most popular mode of transportation in the United States is the automobile. Automobiles should be sheltered from sun, snow, rain, and dust. Because the auto is used frequently, it must be easily accessible. The garage should be an integral part of the living unit or at least attached to it by a breezeway or porch. The choice between garage and carport depends upon climate and construction costs. A garage provides protection against drifting snow and driving rain, but if protection from the sun is the problem, a carport is sufficient.

The garage should be large enough to accommodate the largest vehicle owned by the occupant and to allow the driver and passengers to get in and out of the vehicle. This means a clear depth of 20 feet and a width of 12 feet. Some recreational vehicles, or cars with a luggage rack attached to the top, require larger than average garage doors.

The most popular garage door is that which is manually raised and lowered on a track with a counterbalanced spring. An automatic door opener and closer is a convenience—and may be a necessity for the handicapped or in neighborhoods with a high crime rate. The garage door should blend, not contrast, with the design and color of the house. A pedestrian door facilitates access both to the house and to the outdoors. Local building codes often require a fire barrier between the living unit and the garage. To prevent water from running into it from the driveway, the garage floor should be raised one or two inches, preferably on a concrete slab. The drive that joins the thoroughfare should be as wide or wider than the garage door opening and as short and straight as possible. It should not be located close to the corner of the house, where existing trees or high hedges can block the view. Posts erected to mark the entrance should be one foot beyond each side of the drive. The driver should be able to see along the street a minimum of 100 yards in each direction. If the lot is large enough, a turnaround is desirable. The grade should not exceed 6 per cent, and the surface should slope away from any parking or turnaround area.

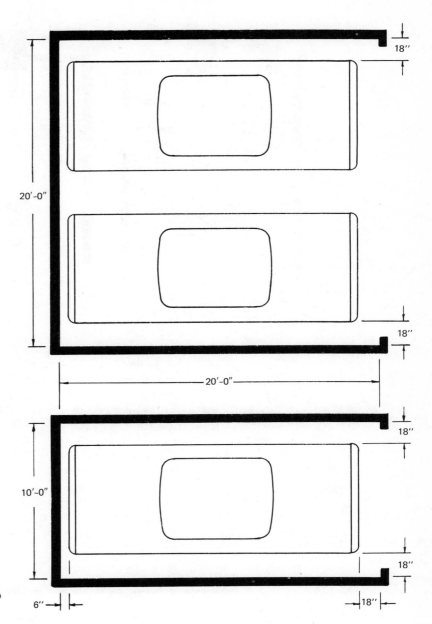

FIGURE 12-5 Minimum dimensions for one and two car garages.

The Semipublic Zone

The activities to which visitors or guests are invited are located in the semipublic zone. Recreation and refreshments are the principal activities.

Entertainment Centers. Entertainment centers often correspond to leisure centers. An analysis of expected leisure activities will deter-

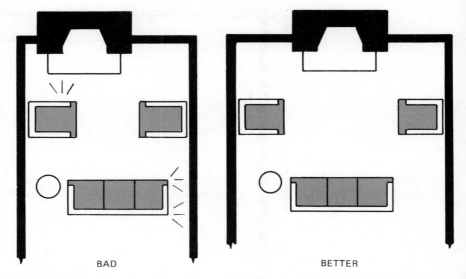

BAD   BETTER

FIGURE 12-6 Planning space for conversation and traffic areas around the fireplace.

mine need. Compatible activities can be placed in one area. Those that have no specific requirements can be accommodated anywhere that is convenient. Should some be compatible with the outdoors, the space required for entertaining within the living environment can be reduced. Outdoor activities give rise to additional requirements, such as the need for protection from sun, wind, and insects.

Only group leisure activities should be located in the semipublic zone. These should be grouped according to the age and life style of the participants, and the amount of exertion and confusion the particular activity generates.

A conversation center is a basic feature; it can, with minor adjustments, facilitate many other quiet leisure activities. In order to have enough space for chairs and passageways for a conversational group-

TABLE 12-1   Size of Living Area

Number of Bedrooms	Living Room (Square Feet)	Living Room Dining Area (Square Feet)	Living Room Dining Area Kitchen (Square Feet)
1	160	210	270
2	160	210	270
3	170	230	300
4	180	250	330

Adapted from *Minimum Property Standards for One & Two Family Dwellings*, Vol. 1, U.S. Department of Housing and Urban Development (Washington, D.C.: U.S.G.P.O., 1973), p. 4–6.

ing, the U.S. Department of Housing and Urban Development requires that one side of the area be at least 11 feet long. This is especially important if a fireplace or a window with a view is used as the focal center.

Active pursuits that give rise to clutter should take place in a family room, a recreational room, or a garden room. A southern exposure assures maximum sunshine, and the proper architectural devices can filter the sun and control wind. Screens and insect repellent will provide protection against pests. Outdoor centers should be coordinated with indoor centers—for example, by use of indoor-outdoor flooring. Outdoor electrical outlets are needed to operate small appliances and provide the lighting for parties; at other times, the outlets can be used to power hedge trimmers and other electrical garden tools.

Refreshment Areas. Inviting friends to share a meal is a favorite method of entertaining and no party is complete without refreshments. The food-preparation area must be screened from the living room and have direct access to the eating area. The semipublic zone may have a dining area in which guests are served formal meals, and/or a refreshment area equipped with a sink, an icemaker, and storage space for food and beverages.

Operative Zone

The operative zone encompasses the work of the household. It is more private than the social zone; guests are welcome in the operative zone only on invitation. The most significant communication between family members occurs here. The operative zone may require natural light or a window view, depending on the amount of time to be spent there, the time of day the work is performed, and the wishes of the occupants. Sometimes, especially in urban locations, only one work area—usually the meal-preparation center—can have a window. Mechanical ventilation is acceptable, and in many multifamily buildings, space for the work of the household is located toward the center "service core" of the building, making possible efficient connections to public utilities.

Kitchens. Ideally, the kitchen should be more than a food-processing and storage plant; it should give reassurance and positive pleasure as well. The design of the kitchen will be influenced by the values, work habits, and living patterns of the family as well as by its social standing and its concern for aesthetic appeal.

Kitchens are basically utilitarian in nature. That does not mean they cannot have style. Kitchens can be coordinated with the decorative scheme of the household through the careful selection of textures and colors for ceiling, walls, and floor, and also through the selection of cabinets and countertops.

FIGURE 12-7 A trend kitchen using the heritage of the Shaker community. Courtesy General Electric.

Laundries.   Another important part of the operative zone is the place clothing and household linens are cleaned and repaired. Usually only the occupants enter this area. Laundry rooms are usually located in the basement, yet a laundry room located on the same level as the rest of the living unit eliminates the need to climb stairs and permits laundry tasks to be coordinated with other tasks. Research has shown that when the laundry room is in the basement nearly half again as much walking is required for other household tasks on days that laundry is done.

Semiprivate Zones

Transitional zones between public and private areas or between operative and private zones are classified as semiprivate. The semiprivate zone is an especially appropriate location in which to accommodate overnight guests, or to provide supervision or aid to other members of the family.

Supervisory and Care Spaces.   A family member who is ill needs privacy for rest and recuperation yet also requires some communication with both the public and the rest of the household. The semiprivate zone is an ideal location: it is convenient to other work areas, so it conserves the time and energy of those who nurse the patient and prepare and serve the meals. To expedite the needs of the patient, the sickroom should have access to personal hygiene facilities often located in the semiprivate or private zones of the house.

Other members of the family—children at play or at study, the elderly and the handicapped—require occasional supervision while pur-

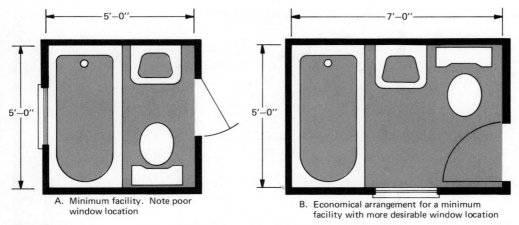

A. Minimum facility. Note poor
window location

B. Economical arrangement for a minimum
facility with more desirable window location

FIGURE 12-8 Minimum bathroom facilities.

suing private activities. In the semiprivate zone, they can enjoy a feeling of seclusion while not being isolated.

Personal Hygiene Facilities. When only one facility for personal hygiene is provided, it is usually located between the sleeping area and the leisure area so that it can be reached from either.

The design of the modern American bathroom evolved primarily from considerations of cost, not of convenience. In fact, the frequency with which each piece of equipment is used varies, as does the amount of time required for each activity and the degree of privacy desired by each family member. Kira believes that a single unit is obsolete and uneconomical if it is intended for use by more than one individual.[1] A partial or minimum facility—with a toilet and a washbasin—is all that is needed in the semiprivate zone, and could be accommodated in a space as small as 5 square feet. Planning guides recommend that a one-person bathroom be 35 square feet, but for anyone to help a child or a handicapped adult, at least 40 square feet is needed.

The U.S. Department of Housing and Urban Development requires that each living unit have at least one bathroom with a lavatory, a watercloset, and a bathtub. Showers, with a minimum area of 1,024 square inches and minimum dimension of 30 inches, can be substituted if additional facilities are installed. For each tub or tub/shower there must be a grab bar, a soap dish, and a water-impervious wainscot rising 6 feet from the bottom of the shower or tub on the walls surrounding the fixture. Soap dishes should be set at each lavatory, and a toilet paper holder beside each watercloset. A mirror, a medicine cabinet (or its equivalent in enclosed storage), and two towel bars are also specified. If income allows, variations in the arrangement and number of facilities are possible.

[1] A. Kira, *The Bathroom* (New York: The Viking Press, Inc., 1976), p. 180.

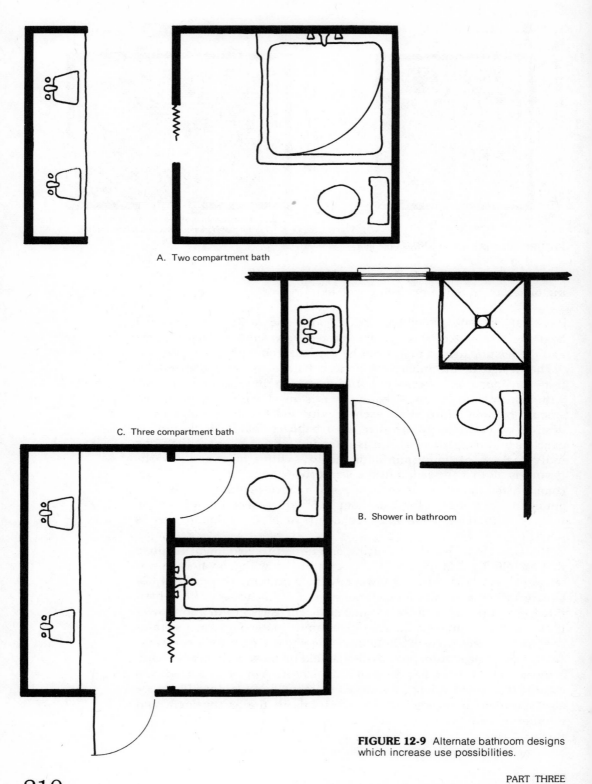

A. Two compartment bath

C. Three compartment bath

B. Shower in bathroom

FIGURE 12-9 Alternate bathroom designs which increase use possibilities.

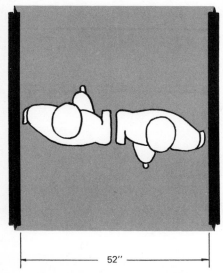

A. Minimum width for circulation

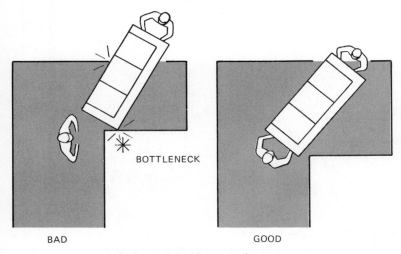

BOTTLENECK

BAD   GOOD

B. Space required for moving furniture
through circulation feature

FIGURE 12-10 Space for circulation.

Doors should be arranged so that they do not strike anyone in the room when they are opened and so that they shield the watercloset. For privacy, a lock with a safeguard to permit unlatching from the outside should be installed. The need for visual privacy tends to exclude transparent window glass in favor of frosted glass, high window vents, or skylights. Windowless rooms, with good artificial light and mechanical ventilation, offer other advantages: drafts are eliminated, cold and dirt are reduced, and wall space is increased. The sounds

CHAPTER 12
ORGANIZATION OF SPACE

Light switch 🔲

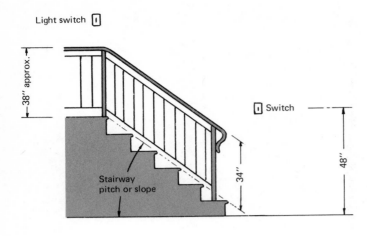

Stairway pitch or slope

38" approx.

34"

48"

🔲 Switch

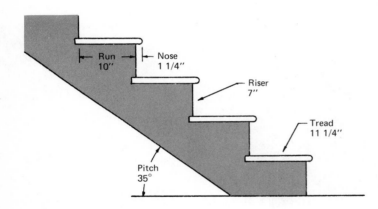

Run 10"

Nose 1 1/4"

Riser 7"

Tread 11 1/4"

Pitch 35°

FIGURE 12-11 Requirements for a well designed stairway.

caused by the use of operation of bathroom facilities can be reduced or eliminated by careful selection of fixtures and their proper installation, and by the use of acoustical ceiling tile, carpeting, and soundproof walls.

Circulation Features

Halls, corridors, and stairs are transitional spaces between the distinct atmosphere of one center and that of another. A divider, a half-wall, or even windows overlooking a patio or lanai provide an illusion of space, as does a wide door at the end of hall or stair. Narrow doorways often cause a sensation of confinement, and have the practical disadvantage of obstructing the passage of large items.

Halls and corridors should be convenient, safe, unobstructed, and as short and free of turns as possible. Floor coverings should be trip-

212

BOTTLENECK

BAD   GOOD

FIGURE 12-12 Improving stairway design.

proof, nonskid, and durable. Wall fixtures for lighting or shelving along side stairs are dangerous because someone ascending may strike his head. As much natural light as possible is desirable.

To provide for a safe ascent or descent under both normal and emergency conditions, as well as for the transport of furniture and equipment, stairs should be planned to accommodate the change in level rather than simply fitted into leftover space. The stairs easiest to climb have 7-inch risers and 11-inch treads, and slope at an angle of 33–40°.

Stairs are especially fascinating to children. A gate at the top and bottom of the stairway will prevent toddlers from venturing there.

In addition, tumble-safe stairs should have uniform risers and treads, adequate light, sufficient headroom, electrical switches at the top and bottom of the flight, handrails with banisters no further than 4 inches apart. Narrow landings and spiral stairways may cause bottlenecks, though spiral staircases are attractive and useful in a large two-story space where they can be seen to advantage.

Private Zone

The private zone is composed of those rooms devoted to those personal activities characterized by the need for privacy: sleeping and resting, dressing and undressing, personal hygiene and lovemaking. It is possible to accommodate all these activities in one room or in one attached to facilities for personal hygiene. A particularly efficient arrangement is a lavatory in the bedroom/dressing room with attached facilities for bathing and eliminating. More common arrangements include a half-bath with toileting and handwashing facilities or a minimum bath with shower. More elaborate arrangements include a bedroom with a dressing room and full bath or half-bath attached or a sleeping-dressing-personal-care suite.

FIGURE 12-13 Methods of arranging sleeping, dressing and personal activities to increase privacy.

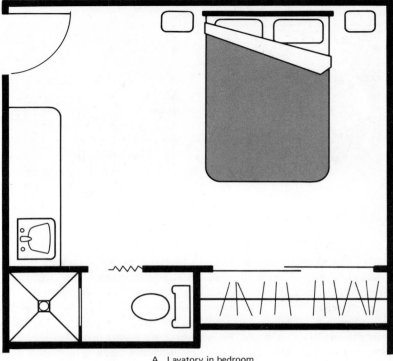

A. Lavatory in bedroom

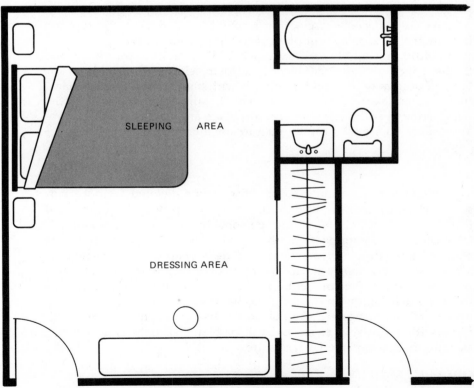

SLEEPING   AREA

DRESSING AREA

B. Bedroom with bath

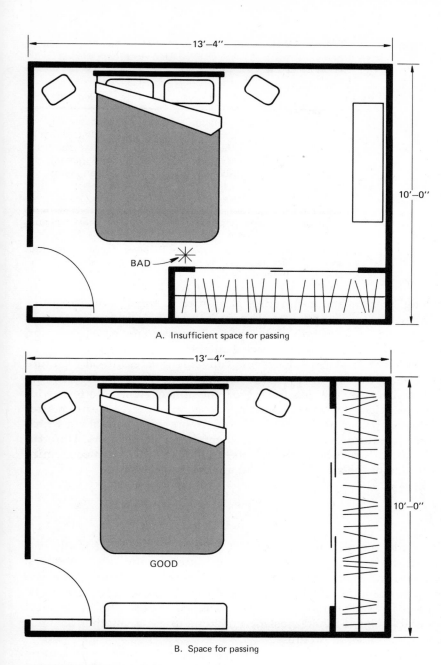

A. Insufficient space for passing

B. Space for passing

FIGURE 12-14 Improving bedroom design.

Most bedrooms have space only for sleeping and dressing, and the minimum size of the bedroom depends on the size of the bed intended for it (see Table 12-2). Separating the dressing area from the sleeping area is advantageous if more than one person occupies the

TABLE 12-2 — Size and Classification of Sleeping Area According to Bed Size*

Room Size (Sq. Ft.)	Classification of Area	Bed Type*
80	Minimum	(Single)
110	Small	Single (std. dbl.)
120	Medium–small	Double (std. twin)
140	Medium	Twin (queen)
170	Above average	Queen (king)
190	Large	King
220	Very large	King

* Largest bed type possible. Those in ( ) indicate minimum space for use and care.

Adapted from *The House: Principles/Resources/Dynamics* by Agan and Lucksinger. Reprinted by permission of the publisher, J. B. Lippincott Co. Copyright © 1965.

sleeping quarters and each retires at a different time. A dressing area also provides a warm place to change clothing if a window is open in the sleeping area. Subdividing space, however, increases cost and often restricts the amount of space available.

An efficient arrangement permits convenient access to all furniture and closet space. The bed or dresser should not be placed below the window because the headboard or the mirror will interfere with draperies, block the view, and impede ventilation. Large rooms reduce layout problems, because they offer more wall space along which to place furniture, windows, doors, heat ducts, or radiators. Unfortunately, as construction costs escalate, builders are likely to economize on the size of the sleeping/dressing areas.

ADJACENCY

A properly zoned house is based on a careful analysis of traffic patterns in the living environment. Major routes are indicated by doors, hallways, and stairs; minor ones, by furniture. The larger the family, the more complex traffic patterns become. Because efficiency is the prime goal, traffic patterns should be planned to be as short and direct as possible and to avoid crossing one zone to get to another or interrupting activities in progress.

A schematic analysis may help. A series of circles, representing rooms, can depict the relationship of areas within the unit. Connecting the circles indicates the location of doors, arches, and so forth. Even a novice can then determine the length of traffic routes from the street to the garage, from the garage or entry to work areas or to private areas. A more exact system is to draw a line on a blueprint to indicate a frequently used pathway, so that the exact distance traveled can be measured and conveniences or obstacles located. One activity

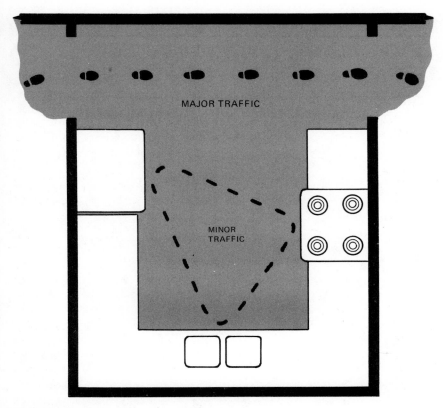

FIGURE 12-15 Methods of indicating traffic routes.

involving the entire living environment is retiring at night. This routine entails many processes—checking the thermostat, letting out pets, visiting children, undressing, washing or bathing, and finally climbing into bed. The route of these movements should be short and convenient with as little backtracking as possible.

Sleeping areas should be located together and have direct access to a hall and to personal hygiene facilities. Bedrooms for young children should be near those of the parents. When one bedroom is separated from the rest, additional space for personal hygiene should be provided.

Since leisure and eating are not mutually exclusive, activities space may be conserved by combining the living room with a dining area. Whether the dining room is separate or combined, it should be close to the meal-preparation center. A service hatch between them may save additional steps.

As the largest amount of household work is performed in the kitchen, many homemakers prefer to have it centered in the operative zone. If the laundry area is adjacent to the kitchen, work activities can be coordinated and plumbing costs minimized. A peninsula can be

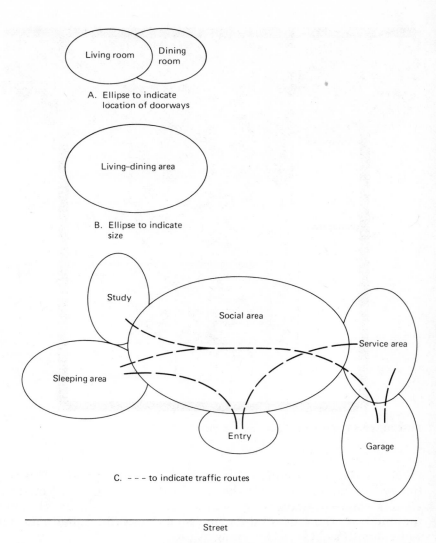

A. Ellipse to indicate
location of doorways

B. Ellipse to indicate
size

C. – – – to indicate traffic routes

Street

FIGURE 12-16 Using schematics for floor planning.

used to separate the meal-preparation area from the laundry area. A
pantry off the kitchen offers the advantage of locating the laundry near
a busy work area but separating the storage and confusion involved in
each task. A family room adjacent to the kitchen makes a pleasant
place to iron but is inconvenient for collecting and redistributing
clothing and household items.

In warm climates, breezeway, patio, carport, or garage are possible
laundry locations if exits are provided near clothes-collection points.
Any of these locations can also be used as a storage place for yard and
garden tools.

Most soiled laundry is collected, and clean laundry stored, in the

PART THREE
THE INFLUENCE OF THE MICRO-ENVIRONMENT: THE INTERIOR

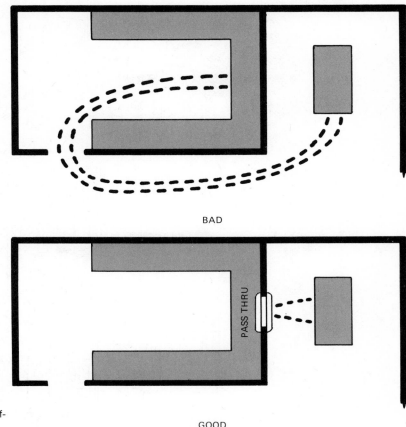

BAD

PASS THRU

FIGURE 12-17 Adjacency for meal preparation and dining areas help increase efficiency for serving.

GOOD

bedroom-bathroom area. A laundry located in this part of the living unit can save many steps; if it is in or near the bathroom, plumbing need not be extensive or costly. If space is limited, a washer–dryer combination or stack-on unit can be used. No additional sink is required because the lavatory of the bathroom is handy and the shower rod can be used for drip drying. Laundry centers in a bedroom, a large hall, or a bath can be successfully hidden by folding doors when not in use.

Food-preservation tasks, in urban homes, are located in the food-preparation area because of the similarity of equipment used. In rural homes, food preservation may encompass butchering, preparing eggs for market, and processing dairy products; a utility room may house these activities as well as the laundry task.

Child care is usually coordinated with other household activities. The design of the living environment can do much to conserve the parental energy required. Since children's needs vary according to age and stage of development, space for their activities needs to be flex-

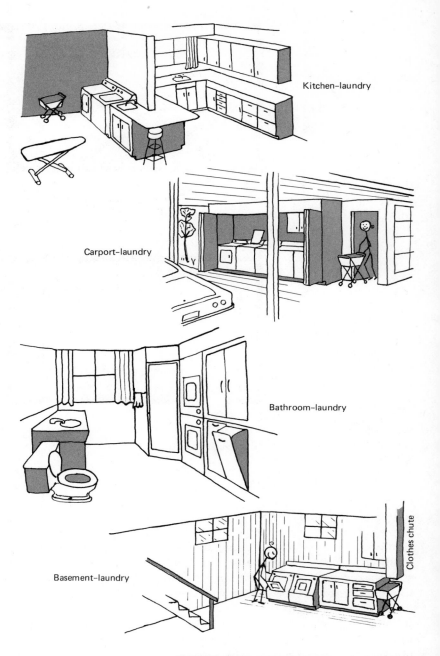

Kitchen–laundry

Carport–laundry

Bathroom–laundry

Basement–laundry

Clothes chute

FIGURE 12-18 Alternate locations for laundries.

ible. For very young children, a play area near the kitchen is preferred. This same area will be suitable for teen-agers' activities and will have the advantage of being near the meal-preparation area, thus facilitating the serving of refreshments.

PRIVACY

Privacy is not a luxury, but a necessity. Its importance to individualism and creativity cannot be underestimated.

The use of space and/or "buffers" between activities grants some extra privacy while extending the budget and often the amount of space actually allotted to an activity. These include spaces for heating and cooling, for heating or softening water, for chimneys, walls, halls, and storage closets that are not part of the activity but must be included in the floor plan. Visual privacy can be obtained by the use of doors or decorative dividers. For acoustical privacy, a buffer that absorbs sound can eliminate use of sound-deadening gadgets. A closet filled with clothes is often an ideal sound-deadener.

One activity that requires complete privacy is personal hygiene. Visual privacy is needed for the entrance to the bathroom. Bathroom sounds, whether human or mechanical, tend to be pronounced, easily identifiable, and embarrassing to both the originator and the listener. Acoustical privacy can be supplied by adding a sound-absorbing buffer to the visual screening. A close-fitting bathroom door will help to prevent some sound from escaping; easily cleaned carpeting also helps. An ideal buffer is a utility closet containing water-heating or water-softening devices. It not only absorbs noise but also reduces cost because the plumbing requirements are similar.

Maximum privacy is necessary when people do not want to be aware of the presence of others. In this extreme case, several devices must be coordinated. The best ones are subtle and inconspicuous, such as placing rooms next to each other that are used at different times of the day. Further separation can be insured by the addition of a chimney wall, a storage partition, or double-entry doors.

ECONOMY

Everyone wants as much as possible for his money. Usually the goal in housing is to have the most accommodations for the least sum or the maximum accommodations for a given sum. This encourages the use of space for more than one activity.

As the center of the work of the household, kitchens are the most popular area for space economy. Many different activities are located there—dining, laundry, children's leisure activities, informal relaxation, and many others.

The business center of the home does not differ significantly from the children's study area, the planning center for meal preparation, or the home office. The top of the dining table offers a large surface on which to spread out work, and can be more comfortable and more spacious than a standard desk.

Invisible elements, such as plumbing and wiring, are other points at

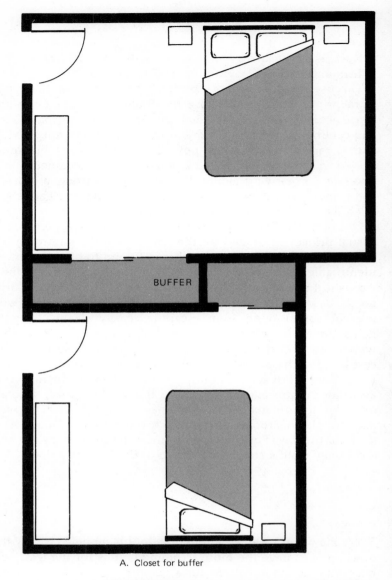

A. Closet for buffer

FIGURE 12-19 Alternate methods for creating buffers.

which to practice economy. Initial and maintenance costs can be kept low if pipes are as few, as short, and have as few bends as possible. A plumbing stack must rise above the roof to carry off odors from the drains and descend into the ground to connect with the public sewer. If rooms that require plumbing are placed back to back, on one wall, or over one another, the plumbing stacks can serve several fixtures.

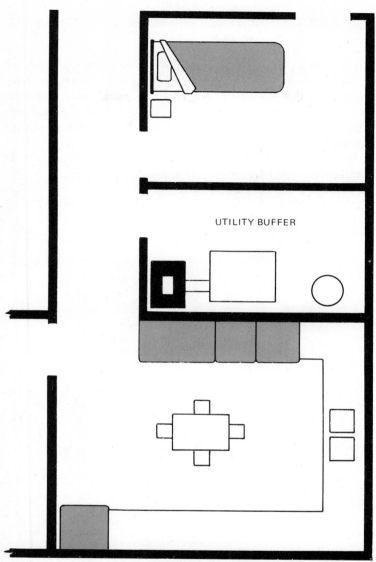

UTILITY BUFFER

B. Utility room for buffer

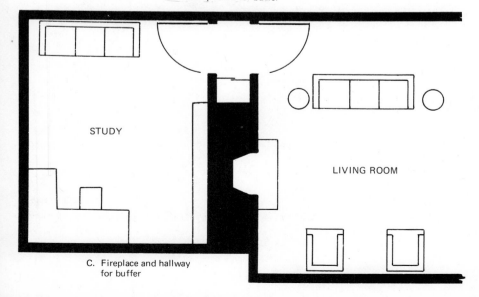

STUDY

LIVING ROOM

223

C. Fireplace and hallway
for buffer

SUMMARY

A living unit should be planned to meet the needs of people within a limited amount of space and to help them maintain low costs, for construction, repair, and remodeling. Extremes in room and area size should be avoided, and areas should be simple in shape, should permit variation in function, and should present a variety of zoning and circulation possibilities.

A utility room, a sufficiently large bathroom, or the kitchen is needed to house domestic equipment or appliances.

Storage or furniture should not be built in.

Circulation space should be treated as a room between rooms not as an access link.

Making Space Livable

LIVABLE space provides a healthful, happy atmosphere. Each generation has its own needs and tastes so that what was good for one is obsolete for another. As Mumford observed,

. . . even the finest urban dwellings of the last century are, for a greater part, obsolete. They were conceived in terms of a limited and now outworn mode of living. . . .[1]

During the last century for example, bathing facilities were considered unnecessary because bathing was considered a health hazard. Twentieth-century beliefs make cleanliness basic to health, and space for personal hygiene a necessity. Yet all the so-called modern conveniences for heating, cooking, lighting, and plumbing were introduced during the nineteenth century. Most of these conveniences are built into today's houses although it is sometimes more economical to install equipment after construction. This discussion is limited to those systems commonly provided as a basic part of the structure.

CLIMATE CONTROL

The climate of the interior environment is controlled: provision is made for sufficient heat, air, and moisture, and for the removal of offensive odors and dust from the atmosphere.

Mechanical systems modify atmospheric conditions by balancing air movement, air temperature, and relative humidity. In general, air must circulate, smell fresh, have a temperature of 17–29°C. (62–85°F.),

[1] Lewis Mumford, *The Culture of Cities* (New York: Harcourt Brace Jovanovich, Inc., 1938), p. 465.

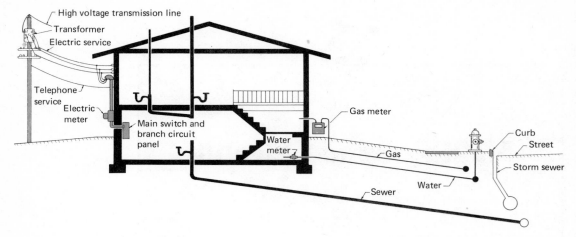

FIGURE 13-1 Utility connections.

and contain just the right amount of moisture. Many combinations provide comfort. Medical specialists and air-conditioning engineers suggest that comfort is based on a ratio of temperature to relative humidity: temperature, 22–30°C. (72–78°F.); relative humidity, 40–60 per cent.

The extent to which mechanical systems are incorporated into the living unit is determined by the natural climate, the cost, and the susceptibility of the occupants to pollen. Heat is required in almost all climates, and air-cooling systems have a high priority where the natural climate reaches extremely high temperatures or remains high for protracted periods of time. In humid or very dry areas, moisture control may be desirable. In most areas, humidifying and dehumidifying systems are designed to cope with small spaces, and are usually installed separately.

Heating

The ideal heating system supplies enough heat to compensate for the body's heat loss, to prevent drafts, to warm floors and walls, and to provide even temperatures from room to room. Fluctuations in temperature, the size and orientation of the house, the number and size of windows, the construction of the walls, the amount of insulation, the type of fuel, and the personal needs and tastes of the family determine heat requirements. Minimum heat levels established by local building codes do not insure an efficient or low-cost system.

Fireplaces. From the earliest times, the fireplace has supplied warmth, light, and heat for cooking. It welcomes the guest, cheers the weary, and warms the soul—or the seat of the pants, depending on the need.

The advent of the wood range, followed by central heating, eliminated the need for fireplaces but not their attraction. Gas logs and heaters or electrically illuminated fittings gave the illusion of an open fire and provided a little heat without the attendant problems of supplying wood or coal, or getting rid of smoke and ashes. The energy crises of the 1970s, followed by the shortage of fossil fuels for central heating systems, prompted new interest in the fireplace. Although still considered a luxury (a well-designed one is about 10 per cent efficient), a fireplace can combat chill in the spring and fall, furnish auxiliary heat for part of a building, heat buildings used only occasionally, or fill in during an emergency when fuel supplies are unexpectedly cut off.

The contemporary fireplace can be both beautiful and useful. The fireplace serves as a focal point for planning furniture arrangement.

FIGURE 13-2 Details of a fireplace.

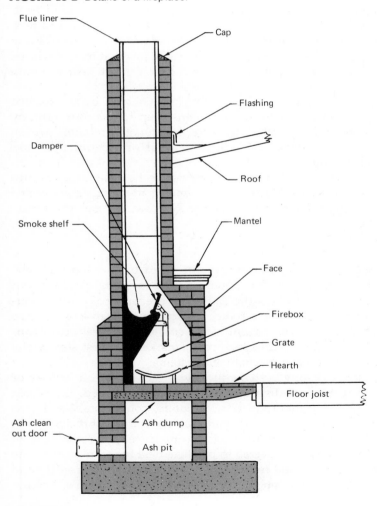

The fire itself adds fascinating light, color, movement, and brilliance to any room. People and objects appear more interesting in its glow; its warmth is considered more enjoyable than that provided by other means; it makes cooking more fun and seems to give a better taste to food.

If a fireplace is to be useful, it must be well designed. Poor fireplace construction and defective or overheated chimneys and flues are a frequent cause of residential fires. Fires can be prevented by keeping the flue clean and using a spark arrester on the chimney. Proper flashing around the chimney on the roof of the house will prevent water leakage that could cause damage to interior walls and ceilings. The fire chamber may be masonry, prebuilt metal with or without a heat circulator, or a prefabricated freestanding model wide enough for firewood 2 feet long. Only prebuilt factory models are guaranteed not to smoke. A fireplace located in the center of the house generates heat more efficiently because the chimney heats quickly and cools slowly, and because other rooms also benefit from the chimney's retained heat. Fireplaces located higher than floor level are more convenient to tend but provide less heated air to floor areas. The damper that controls the draft should have a movable valve plate or adjustor that may be closed when the fireplace is not in use, in order to prevent heat loss and reduce floor drafts.

Kindling, fuel supply, and fire-tending tools should be stored near the hearth. Built-in or traversed fire screens keep sparks from igniting combustibles near the hearth, and solve the storage problem. An ash dump with cleanout located outside or in an ash pit permits easy removal of dirt and mess.

People living in multifamily units or mobile homes can use simulated portable fireplaces. Recent improvements in design give them a more realistic appearance, guarantee the BTU rating, and make them easy to install.

Central Heating.   Central heating was initiated by the Romans, who invented elaborate systems for moving heated air through floors and walls. The Franklin stove was the American precursor of central heating. Placed in the center of the room, it radiated enough heat to keep one room comfortable. The advent of the coal-fired central boiler connected to radiators installed in each room marked the first step in the development of automatic mechanized systems.

Modern central heating systems include a fuel burner, a furnace or boiler in which the heat-distributing medium is warmed, pipes and ducts, room heating units (registers, radiators, convectors, baseboard units, or concealed panels), and temperature controls. Efficiency depends on the method of installation, the fuel used, and the type of operation. The system is expected to produce heat for months at a time with little maintenance and repair. Those systems that meet safety and performance standards often have a seal of approval from a heating

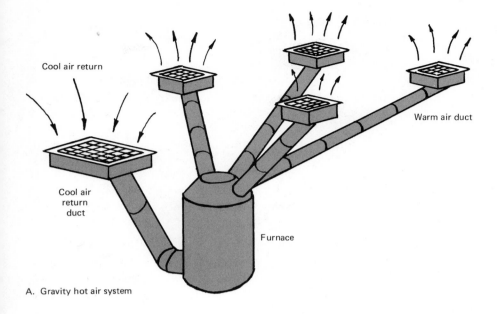

Cool air return

Cool air return duct

Furnace

Warm air duct

A. Gravity hot air system

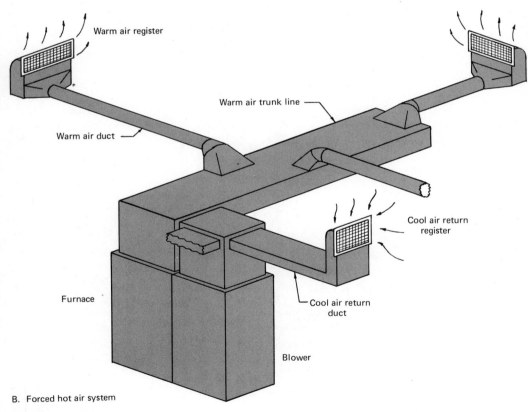

Warm air register

Warm air trunk line

Warm air duct

Cool air return register

Furnace

Cool air return duct

Blower

B. Forced hot air system

FIGURE 13-3 Hot air systems.

CHAPTER 13
MAKING SPACE LIVABLE

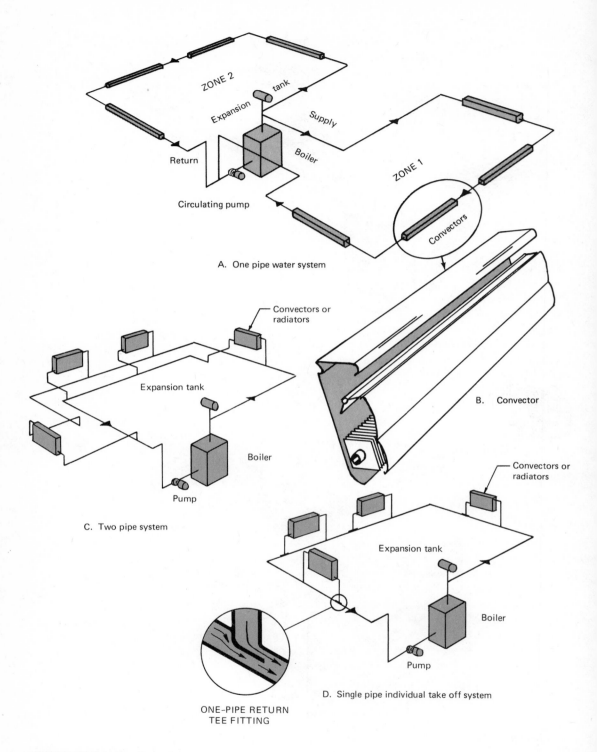

A. One pipe water system

B. Convector

C. Two pipe system

ONE–PIPE RETURN
TEE FITTING

D. Single pipe individual take off system

FIGURE 13-4 Hot water systems.

trade association or technical society. Installation must meet local ordinances.

Air, steam, or hot water can be used as the medium for transporting heat to the various rooms of the residence. The medium is heated in a space around or near the burner and circulated through ducts or pipes. (Floor furnaces without ducts are sometimes used in moderate climates.) Warm air enters the room through radiators or registers installed in the ceiling, wall, or floor. Cold air or water descends to the furnace through return ducts or pipes. Movement occurs from force of gravity, or a blower, fan, or pump. Gravity systems are quiet, easy, and economical to install, and most suitable for small houses. A fan or pump helps give more equal distribution of heat throughout large houses.

Air systems sometimes need a filter to clean dirty air and a humidifier to add moisture to dry air. Properly adjusted, the system does not create dirt or dust but may stir up and redistribute dirt or dust that is already present. Small ducts can be used for both heating and cooling and provide a more flexible system than one with large ducts that can be used only for heating. Outlets should be located under windows or around the perimeter to keep the floor warm. Several types of hot-water systems are available. A one-pipe series has the advantage of low-cost installation, but rooms at the farthest point from the furnace may not be as warm as those closer to the source of heat. Although installation of several hot-water loops is more expensive, such a system is more efficient; individual regulation at each radiator improves the situation still more. The best system, and also the most expensive system to install, has one pipe to deliver the hot water to the room radiators and another to return the cold water to the boiler.

Steam heat is similar in operation, the main difference being that steam rather than water is the heat-distributing medium. Water changes to steam in the boiler, rises to the radiators where it condenses into water as it releases heat, and returns to the boiler. The system is simple to maintain and operates economically because motors or electrical connections are unnecessary. Unless the house has a basement, a pump is needed.

A radiant hot-water system pumps heated water through coils of pipe embedded in the floor, walls or ceiling (floor installations are most common). Its major advantages are the absence of visible radiators or baseboard units, and freedom from drafts. Among its disadvantages are a slow response to changing temperatures, a floor temperature often too high for comfort, and as much as a 50 per cent decrease in efficiency because of floor coverings and furniture.

Automatic temperature controls or thermostats are basic to any heating system. One thermostat is usually sufficient to control the heat for the entire living unit although individual room thermostats can be appropriate. For maximum benefit, the thermostat should not be affected by any other heat source, such as a fireplace or sun streaming through a picture window. Sometimes a thermostat's response setting varies too much to allow an even temperature. A simple adjustment can nar-

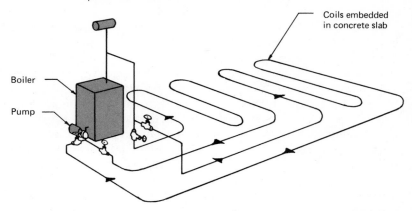

Expansion tank

Coils embedded in concrete slab

Boiler

Pump

FIGURE 13-5 Radiant hot water system.

row the range of a bimetal thermostat. Other types of thermostats are not adjustable and must be replaced by a more sensitive instrument.

Although solid fuels (coal and coke) are dirtier to handle, there is little significant difference among fuels in terms of the safety and cleanliness of the heat they produce. Although the kind and amount of storage required will affect convenience, efficiency, and cost, those fuels that are most available are usually least expensive. Most fuels are between 55 and 100 per cent efficient, with bituminous coal consistently lower and electricity the highest. Oil, gas, and anthracite coal or coke are approximately 80 per cent efficient. Too much or too little air entering the combustion chamber affects the relative completeness of combustion, and heat can escape through the front of the furnace or boiler, up the smoke pipe, or the chimney, all of which reduces efficiency.

The amount of storage required for different fuels varies. Natural gas and electricity are supplied as needed by a local utility. Tanks (thus space) must be supplied for gas under pressure, manufactured gas, and oil. No more than 500 gallons of fuel oil may be stored in a basement. Larger tanks must be located outside, usually buried. No more than 125 pounds of liquid petroleum may be stored in tanks adjacent to the living unit; larger tanks must be located as much as 25 feet away from the house—the larger the tank, the greater the required distance from the building. Coal requires storage bins in the basement or in an outside shed. The closer it is to the point of use, the less time and energy need be devoted to keeping the heating system fueled. A larger storage area means that fuel may be purchased during off-seasons when prices may be lower.

It is difficult to compare fuel costs because the various fuels lack a common measure. Solid fuels are sold by the ton; liquids, by the gallon; gas, by cubic feet. For the consumer, a comparison of fuel bills for equally satisfactory living units is more helpful than heating cost

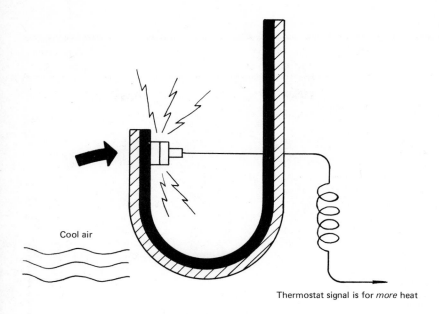

Cool air

Thermostat signal is for *more* heat

A. On position

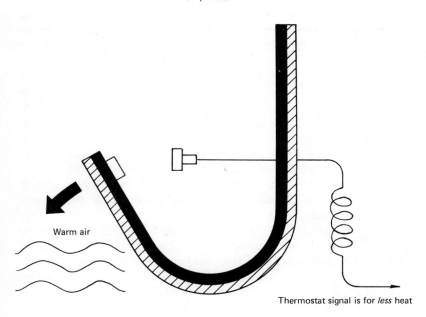

Warm air

Thermostat signal is for *less* heat

B. Off position

FIGURE 13-6 Operation of an automatic control for a heating system.

TABLE 13-1   Comparison of Heating Systems

Considerations	Gravity	Forced Air	Hot Water Baseboard	Radiant Floor
Air				
Fluctuation, Room to Room	Large	Medium	Small	Very Small
Fluctuation, Floor to Ceiling	Large	Medium	Small	Very small
Response	Fast	Fast	Slow	Slow
Humidification	None	Yes	None	None
Ventilation	None	Good	None	None
Stagnant Air Pockets	Yes	None	Possible	Possible
Surface Temperature				
Floor	Cold	Warm	Warm	Very warm
Ceiling	Hot	Medium	Medium	Medium
Walls	Medium	Medium	Warm	Warm
Windows	Cold	Medium	Medium	Medium
Temperature of Heating Medium at Discharge or Surface	High	Very low	Low	Very low
Cleanliness				
Dust Circulation	High	High	Low	None
Dust Removal	None	Filters	None	None
Noise	Quiet	Medium	Quiet	Very quiet

Adapted from E. Wilson, *Heating Systems for the Home.* E.M.2733 Cooperative Extension Service, College of Agriculture, Pullman, Wash., June 1975, p. 8.

calculations. In general, fuel oil is considered least expensive in southeastern and northwestern United States, electricity is considered high in all areas, and natural gas is most commonly used in all regions. Coal, heavy and dirty to handle, is currently the least used residential fuel. An electric heating system is compact and requires no furnace room, ducts, flue, or plumbing. It is said to be the most versatile, convenient, and controllable, but lack of an on-site emergency supply makes the availability of an alternate method of heat desirable in case the supply of electricity is interrupted.

The shortage of fossil fuels in the 1970s initiated a search for new energy sources. Wind, thermoheat, and solar energy have all been suggested. Most progress has been in the area of solar energy. Weather records from representative communities throughout the United States show that even during the winter the sun shines about 38.8 per cent of the total possible daylight hours. Even when the sun is not actually shining, some solar heat is available. To convert solar heat for residential application, it must be collected, transmitted to storage, recovered from storage, and redistributed where and when needed at minimal loss. The heat pump traps heat from the atmosphere and operates on the same principle as the refrigerator. Circulation may be provided by electric motors or generated thermodynamically.

Solar collectors, placed in the attic or on the roof, trap heat from

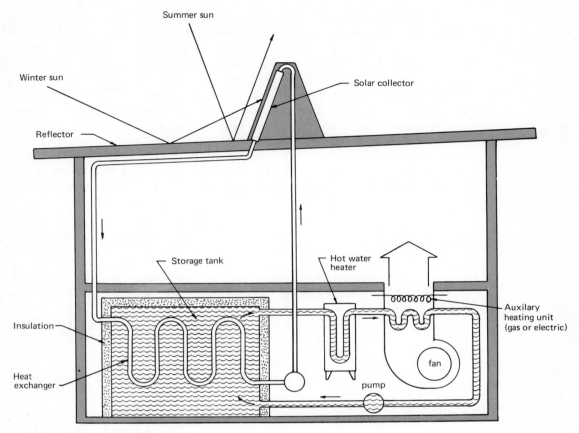

FIGURE 13-7 Solar heating system.

both direct and diffused rays and transfer it to a liquid that carries the heat to a storage area of crushed rock, chemicals, or water. When needed, the heat is distributed throughout the residence. To date, these systems can provide approximately 75 per cent of the home heating requirements and store as much as a three-day supply to use on overcast days. Operationally, solar heat is not yet competitive with oil or natural gas. The disadvantages of solar heat are the high cost of installation and the need for stand-by furnaces or heaters.

Cooling

The ideal cooling system controls temperature, humidity, and air movement. Forced air movement is as old as time: elaborate feather fans appear in Egyptian hieroglyphics. Until recently, however, cooling was considered a personal, not a housing, problem and most women solved it by carrying a fan as part of their costumes.

Natural Ventilation. Natural ventilation through advantageous window and room placement was the usual defense against summer heat. It remains the most economical solution. The first consideration in planning the location of windows is to take advantage of whatever natural air movement is available. Guidelines published in current *Minimum Property Standards* attempt to insure natural air movement by requiring a ventilatory window area equal to 4 per cent of the floor space in each room. When this requirement interferes with visual effect, sliding doors are an alternative.

Mechanical Systems. When there is no natural air movement or the humidity and temperature are excessive, mechanical air conditioning

FIGURE 13-8 An evaporative cooler.

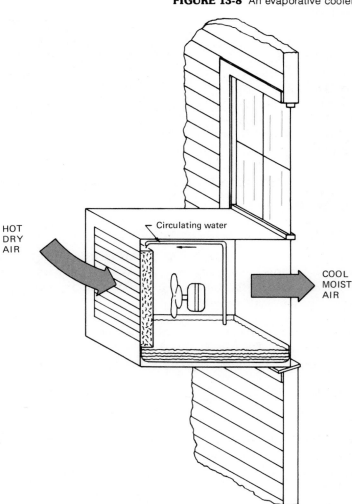

HOT
DRY
AIR

Circulating water

COOL
MOIST
AIR

is necessary. When electricity first became common, large fans were attached to electric motors and installed in the ceiling to stir the air. Today, small exhaust fans are frequently installed as an integral architectural feature in activity centers where heat or moisture is excessive. Fans used to circulate heated air in the winter can be used to circulate cool air in summer if the heating system is located where the summer heat does not penetrate readily. A large window or attic fan that exhausts warm or hot air from a room, attic, or an entire house helps to reduce interior air temperatures— but only if the outside air is cooler. However, such fans can also introduce dust and humid air or may cause disruptive noise. Their optimum size depends on the floor area and the number of times the air is to be exchanged. Whether these fans reduce energy costs is unknown; tests, to date, have been inconclusive.

In hot, dry climates an evaporative cooler is successful. A typical installation has a fan that draws outdoor air through a moistened pad into a cabinet where the air is cooled. The cool air is circulated through ducts or directly into the room. Provision must be made for disposal of any excess water used to moisten the filter pad.

A refrigeration system is the most positive method of cooling the air. The more common of the two available types is the compression–expansion system, which may be installed in a single room or an entire building. Sometimes the ducts and fan that distribute the warm air in the winter can be used. Correct installation and maintenance will insure quiet, dependable service. The unit can be more efficient if

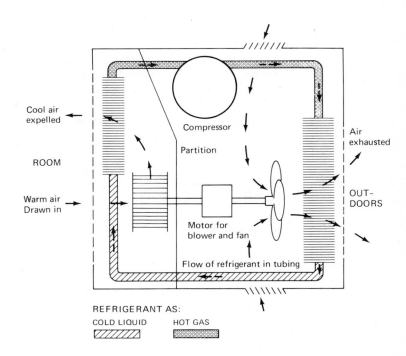

FIGURE 13-9 A refrigeration-type air cooling system.

Cool air expelled

ROOM

Warm air Drawn in

Compressor

Partition

Motor for blower and fan

Flow of refrigerant in tubing

Air exhausted

OUT-DOORS

REFRIGERANT AS:

COLD LIQUID   HOT GAS

the air entering it is cool, so outdoor compressors should be located in a cool place, usually the north side of the building. Surrounding the refrigeration unit with a solid fence or shrubbery provides shade and reduces operational noise. A thermostat that maintains a narrow air temperature differential will reduce the amount of operation and lower costs. Open doors and windows decrease the efficiency of a cooling system by increasing the volume of air.

Insulation. Neither heating nor cooling systems can be efficient without adequate insulation, which controls the passage of heat. In a world of limited energy resources, insulation is increasingly important for it reduces costs while conserving energy. Moreover, insulation also helps to control moisture and sound.

Insulating materials are rated according to thermal resistance or *R* value, which is proportionate to the thickness of the insulating material—the higher the *R* value, the greater the ability of the insulation to retain or exclude heat. In order to be eligible for Federal Housing Authority loans, houses must meet established standards for insulating materials between floors, walls, and ceilings. Fiberglass sheets designed to fit between framing are most frequently used because of their high insulating qualities, low cost, and resistance to vermin and moisture.

Humidity

The control of moisture in the air is as important as the control of temperature. Lack of sufficient moisture can cause physical discomfort, build up static electricity, loosen furniture joints, or cause structural beams to warp. Growing plants add water to the atmosphere, but the most effective method is to add a humidifier to an existing hot-air heating and cooling system. The amount of water required is determined by the type of construction and the size of the area to be humidified.

Houses without a vapor barrier should not be humidified, for over-humidification may cause the peeling or blistering of paint, as well as rust, mildew, and other damage. A good sign that overhumidification exists is condensation or frost on the inside of windows. Like a humidifier, a dehumidifier can be attached to a hot-air heating and cooling system.

Removal of Air Pollutants

Many people are sensitive to dust and pollen. Most forced hot-air systems include a filter of aluminum or plastic mesh, which removes about 8 per cent of the dust particles from the air. Efficient operation of forced air systems is dependent on periodic replacement of filters.

Electronic air cleaners are more effective, and these too can be added to the central air system to remove pollens, smoke, fumes, and other

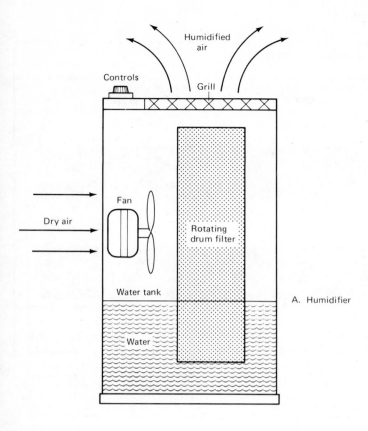

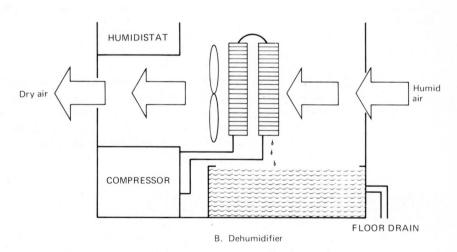

FIGURE 13-10 Systems for controlling moisture in the air. Humidifier drawing courtesy of Hoover Company.

TABLE 13-2

HUMIDIFICATION SELECTION GUIDE

Find your humidification requirements by first determining the size of your home and its type of construction. Then read across to the necessary humidification requirements. For example, if you have a 1500 square foot home with average construction, you have a humidification requirement of **at least** 7.7 gallons/24 hours.

CONSTRUCTION OF RESIDENCE	SIZE OF RESIDENCE IN SQ. FT.					
	500	1000	1500	2000	2500	3000
Tight (Well insulated, Vapor Barrier, Tight Storm Doors and Windows with Weather Stripping, Dampered Fireplace)	0.1	2.1	4.2	6.3	8.4	10.4
Average (Insulated, Vapor Barrier, Loose Storm Doors and Windows, Dampered Fireplace)	1.2	4.4	7.7	10.9	14.1	17.4
Loose (Little insulation, No Storm Doors or Windows, No Vapor Barrier, Undampered Fireplace)	2.5	6.9	11.4	15.9		24.8

NOTE: If there is uncertainty as to the type of home construction, the values shown in the average category (the unshaded area) may be used.

An amount of approximately 2 gallons per 24 hours provided by internal sources of humidity (based on a family of four) has already been deducted from the above values.

To prevent overhumidification, make certain you properly adjust the humidistat, preferably when there is a major change in outdoor temperature. Condensed moisture or frost on inside windows is a good sign that your controls are set too high. You can place your humidifier almost anywhere in the living area as long as the moist air can circulate freely throughout the house. Avoid placing the unit near cold, outside walls or in the bathroom, kitchen, or laundry area. When your humidifier first begins to operate, it may run constantly for a day or so in order for dry furniture, drapes, etc. to absorb moisture. Normal changes in indoor and outdoor conditions will cause the unit to cycle on and off to maintain necessary humidity levels. When determining the square foot area to be humidified, include only those areas where normal, daily living occurs.

Reprinted by special permission from 1976 AHAM Directory of Certified Humidifiers by Association of Home Appliance Manufacturers.

pollutants by magnetic force as air passes over a series of collector plates and through filters of various sizes. Periodically these plates and filters must be washed. The efficiency of electronic cleansers depends on the volume and velocity of the air passing through them, so it is important not to increase air volume by opening doors and windows when the system is in use.

SANITARY CONDITIONING

Sanitary conditioning emphasizes the prevention of contagion. It has been an important factor in the formation of American housing policies throughout the country's history. Many health and safety regulations have been enacted at both federal and local levels.

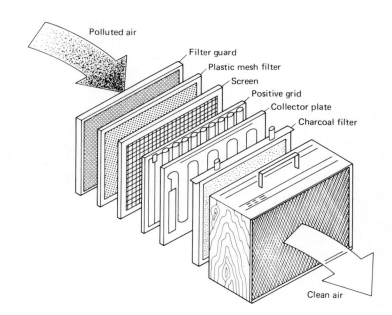

Polluted air

Filter guard
Plastic mesh filter
Screen
Positive grid
Collector plate
Charcoal filter

Clean air

FIGURE 13-11 An electric air cleaning system Courtesy of the Hoover Company.

Water Supply

The human body is 55–70 per cent water, and water is also an essential part of most body functions. Too little water causes some form of dehydration, the symptoms of which range from weight loss to mental confusion. Water is also needed as a cooking medium, for cleaning the body and laundry. Unsafe water is an invitation to disease.

It is not surprising that a good source of water is a prime factor in selecting a place to live. The Nile River supplied the Egyptians; the springs of an oasis supplied the nomads of the desert; and in North America, the Plains Indians always camped at the junction of two streams, using one for a water supply, and the other for disposing of human waste. The discovery of underground water made it possible to live away from natural supplies. Wells became the central feature of the town square or plaza. Until about 1850, individual householders in the United States were responsible for supplying water to their residences. Individual wells and rain water (collected from the roof and piped into cisterns or barrels) were prime sources.

Most metropolitan areas today have a public water supply, the standards for which are set and maintained by local and state health officials. In rural areas, private wells must conform to the specifications set by local health officials. Rain water is still collected and stored, and although inconsistent in quality, often proves desirable for washing clothes, maintaining lawns, or augmenting major water supplies during a long, dry period.

Regardless of the source of supply, there should be an emergency shutoff valve before water enters the living unit. There are usually two such valves for a single detached house: one at the junction to the public system, usually at the front near the street, and a second one near the water meter when one is required (some utilities charge a flat rate or a per-fixture fee).

Pipes that carry water through the structure should not leak, make noise, reduce pressure, or impart any color or taste to the water. Most building regulations require copper pipe or flexible copper tubing, which are less likely to leak because joints are soldered and because copper is impervious to the corrosive materials often found in water. Some codes permit the use of galvanized steel or wrought iron. Plastic pipe is available but it is not yet permissible in many areas.

When public supply is obtained from deep wells, many minerals may be dissolved in it; calcium, magnesium, sulfates, bicarbonates, and iron are the most common. Although not harmful to health, they cause laundry problems or give water an offensive taste. Equipment designed to remove these salts can be permanently installed or rented to treat all or part of the home water supply.

Short pipes to transfer the heated water from heat source to point of use conserve fuel. To eliminate as much heat loss as possible the water heater should be placed at a central location. Pipes longer than 15 feet should be insulated. Water can be heated by one of several methods. It is possible to combine the hot-water system with the furnace. This provides a fast recovery rate, but it may also necessitate running the furnace year round or having separate connections for summer and winter. A more common solution is to install a separate tank fired by either gas or electricity. Electric heaters are generally larger and do not have a fast recovery rate, making them more suitable as "peak load" installations for heating water only at night or during the early morning hours when general usage is low. Gas heaters recover faster and, depending on family size and need, a small tank holding between 30 or 40 gallons of water is often sufficient (see Table 13-3). Although oil heaters are also available, they are expensive and installation costs are high, especially if oil has not been previously installed as a heating or cooking fuel. While final selection must be based on the relative fuel costs in the area, using the same fuel for heating water as for heating the air may be the most expedient decision.

TABLE 13-3		Size of Gas Hot Water Storage Tank per Household
Bedrooms	Bathrooms	Water Capacity
1–2	1	40
3–4	2	50
4–5	2	75
4–5	3	100

Adapted from *Enough Hot Water . . . Hot Enough* (Arlington, Va.: American Gas Association), p. 5.

Each detached dwelling should have an outside water faucet. The U.S. Department of Housing and Urban Development requires two, located on opposite sides of the house. In areas where temperature drops below freezing, each faucet should have an individual shutoff valve to prevent pipe damage.

Sewage Disposal

Disposal of human waste received little attention until the link between contagious diseases and lack of sanitation was discovered. Boston was the first city in the United States to have a sewer system. In most metropolitan areas today, sewage disposal is an expected municipal service. When a city sewer system is available all structures must be connected whether or not a satisfactory individual system has been installed.

The sewage system depends upon gravity. Water flushes the waste from the drain of each fixture within the structure to the public sewer. Waste pipes do not need to withstand pressure but must be larger than water pipes because they carry solid waste. Cast iron, plastic, or tile are commonly used. The U.S. Department of Housing and Urban Development recommends pipes 3 to 4 inches in diameter for toilet drains, 2 inches in diameter for showers, and 1½ inches in diameter for all other fixtures. Each plumbing fixture must have a trap (curved pipe) to provide a water seal and prevent seepage of sewer gas from the waste pipes into the house. Some municipalities require a grease trap to prevent clogging caused by waste build-up on the inside of pipes. Vent pipes through the roof for each stack or vertical drain line help prevent sewer gas odors from entering the house.

Waste pipes often suffer from clogged drains and traps. This can be relieved if a crumb cup or stopper is used with each fixture that has a small diameter drain pipe. Although garbage disposal units are a convenience in the handling of food waste, some municipalities and many septic tank systems are not designed to handle either the volume or type of waste produced; regulations should be checked prior to installation of these appliances.

Individual waste systems are like a miniature public waste disposal system. Lines carry the waste from the house to a central collection area (septic tank), the site of which is determined by the size of the house and family. The average septic tank has a capacity of 900 gallons and holds the solid waste until it is decomposed by bacteria, while the liquid moves to a leech bed from which it seeps into the soil. When space is limited, a cesspool can substitute for the leech field. In this case, the liquid waste seeps out of a tank made of concrete, brick, or stone. Because it does not disintegrate waste as effectively as does a septic tank, a cesspool is not generally recommended. One of the first signs of trouble is odor. Often the solution is to pump out the system and start the cycle anew.

LIGHT CONDITIONING

Maximum physical comfort and safety, and optimum emotional, aesthetic, and social satisfaction depend on light. Interior lighting plays a functional and psychological role in human activities. Eating, for example, requires enough light for the food to be visible (functional) as well as light to make the dining space appear attractive, complement the china and crystal, make the food appear appetizing, and be flattering to the diners (psychological).

The luminous environment is composed of three qualities of light; all must be present for light to be both functional and decorative.

Focal glow, or light coming directly from the source, attracts the eye, commands attention, creates interest, and helps to separate the important from the unimportant. More often it is supplementary or portable, provided to make possible high visual concentration. It is exemplified by a pool of light from a campfire, a light burning at the window, or a gleam from an open door at night.

Ambient luminescence is indirect light used for general functional lighting. Glareless and shadowless, it minimizes form, bulk, and the importance of things and people. Examples are the luminous haze on a mountain top, an overcast snowy morning in the open country, or a reflector over a center light.

Brilliants, the jewels of the living environment, excite the optic nerve, stimulate the spirit, alert the mind, and quicken the appetite. Exciting as well as entertaining, they are the sunbeams on a tumbling brook, the magic of the lights on the Christmas tree, or the splash of light from a crystal chandelier.

The way light is created and combined may vary. For eye health, light intensities, measured in lumens or units of light energy, are important. One determinant of light energy is the color and texture of the reflecting surface. In general, the higher the reflection, the higher the utilization of light. White is able to reflect approximately 94 per cent of the light whereas black absorbs all but 2 per cent.

Surfaces that are rough or dull diffuse light more evenly; smooth and shiny surfaces tend to cause glare. Light intensity decreases rapidly as the distance from the light source increases. For good home lighting, a ceiling should have a highly reflective surface (60–90 per cent); walls should be in the middle range (35–60 per cent); and the floor surface should absorb or diffuse most of the light (15–35 per cent).

Shifts in brightness from one area to another cause eye fatigue and should be avoided. Even light distribution is more desirable, but lack of varying intensities makes a monotonous and uninteresting living environment. Best results are obtained when light levels conform to the functional level for the task for which the area is designed. According to research from General Electric Company, 70 lumens per square foot of floor space is considered average.

TABLE 13-4   Light Reflectance of Various
Colors and Finishes

Color	Reflectance (Per Cent)
Dull or Flat White	75–90
Tints	
Ivory	75
Pink or Yellow	75–80
Light Green, Blue, Orchid	70–75
Beige or Gray	70
Medium Tones	
Tan, Yellow Gold	55
Gray	35–50
Turquoise, Blue	42–44
Chartruese	45
Gold, Pumpkin	34
Rose	29
Deep Tones	
Cocoa Brown, Mauve	24
Green and Blue	21
Gray	20
Olive Green	12
Navy, Forest Green	5–10
Wood	
Birch	35–50
Maple, Oak	25–35
Cherry	10–15
Black Walnut, Mahogany	5–15

Adapted from *Planning Your Home Lighting*, House and Garden Bulletin 138 (Washington, D.C.: U.S.G.P.O., 1968), p. 4.

Natural Light

Natural sources of light are the sun during the day and the moon and stars at night. In early shelters, openings to admit natural light also permitted the entrance of wind and rain, insects, and predators. During the Middle Ages, window openings were covered with horn or canvas, which permitted the entrance of little light. It was not until the advent of glass that it became possible to utilize natural light in structures. The amount of natural light that enters a living environment is determined by the kind, number, and size of the openings, the weather, and the time of day.

The size of the window is important. The U.S. Department of Housing and Urban Development requires a window area equal to 10 per cent of the floor area.

The larger the window area, the more evenly the light is distributed. Small windows may cause a brilliant patch of light that contrasts with the surrounding dimness. Light from short windows close to the ceiling and from clerestory windows is more evenly distributed, though such windows eliminate the pleasure that could be obtained from viewing outside scenery. Shadows form when windows are concentrated on one side of the room. As a rule, a well-designed room has no floor area that is more than one and a half times the ceiling height away from the window wall.

Direct sunlight and reflections from water or sky cause glare; landscaping, architectural features, light-refracting glass, or interior barriers such as curtains, draperies, and shades give effective relief.

Artificial Light

The first source of artificial light was undoubtedly the cooking fire; torches made of pine knots or faggots were portable light sources. The need for light without heat resulted in the development of two systems of artificial light still used today: candles and liquid fuel lamps.

The Etruscans are credited with inventing the tallow taper with an embedded wick. Both molded and hand-dipped candles were used in the American Colonies. Candles are still considered appropriate for decorative, romantic, religious, or emergency purposes. The original lamp was liquid fuel to which a wick was eventually added to control intensity and lengthen burning time. But lamps, like candles, gave poor light and constantly had to be replenished.

Today, the major source of artificial light is electricity. The high-intensity lamp has a long life and high efficiency but is seldom appropriate for residential lighting. The fluorescent tube gives more light per watt than the incandescent bulb, lasts longer, and distributes light more evenly. Several types of fluorescent tubes are available and care must be taken to select one that does not distort colors, particularly if

TABLE 13-5   Efficiency of Common Artificial Home Lighting Sources

Watts	Incandescent	Std. Cool	Std. Warm	Deluxe Warm	Std. Cool	Std. Warm	Deluxe Warm
		(Without Ballast Loss)			(Including Ballast Loss)		
		Lumens per Watt					
15	—	53	53	33.6	28.5	28.5	18
18							
20	—	65	65	41	50	50	31.5
25	9.4						
30	—	76.6	78.6	49.6	50	51	32
40	11.4	78.7	78.7	53.7	60.5	60.5	41
60	14.5						
75	15.9						
100	17.5						
150	19.2						
200	20						

(Columns 2–4 grouped under *Florescent* — *Std. Cool*, *Std. Warm*, *Deluxe Warm* (Without Ballast Loss); columns 5–7 — *Std. Cool*, *Std. Warm*, *Deluxe Warm* (Including Ballast Loss).)

Adapted from *Artificial Light Sources*, G.E. 9200X, General Electric, Cleveland, Ohio, September 1976.

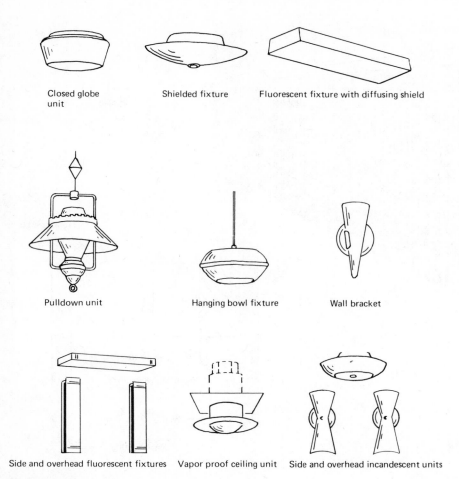

Closed globe unit

Shielded fixture

Fluorescent fixture with diffusing shield

Pulldown unit

Hanging bowl fixture

Wall bracket

Side and overhead fluorescent fixtures   Vapor proof ceiling unit   Side and overhead incandescent units

FIGURE 13-12 Common wall and ceiling fixtures.

it is to be used in an area where food is served. Because fluorescent tubes emit ultraviolet light, which may be irritating to the eye, shields or diffusing lenses are recommended; these tend to restrict fluorescent tubes to general rather than focal lighting.

In today's homes, general or functional lighting and the electrical outlets to operate portable lamps for high-intensity or task lighting are provided as an integral part of the structure.

Fixed Lighting.   Half the artificial lighting in today's structures is built into place. Usually reflected off walls and ceilings, it produces a low-intensity, glareless light. Commonly, a light base containing a group of incandescent bulbs or a fluorescent tube and covered with a glass reflector is affixed to the center of the ceiling. Some of these fixtures are designed to coordinate with the style or atmosphere to be created and are controlled by switches at or near the entrance to the

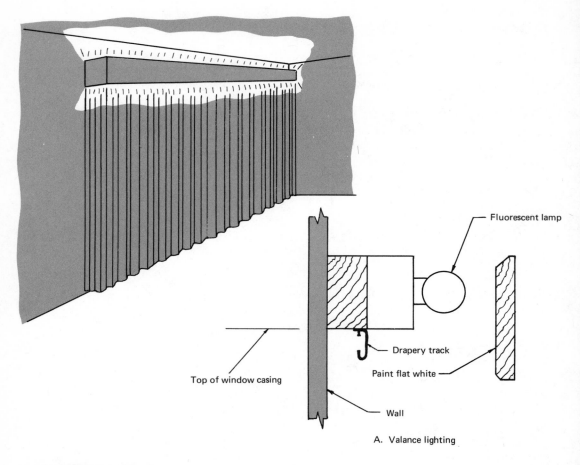

Fluorescent lamp

Drapery track

Paint flat white

Top of window casing

Wall

A. Valance lighting

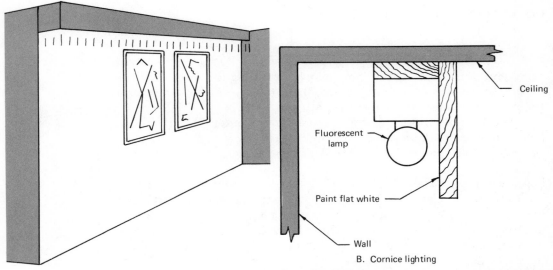

Ceiling

Fluorescent lamp

Paint flat white

Wall

B. Cornice lighting

FIGURE 13-13 Common types of structural lighting.

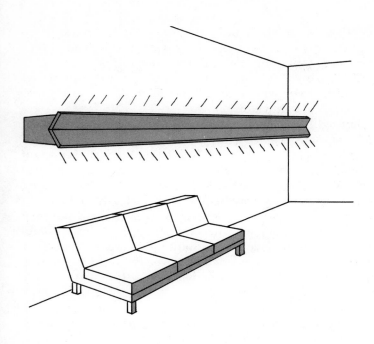

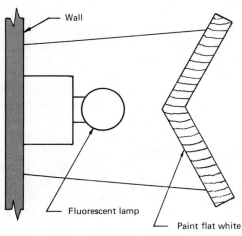

C. Wall brackets

room. Dimming switches vary light intensity and add flexibility to room lighting systems.

The central lighting fixture provides background light. It is frequently replaced by structural lighting. The three most common types of structural lighting are these:

1. *Valance lighting.* Installed at the top of windows, valance lighting provides upward light that reflects off the ceiling and contributes to general lighting, and downward light that accents window treatments.

2. *Cornice lighting.* Mounted at the juncture of the ceiling and the wall so that light is directed only downward, cornice lighting gives dramatic interest to anything on the wall underneath.

3. *Wall brackets.* Like valance installations, wall brackets are placed on an interior wall to give visual impact to an architectural or decorative feature located either above or below.

Other structural lighting installations that add to functional lighting are cove lights, luminous wall or ceiling panels, soffit lights, and recessed wall or ceiling lights. Cove lights, located on the wall, reflect off the ceiling and make it seem lower. Luminous wall panels make effective room dividers. Ceiling panels are best suited to a low ceiling because they give the effect of more height. Recessed lights add a decorative accent or augment existing light in a work or reading area; they are less expensive if planned when the structure is in the blueprint stage or when a ceiling is lowered. Soffit lights are installed at or beneath an architectural beam designed to lower the ceiling, cabinet, or bookshelf, and are especially effective where high-intensity light is needed over a kitchen or bathroom sink.

Wiring. Electrical energy travels with almost the speed of light along the course of least resistance. Its distribution is directed by copper or aluminum wire incased in an insulating material that offers a high resistance to the flow of electricity and thus prevents it from leaving the wire.

Electricty is brought from external service lines through an electric meter to a distribution panel containing fuses or circuit breakers. If a primary service line has a high pressure rating, a transformer is located between it and the branch line that feeds the building. Since 1959 the National Electric Code has recommended a minimum of 220–240 volts for home service so that at least 100 amperes service is available.

The distribution panel controls the routes or circuits over which the electricity travels, the number of which is indicated by the number of fuses or circuit breakers in the distribution panel. Many older homes still have only four circuits, but the U.S. Department of Housing and Urban Development, and most building codes, recommend a 100–150 ampere service. The typical panel will have 12 to 16 fuses or circuit breakers. An even larger service entrance is required when electric heat or central air conditioning is installed.

A disconnect switch in the distribution panel makes it possible to turn off the entire system during an emergency, such as a fire or when lines must be repaired. Each circuit carries its part of the electrical load and has its own protective device in case of inadequate wiring or overload. Fuses contain a piece of metal that melts when excess electricity flows through it. Each time the fuse blows (or the metal melts), the fuse must be replaced. Circuit breakers work on the same principle but have a disconnect switch that can be reset manually and does not require replacement.

250

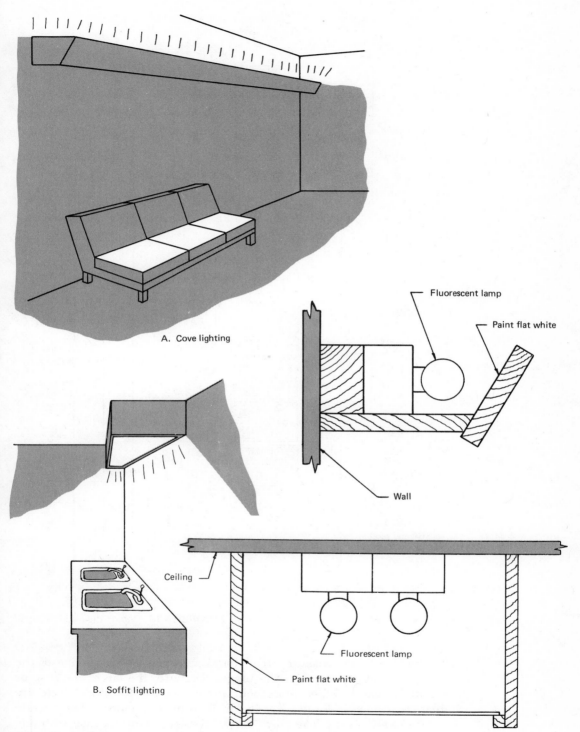

A. Cove lighting

B. Soffit lighting

Fluorescent lamp

Paint flat white

Wall

Ceiling

Fluorescent lamp

Paint flat white

FIGURE 13-14 Unusual types of structural lighting.

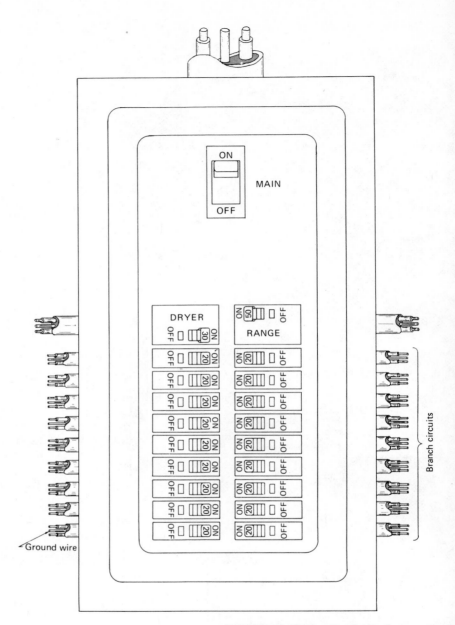

FIGURE 13-15 Electric distribution panel.

The size of the fuse or circuit breaker is related to the size of the wire used for the circuit. The bigger the wire, the larger the fuse or circuit breakers. When household appliances call for more electricity than is available, lights may flicker or dim, appliances may operate ineffectively, or the fuse may "blow." Replacement of a fuse with one of larger size may permit operation but creates overheated wires and

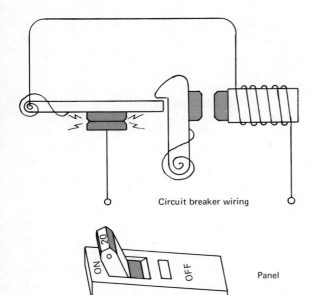

Circuit breaker wiring

Panel

A. On position of circuit breaker indicating safe operation

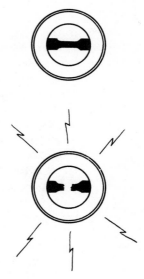

C. Screw type fuse

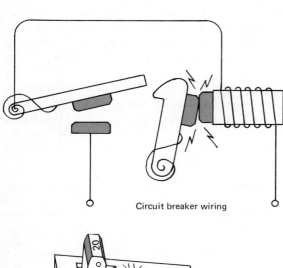

Circuit breaker wiring

Panel

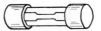

D. Cartridge type fuse

B. Off position of circuit breaker indicating circuit overload or safety problem

FIGURE 13-16 Operation of fuses and circuit breakers.

CHAPTER 13
MAKING SPACE LIVABLE

the possibility of fire. This practice is both uneconomical and unsafe. Newer installations have special fuse sockets so that only the correct size may be used. Special fuses called *fustrons* are available for those instances when a momentary overload may occur as the result of an initial surge of power required to start a motor.

There are three types of circuits: general, appliance, and special. For general circuits, the National Electrical Code requires three watts of power per square foot of floor space. A small house should have a minimum of three general circuits with one circuit open for expansion. Lighting fixtures and receptacle outlets for lamps and appliances not generally in the kitchen are connected to a general circuit. Appliance circuits provide power for the portable appliances used in the food-preparation area and other work centers. The National Electrical Code recommends at least two circuits of this type—one located in the food-preparation center and the other in the laundry area. Special circuits are needed for each individual appliance installed more or less permanently, such as the range, the dishwasher, the dryer, and power tools. Often it is desirable to have a special circuit for refrigerators and freezers.

The amount of service supplied can be calculated from the number of circuits available (see Table 13-6). Each household item requires a different amount of electric power. As a general rule, it takes more energy to produce heat than light. An electrical motor requires an initial surge of power to overcome inertia, but once in motion requires significantly less energy. Because circuits can carry only a limited amount of electricity, it is unsafe to operate appliances whose total draw on a circuit exceeds the amount of electricity available (see Table 13-7).

The problem of inadequate wiring often begins with inadequate voltage (the force or pressure with which electricity flows) or inadequate amperage (the rate at which electricity travels). The problem is

TABLE 13-6 Wattage Supplied by Various Service Loads

Wattage	Typical Number Circuits	Amp. Service
6,900	4	30
13,800	6–8	60
23,000	12–16	100

Adapted from, with permission of the Realtors National Marketing Institute®, *Houses: The Illustrated Guide to Construction, Design and Systems* by Henry S. Harrison. © Copyright 1973, 1976 by the Realtors National Marketing Institute® of the National Association of Realtors®. All rights reserved. Chicago. P. 315.

TABLE 13-7

TABLE 13-7   Typical Wattage and Circuit Recommended for Selected Household Items

Item	Average Wattage	Type of Current	Fuse	Outlets
Clock	2	General purpose	15–20	2-prong
Electric Blanket	190			
Hair Dryer	260			
Fan (Window)	85			
Fan (Roll-about)	200			
Heating Pad	60			
Light bulbs	25–300			
Radio	75			
Sewing Machine	75			
TV (Black/White)	260			
TV (Color)	315			
TV (Instant Start)	add 50			
Blender/Liquifier	350	Appliance	20–25	3-prong
Coffee Maker	800			ground outlet
Iron	1,100			
Roaster	1,325			
Toaster	1,150			
Vacuum cleaner	700			
Waffle Iron	1,100			
Room Air Conditioner	1,200	Special purpose	20	3-prong
Automatic Washer	600			ground outlet
Dishwasher	1,200			
Refrigerator	265–435			
Freezer	350–440			
Trash compactor	600			
Automatic Dryer	4,500	Special purpose	30–60	3-way
Range	12,000			
Water Heater	4,500			

Adapted from *Electrical Appliance Reference* (Butte, Mont.: Montana Power Co., 1977).

compounded by an insufficient number of circuits and too few wall outlets. The use of fuses with a higher rating than called for is a sign that a living area is underwired. Extension cords and monkey plugs are a sign of a deficient distribution system.

Before 1960 receptacles that received two-pronged plugs were acceptable. Today, receptacles for three-pronged plugs are recommended. The extra prong is for grounding, which reduces shock hazard. Special waterproof receptacles with caps and a ground fault circuit interrupter (another safeguard against shock) should be installed in locations where a large amount of water is used near or in conjunction with the electrical outlets. Special three-way outlets must be supplied for 220–240 voltage equipment such as ranges and clothes dryers.

The U.S. Department of Housing and Urban Development requires that general outlets be placed so that no point along a wall will there be more than 6 feet from an outlet, that three wall plugs be installed (regardless of room size) if there is not a central lighting fixture, that

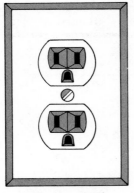
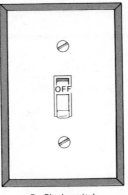

A. Double outlet plug with ground

B. Single switch

C. Outlet plug for 220 service switches and outlets

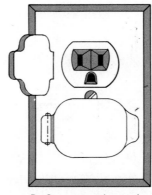
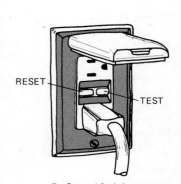

D. Common outdoor outlet

E. Ground fault interrupter

FIGURE 13-17 Electric outlets and switch.

two outlets be available over counters in the kitchen and one next to the mirror in the bath.

Wall switches control permanently installed light fixtures, and often wall outlets as well. One should be able to take any traffic route through the living unit and turn on a path of light ahead while turning off those in the area just traversed. A variety of special switches can be obtained. Silent switches are usually expensive; those that glow are easy to locate in the dark. Switches with light indicators are helpful reminders that heating appliances need to be disconnected. Automatic door switches that turn closet lights off or on as the door is opened and closed are also helpful.

Special Equipment

Low-voltage electrical equipment, such as television antennae or cables, high fidelity speakers, intercommunication systems, controls for garage door openers and telephones, requires special outlets. If installed during construction, low-voltage wiring can be hidden (a sign of quality housing). The outlet plugs for low-voltage equipment can be identified by a single-hole face plate. Service is supplied to the individual structure from aerial or underground utility right-of-ways.

ACOUSTICS IN THE LIVING ENVIRONMENT

Sound conditioning increases comfort and privacy. Irritating sound can build stress and nervousness, impede sleep, lower productivity, and interfere with communication. High levels of sound during childhood or adolescence can cause hearing loss in middle age, whereas loud or unexpected noise is a known cause of accidents.

To control sound, the characteristics of sound must be understood. Sound travels in pressure waves from a vibrating source. These sound waves move rather slowly in comparison to light waves. They vary in frequency from ¾ inch to about 60 feet and move in a harmonic, periodic, or random manner. Low-frequency waves spread out in all directions from the source, dropping in intensity as they travel. High-frequency waves tend to confine themselves to a narrow beam in front of their source. Harmonic waves are like the waves produced by a stone dropped into calm water; with no interference, the waves spread until dissipated. Sound waves travel in straight lines, and thus may be absorbed, reflected, or transmitted. They will be absorbed by a soft and resilient object, and reflected by a hard or smooth surface. When sound is reflected toward its source, it intensifies, raising noise levels; if it is reflected into a new area it may seem loud or unexpected. If the waves cause an object to vibrate, they are transmitted; this occurs most often when the material is stiff, hard, or thin.

Sound level is measured in decibels. A zero decibel level is barely perceptible sound. The decibel scale is logarithmic; thus a 10-decibel increase corresponds to a ten-fold increase in sound intensity (see Table 13-8).

Absolute quiet is difficult to attain, but people can adapt to a general noise level of about 30 decibels. To keep noise at this level, it is necessary to calculate the probable noise produced by natural sounds, machines and appliances, outside traffic, and the activities taking place in a particular area.

Both structure and floor plan can eliminate outside noises and block those on the inside. A good floor plan makes it possible to incorporate a sound buffer. Seven factors affect the amount of sound reduction necessary.

1. If background noise is loud, the noise created may not be heard by others and therefore is nonirritating. (This has its limits and the sound must be constant to be effective.)

2. The louder the noise, either background or created, the greater the need for sound reduction.

TABLE 13-8   Decibel Levels and Corresponding Threshold
Feeling of Common Sounds

Sound	Decibels	Description
Thunder	140	Threshold of pain
Shotgun Shot		
Jet Aircraft—		
Landing, Taking Off	120	Painful to the ear
Subway Train	100	Deafening
Noisy Kitchen		
Power Mower	95	
Food Blender	90	
Unmuffled Truck		
Vacuum Cleaner	87	
Garbage Disposal	80	Very loud
Knife Sharpener		
Dishwasher	70	
Typical Conversation		
Average Radio, TV		
Conversation	60	Loud
Average Office	50	Moderate
Average Living Room		
Refrigerator	45	
Bedroom at Night	30	Faint
Whisper	20	
Rustle of Leaves	20	
Breathing	10	Threshold of Audibility

Compiled from material in *The House and the Art of Its Design,* p. 153. Reprinted by permission of Reinhold Corporation, 1956.

"Noise Control," *House and Home* (April 1958), p. 128, and *Noise Abatement and Control, VII, Physiological and Psychological Effects* (Washington, D.C.: U.S. Environmental Protection Agency, U.S.G.P.O., 1971), p. 102.

3. Because each noise has its own wave length some materials are more effective than others in reducing certain sound waves. A wall that might be adequate for reducing the transmission of the human voice might not block the thump of an air conditioner.

4. People accept noise in a kitchen, have little reaction to sound in an entryway, but expect sleeping areas to be quiet. Keeping noisy centers next to each other reduces the need for sound control and lowers cost.

5. The ratio of the area of a common wall (a wall separating two living units) to sound-absorbing surfaces in the room where noise is produced is significant. The more carpet, draperies, and upholstered furniture in the room, the more sound is absorbed and the less is transmitted elsewhere to an adjacent room.

6. The more distant the source, the more sound the structure absorbs or blocks out. If a television set is on in one room and a reader is sitting in another but along the same wall, the distance between the noise source and the person to whom the sound may be irritating is short.

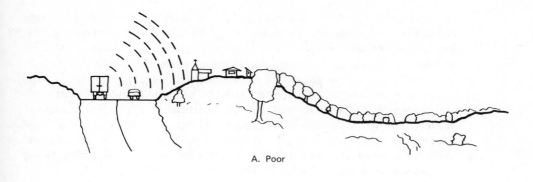

A. Poor

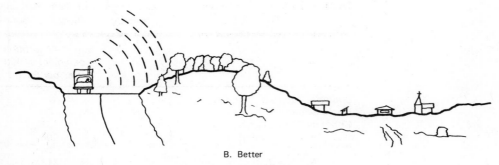

B. Better

FIGURE 13-18 Selection of a good site can reduce road noise.

7. The higher the ratio of common wall area to floor area, the more sound the common wall will transmit. Adjacent areas should have short common walls.

Sound conditioning begins with the natural environment. Trees and shrubs placed at the property line deflect and absorb street noise. A patio or yard wall should be placed closer to the dwelling and be slightly higher. Both of these methods can block out light, so it is usually unwise to rely on either for significant street noise reduction.

Picture windows facing the street permit the entrance of a great deal of noise; just how much depends on the type of glass. Window glass with a coefficient of 0.18 at 500 cps (cycles per second) absorbs much more sound than plate glass with a coefficient of 0.04 at 500 cps (see Table 13-9). When outside noises are loud, materials used for walls and roof should have a high sound-loss rating and a roof design that deters transmission. A truss roof will transmit slightly more noise than one with rafters because there is more direct connection between roof and ceiling beams. As noise enters through windows and doors, double windows and storm doors help in sound reduction.

The organization and design of the living unit will affect the sound level. Noisy areas should face the street. If a quiet area must face a street, a more solid exterior wall should be chosen. The side of a house containing the most windows and doors should face the interior of the lot; the street side should have limited window area, and the house should be placed as far from the street as possible. Small courtyards and enclosed stairwells create reverberation. Ideally, stairwells and courtyards should have an open side to permit sound to escape. A stairway with a landing that changes direction helps diffuse sound waves, as do hallways that change direction, doorways that are staggered, windows that are positioned so that there is an unequal distance from an inside corner, and casement window openings along one wall that open in the same direction.

The materials used for walls, floors, heating ducts, and plumbing determine the extent to which sound is transmitted. Floors transmit

TABLE 13-9   Sound Characteristics of Common Materials and Construction Techniques

	Sound Absorption Coefficient @ 500 Cycles per Second
Building Materials	
Brick, Common	.03
Concrete Block, Coarse	.31
Painted	.06
Glass, Plate	.04
Window	.18
Marble or Glazed Tile	.01
Plasterboard, Ordinary	.03
Acoustic	.20–.30
Plywood Paneling, ⅜"	.17
Wood, Painted	.03
Construction	
Walls	
Gypsum Board on 2×4's, 16" o.c.	.05
Plaster on Tile or Brick	.02
Plaster on Lath (Rough)	.04
Plaster on Lath (Smooth)	.03
Floors	
Concrete or Terrazo	.015
Linoleum, Asphalt Tile, or Cork on Concrete	.03
Wood	.10
Parquet on Concrete	.07
Furnishings	
Draperies	.40–.75
Furniture per Sq. Ft. Floor Area	
Cloth-Covered Upholstery	.80
Leather-Covered Upholstery	.60
Pew	.75
Metal or Wood Seats	.22

Adapted from Robert C. Weast, Ed. *Handbook of Chemistry and Physics,* 57th ed., [© CRC Press Inc. Cleveland, 1976], pp. E39–40. Used with Permission of CRC Press Inc.

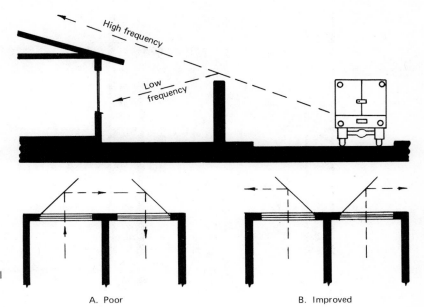

FIGURE 13-19 Use of wall or fence to deflect street noise.

A. Poor   B. Improved

sound both up and down so that rooms above and below are affected. A heavy, multilayered floor may reduce sound level by as much as 50 decibels. Further sound reduction is possible if joists, studs, and plates serve only one living center.

Interior walls separate living areas on the same level, and floors separate different levels. As a general rule, when the thickness of the wall is doubled, sound transmission is reduced five decibels. An interior wall can also reduce sound by containing air spaces between a number of layers. The brick of the fireplace when plastered on one side can

FIGURE 13-20 Window arrangements that deflect sound from interiors.

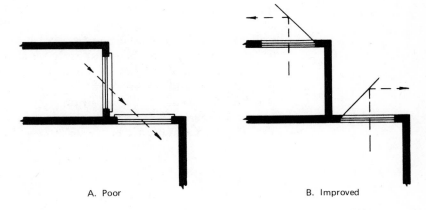

A. Poor   B. Improved

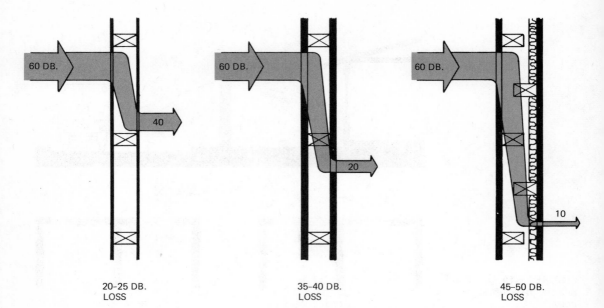

| 20–25 DB. | 35–40 DB. | 45–50 DB. |
| LOSS | LOSS | LOSS |

FIGURE 13-21 Construction techniques that reduce sound transmission.

reduce noise about 50 or 60 decibels. Closets are effective because they keep noise sources and listeners away from walls. In addition, the clothes stored in closets absorb sound. For maximum noise reduction, rooms must be sealed against sound leakage at the floor, ceiling, and outside wall.

Ducts and plumbing within the walls are a potential noise source. Ducts may act as megaphones, broadcasting sound from one room to another; insertion of a sound trap will keep sound waves from bouncing down their length. Drain pipes and water pipes should be isolated and insulated.

Selection of noiseless or near noiseless equipment also helps keep sound levels low. Quiet water closets, screen diffusers for water traps, and silent electric switches are available. Other equipment, such as telephones, doorbells, and buzzers can be adjusted to individual requirements.

If all measures fail, the application of sound deadeners may be in order. Reverberation can be cut sharply by acoustical ceilings. Carpet, cork, rubber, and vinyl can be used on floors. Acoustical paints or wallboard help reduce sound transmission through walls. Sound can be further diffused by the addition of cabinets, bookshelves, and counters. Draperies or curtains will absorb sound. As a last resort, equipment with moving parts can be mounted on cork or rubber pads.

Many local building codes are designed to eliminate hazards in the living environment. Still, each year there are an estimated 4.5 million home accidents of which 30,000 result in death and 2.5 million in bodily injuries. More disabling injuries occur in the home than in industry or on highways.

Fire Hazards

The leading causes of home fires are smoking, defective or misued home appliances, and faulty electrical wiring. Other common hazards are defective chimneys and heating equipment, combustible roofs, and improper use and storage of combustible fuels. In order to prevent the spread of fire, building codes contain regulations concerning the location of the building on the lot and the use of fire protection around chimneys, at ceilings or floors and between common walls of multifamily structures. Special attention should be given to providing a concrete or other masonry support for a fireplace and a separate flue for each fireplace. Special precautions are listed for areas where extremely combustible equipment is housed; such precautions usually stress that materials should resist the spread of fire for a minimum of two hours.

A method of escape from each room, especially bedrooms, is necessary. Spread of fire to other parts of the house can be delayed or even prevented if rooms, or at least a section of the structure, can be closed off.

Some provisions for detecting, fighting, and preventing small fires at home (especially important in rural areas) include alarms, extinguishers, sprinkler systems, and protection against lightning. The most common, the fire extinguisher, is best located at a doorway in the kitchen, where so many fires occur.

Accident Hazards

According to the U.S. Department of Housing and Urban Development, 178 identified home safety hazards are not covered in most building codes. Such regulations as do exist were judged inadequate in providing accident protection.

Guilford contends that regardless of built-in safety, accidents will not decrease until there is a change in human behavior.[2] In her study, although every worker was confronted with exactly the same environment and performed the same task, some participants had many accidents and others had none. The difference seemed to be attributable not to the environment but to the individual. Alteration of the struc-

[2] J. S. Guilford et al, *An Experimental Study of Home Accident Behavior* (Los Angeles, Calif.: American Institutes for Research, 1965), p. 149.

ture and its design seems to reduce only a small fraction of the hazards. The most advantageous arrangement for a living unit is one in which traffic patterns are free of obstruction, and rooms have only the furniture and equipment needed for the number of people to be served and are convenient for the intended use. Checklists from national safety organizations help identify potential hazards but these are usually inadequate because of changes in technology and life style.

Stairs. Although two thirds of the falls within the home occur on stairs (1,800,000 per year), most are the result of human error. Slippery surfaces, inadequate design, and poor lighting are contributing factors. Safety treads, carpeting, or an application of abrasive paint can reduce slipperiness. A rough-surfaced material (brick, stone, or exposed surface aggregate), cleats, abrasive strips, cleating elements in treads, or broom finishing reduce the possibility of accident on concrete steps. Lights should be placed near the midpoint of the stairs with switches at head and foot.

Bathrooms. Most injuries are related to tubs and showers because materials for fixtures become slippery when wet. In addition, the bottoms of bathtubs and shower stalls slant to aid drainage. To decrease bathroom hazards flat bottoms and slip-resistant surfaces should be used.

Windows. Safety in operation and maintenance is often overlooked when planning or selecting windows. Horizontal sliding or crank-operated casement and awning type windows reduce the possibility of accidents, especially when windows are located over counters, fixtures, or other obstructions. On the other hand, these windows may create a hazardous situation when they open into a traffic lane either within or outside the house. This can be overcome by the installation of planters, protective walls or screens, or shrubbery underneath the projecting window. Windows that can be cleaned and repaired from ground level—or, better yet, from the inside—are recommended.

   Window walls create beautiful vistas, but safety glazing and care in placement are necessary to insure they do not become yet another safety problem. Highly hazardous window locations include stair landings, or the foot of staircases.

Doors. Poor planning and installation of doors cause 25 per cent of home accidents. Sliding glass doors and glass doors on shower and bathroom enclosures produce the majority of door-related accidents. Safety glazing is the best protection against broken glass, but application of decorative decals, especially at adult eye level, will prevent collisions. Proper installation will insure ease and dependability of operation. Doors should swing into a room and open to a 90° angle.

No two doors should come in contact. Double-hinged doors are a poor choice when there are children, senior citizens, or handicapped members in the household.

Floors. Floor coverings should be compatible with their use. Carpeting is the most practical residential floor covering, but where water spillage occurs frequently and carpeting may not be acceptable, a nonglazed or slip-resistant material should be used. On exterior patios or porches, where there are potential wet or icy conditions, floor surfaces should be sloped to provide good drainage and have a roughened finish.

Electricity. Seven per cent of home accidents are related to electrical devices, but adherence to the National Electrical Code or similar standards will eliminate most of the accident potential.

Exteriors. Proper grading, terracing, drainage systems, and vegetation can reduce accidents in the garden. Landscaping should provide safe and convenient access to the living unit. Outside lighting should provide a clear view of the passage to and from the house. Post lamps, mushroom surface lights, and floodlights all produce good exterior lighting. Slopes for drainage should have no more than a 10 per cent grade. If the grade exceeds 10 per cent, a series of low retaining walls or terraces should be utilized with railings, shrubbery, flower beds, planters, or hedges located at the top of each wall. The greatest danger from trees and shrubs comes from toxic berries, roots, stems, and leaves; such toxic plantings should be eliminated, especially if children are part of the household (see Table 13-10).

Other hazards come from tree litter, which produces slippery conditions underfoot, or foliage, which obstructs view or blocks light.

Fences and walls can provide protection and privacy. All fencing should be free of sharp edges, pinch points, and post crowns. The most popular, the chain-link fence, should be installed with the sharp edge toward the ground or removed altogether. Fences with interstices large enough to permit a child to be caught should be avoided. Gate latches are best installed at least 4 feet above ground.

Storage. The greatest asset in the creation of an accident-free living environment is adequate storage; it can reduce falls by reducing clutter. Cabinets and containers designed to hold poisonous cleaning agents, pins, razor blades, scissors, matches, and pressurized or combustible materials should be supplied with locks. Shatterproof glass shelving in medicine chests and display cases is recommended. Storage areas more than 3 feet deep should have an artificial light that does not come in contact with any flammable material.

TABLE 13-10 Toxic Plants, Shrubs, Trees

Plant	Foliage or Leaf	Bark	Berry or Fruit	Flower	Sprouts, Stem, or Branch	Seeds	Pod
Azaleas	X		X	X	X	X	X
Black Locust	X	X			X		
Bleeding Heart	X						
Buttercup	X	X	X	X	X	X	X
Cherry (Wild and Cultivated)	X				X		
Dieffenbachia	X	X	X	X	X	X	X
Elderberry	X	X		X	X	X	X
Elephant Ear	X	X	X	X	X	X	X
Jack-in-the-Pulpit	X	X	X	X	X	X	X
Jessamine			X				
Lantana Camara (Red Sage)			Green				
Larkspur					X	X	
Laurels	X	X	X	X	X	X	X
Lily of the Valley	X			X			
Mayapple	X	X	X				
Oaks	X		X				
Oleander	X				X		
Poinsettia	X						
Rhododendron	X	X	X	X	X	X	X
Thorn Apple (Jimsen Weed)	X	X	X	X	X	X	X
Water Hemlock	X	X	X	X	X	X	X
Wisteria						X	X
Yew	X		X				

Adapted from *Designing for Home Safety: A HUD Handbook,* U.S. Department of Housing and Urban Development (Washington, D.C.: U.S.G.P.O., 1975), pp. 9–12.

SUMMARY

Everyone wants a comfortable living environment. Keeping air temperatures, light, and sound at proper levels promotes human well-being. Proper equipment, materials, and construction techniques will maintain acceptable levels.

Air temperatures can be modified by using fossil fuels, electricity, or solar energy to heat, cool, and circulate air or water. Moisture can be controlled by humidifiers and dehumidifiers; filters or air cleaners are helpful in removing dust and dirt, ridding the air of odors or harmful pollens. With proper automatic controls it is possible to maintain constant temperatures. In general, electricity is expensive; gas, most common; solar energy, just emerging from the experimental stage.

Outlets and circuits are needed to operate large electrical household equipment, large and small appliances, lamps and structural lighting

266

fixtures. Most codes require 100 ampere service. Most structural lighting is functional but can be used to achieve dramatic effects, to make rooms appear larger, to spotlight pictures, or to create a pleasant view. Structural lighting added in the blueprint stage is less expensive.

Most acoustical control is needed between levels or activity centers. The more layers of material or air through which sound must pass, the more sound is absorbed. Hallways and stairways that change direction, staggered doorways and window openings, also discourage transmission of sound.

Water and sewage systems provide sanitation within the living environment. In urban areas these systems are controlled by public officials. There are still rural locations where the source of water and the storage and disposal of waste are determined by the individual. In the latter case, care must be taken so that waste does not contaminate the water supply.

Building codes regulate materials and construction techniques to provide protection from natural hazards. Both fires and accidents can still occur because of poor design. Most accidents are caused by structural features related to circulation within the living environment—stairs, doors, and windows—or by the use of plants and trees that have poisonous stems, leaves, or flowers.

consumer considerations

Everyman a property owner . . .
none a master.

Victor Hugo

14

Acquisition Variations

HOUSING plays a leading role in the economy of the United States. It represents about one half of the national wealth. The 69 million housing units available for occupancy in 1970 represented an increase of 11 million homes over the previous decade. Even then supply did not exceed demand. Future needs are too often difficult to estimate. Much depends upon an individual's marital status and age. There are typically several moves during the progression of the family cycle—from a furnished or unfurnished apartment to a secondhand house to a new and larger house (which may be remodeled, expanded, or sometimes custom-built) to a smaller dwelling in a more central location to a residence that provides custodial care.

It is important for some to sink roots deep into a particular community. Others desire flexible housing arrangements. Housing also has social consequences: both disease and crime have been attributed to substandard living conditions.

To build a house requires considerable capital. Housing is one of the most important purchases the family or individual can make. The price of the average new home in 1977 ranged between $44,000 and $50,000—the actual amount depending on location, materials, and workmanship. The 1970 U.S. Census report indicated that homes in urban areas were more valuable than those in rural areas and those in the western United States were worth more than those in other regions of the country.

271

HOUSING SELECTION

A shopping expedition for a home should begin with a consideration of the needs and preferences of those who are to use it, a determination of the amount of money available, and and an appraisal of the housing available on the local market. It is unlikely that a single dwelling unit will fit all needs perfectly. Some of the best dwellings have deficiencies and some of the worst have desirable features. A checklist of housing needs and desires and a determination of how much can be spent will make the decision easier.

Needs and Preferences

For some people a house is simply a headquarters, a place to begin and end the day's activities; for others, it is a place to relax away from the pressures of everyday life; for many it is the center of all activities. The first step in selecting family shelter is to list the activities in which each family member participates. The checklist can be used to evaluate the ability of each available dwelling unit to meet the design requirements for each family member. A second approach is to use a checklist developed by a housing specialist. Many are available. Some are designed to cover the entire house; others serve for a specific room or area, such as the kitchen. The least acceptable conditions should be equivalent to the U.S. Department of Housing and Urban Development's Minimum Property Standards so that a loan (if necessary) will be approved by the Federal Housing Administration.

Cost Considerations

Each family differs in income, characteristics, values, and priorities. Some prefer to buy a large car and a small house whereas others prefer the opposite. Usually, no more than 20–25 per cent of the monthly income or two and one half times the annual income should be spent for housing. Many families spend much more; others, considerably less. In general, the proportion of income spent on housing declines as income increases. The share of income spent for housing is also affected by the size of the family, the ages of the various members, whether or not they belong to a minority group, and even the way in which housing is acquired. Table 14-1 shows a plan for determining housing expenditures.

The Local Housing Supply

Regardless of family needs or desires or income, decisions will be influenced by the local housing supply. Usually the local housing market includes both incorporated and unincorporated areas that have central shopping, residential suburbs, and/or fringe developments.

TABLE 14-1   A Family Budget for Housing

Income from All Sources	Head of family	_____
	Spouse	_____
	Other	_____
	Total	_____
Living Expenses Other than Housing	Food	_____
	Clothing	_____
	Medical Care	_____
	Insurance (car & life)	_____
	Recreation	_____
	Social security & other retirement	_____
	Taxes: Income	_____
	Personal	_____
	Gifts	_____
	Transportation: Car	_____
	Other	_____
	Personal Care	_____
	Other	_____
	Total	_____
Operational Expenses for Housing	Insurance: Fire	_____
	Liability	_____
	Utilities: Electric	_____
	Gas	_____
	Phone	_____
	Water	_____
	Other	_____
	Furniture	_____
	Total	_____
Capital Money for Housing	Total income	_____
	Less total expenses	_____
	Available for Housing	_____

Frequently, topographical characteristics, transportation routes, and facilities are important factors. The kind and number of housing units within this area will limit housing choices. In general, large communities tend to have more vacancies than small ones. Those with a high proportion of multifamily structures have more living units than areas with only single detached houses. Communities with a high proportion of rental units tend to provide more choice than those with a high number of owner-occupied units.

ECONOMIC CONSIDERATIONS

The decision to rent or to buy is often dictated by the local market: there may be nothing suitable for rent, or conversely, nothing suitable to purchase. Personal credit ratings, status, or lack of a down payment may limit options.

Any consumer decision involves an innate desire to get the most for the least cost. The amount of money involved in purchasing a place to live is considerable. Homeowning costs are less if a person remains in one place more than four years. If a transfer or move is expected within that time, it is difficult to justify home ownership.

It is difficult to compare ownership costs and rental figures. Differences in types of dwellings, locations, floor plans, age of buildings, and other factors tend to cloud the issue. In general, there is a slight financial advantage to the renter. The difference can be even greater if any utilities are included in the rent. Some people argue that taxes and interest on the loan decrease the difference because of current income tax regulations. This advantage does not accrue unless deductions are itemized and amount to more than 15 per cent of the income. A more accurate method of attaining cost comparisons is to consider three types of cost: the one-time charges required to move in, monthly payments, and alternate uses of investment dollars.

Initial Costs

Both rental and purchase require one-time initial charges: renters must provide security deposits; buyers must make a down payment in order to obtain a loan and pay closing costs and sales taxes on the property transfer. Money to purchase major equipment or furniture and the cost of moving belongings to the site will be needed for either type of transaction.

Monthly Costs

Both renters and owners have monthly payments—rental fees or loan repayments and interest. Monthly charges are paid for parking a mobile home and by those in condominiums or cooperatives. Owners also have to meet the monthly costs of property taxes, insurance, repair, maintenance, and replacement. These charges are required only periodically, but they should be averaged to give a more realistic assessment of costs. Some financial institutions add property tax and insurance costs to loan payments to assure payment when due; this is a requirement of many FHA-insured loans. Both owner and renter must also consider the costs of utilities and trash collection.

Other Dollar Considerations

Cost comparisons should take into account alternative investment of the sum used for a down payment, from which earnings would accrue. Interest paid on a loan must be considered as lost because it earns nothing. Also to be taken into account is the depreciation or appreciation of a house. Accurate estimates are difficult because the main consideration is an estimation of resale value. Houses have recently been rising more than 5 per cent per year in value. Mobile homes usually depreciate. Changes occur rapidly and it is wise to check with someone who is familiar with financing in the local area (see Table 14-2).

274

TABLE 14-2　　　　　　　　　　　　　　Work Sheet for Cost Comparisons

	#1	#2	#3
Basic Information			
Selling Price			
Rate of Interest for Loan			
Financing Available for Number Years			
Percent Amount of Down Payment			
Initial Costs			
Deposits			
Down Payment			
Loan Closing Costs			
Land Costs			
Furnishings/Equipment			
Moving			
Total			
Monthly Costs			
Basic Rent			
Land Fees			
Loan Repayment and Interest			
Property Tax			
Insurance			
Utilities			
Repair/Maintenance/Replacement			
Total			
Other Dollar Considerations			
Total Initial Costs			
Total Monthly Costs (120 months)			
Total Ten Year Cost			
Property Owned			
Total Savings			
Amount in Account			
Compounded Interest			
Income Tax Savings			
Federal			
State			
Resale			
Estimated Selling Price			
Selling Expense			
Cash After Sale			
Money for New Home			
Sale of Property			
Plus Money in Savings			
Total			

Adapted from *Comparing Costs of Housing,* PNW 139, A Pacific Northwest Cooperative Extension Publication (Oregon, Washington, and Idaho: 1974) pp. 2–3.

RENTING

There are more renters in America in the 1970s than ever before, but the proportion of renters has declined steadily since 1940. The 1970 U.S. Census showed that about 36 per cent of the white population and 58 per cent of the blacks rented shelter. Two major factors are responsible for this significant percentage of renters in the population. Those who rent often lack sufficient funds for a down payment on a home—low-income families include the newly married, couples with young children, some elderly couples, and young single adults. Demographic trends show that the postwar babies are now marrying and establishing independent households. This creates a demand for more rental units. The other factor is a social change that has made it acceptable for the single adult to live alone, and for the young married couple to postpone child-bearing or to limit themselves to one child.

Renting is more prevalent in the central cities than in the suburbs, rural areas, or small towns, because the central cities have a higher proportion of people who prefer to rent. There is no location, however, where rental units cannot be obtained.

Advantages

There are many reasons for renting. Many people find it provides a way of life they enjoy.

There is no long-term financial investment when renting. Unless there is a "no escape" clause in a rental or lease agreement, the individual can leave at any time. This makes it easier to grasp an unanticipated opportunity elsewhere, and to adjust to changes in income, family size, neighborhood and market values, or to get away from an unsatisfactory situation.

Costs are clearer for those who rent. The fixed price for the use of the premises may include some of the operational costs such as heat, water, and waste disposal as well as decorating services. Money can be invested in furnishings, which can be moved when the renter moves. This makes it easier to control living expenses and simplifies budgeting.

Renting may save time. The renter's considerations can be limited to costs related to the actual living environment and transportation. There is no need to obtain information about real estate values, taxes, special tax assessments, loans, and the legal complications of ownership. The renter is also freed from maintenance problems. Some leases and rental agreements prohibit the tenant from decorating or remodeling—which enables him to resist spending time and talent on home improvements.

Rental units often offer greater security. Except for vacation hideaways, rentals are usually not located in isolated places. With rising

Costs	Information		
	Amount	When Due	Type and Condition
Basic Fee			
Security Deposit			
Total from Part II			
Grand Total			
Services and Maintenance			
Utilities			
Electric			
Gas			
Heat			
Television			
Telephone			
Water			
Sewer			
Refuse Disposal			
Decorating			
Window Cleaning			
Repairs			
Facilities			
Entrance			
Mail			
Deliveries			
Elevator			
Lobby			
Laundry			
Recreation			
Storage			
Parking			
Appliances			
Range			
Refrigerator			
Dishwasher			
Other			
Installation Charge			

crime rates, more attention is paid to security provisions for dwellings, especially in first-class multifamily units. There are doormen, night watchmen, and janitors to maintain surveillance. Other units have television surveillance of doorways, hallways, and parking areas. Individual security arrangements are provided in both individual and central entries. In some instances, the landlord will make repairs and provide security when the renter is absent. In addition, buildings must conform to safety standards that assure proper attention to fire escapes, fireproofing, light, and ventilation.

In rental units, central services like mail, laundry, storage, and parking make it possible to meet people more easily. Recreational facilities and day-care centers provide an opportunity to establish friendships with people who have mutual interests. Social directors are sometimes employed to arrange recreational activities for the occupants of rental units.

Rental also frees funds for other investments. Small monthly savings can be substantial over a period of time, and a small additional amount can be realized monthly because rental costs are likely to be less than for owning a home. If a wise, methodical investment program is followed, this money can be used to increase capital.

Units Available for Rent

Any type of single or multifamily dwelling unit can be rented. Options are limited only by the availability of rentals on the local market and the money the family sets aside for a place to live. In times of scarcity, the renting family may face high rents or overcrowding. When houses are plentiful and financial arrangements difficult, there is the possibility of renting with an option to buy; sometimes there is even the opportunity of including part of the rental payments toward the purchase price.

A renter's checklist differs from that of a buyer. It includes consideration of condition and appearance, layout and design, special services, price, and the specifics of the rental agreement. Particular points should be considered.

What is the total cost per month necessary to obtain the services desired? Basic rent may be only the starting point. Special charges are made for some repairs and services. Under normal conditions the individual has the use of the space and someone else takes responsibility for redecorating and repairs. Usually the landlord or his manager is responsible for building maintenance, major plumbing, and electrical and structural repairs. As efficiency is gained by installing central facilities rather than providing individual services, the rent usually includes the fee for some utilities. This is especially true as the number of units within the building increases. The landlord assumes less responsibility in single detached houses. It is important to understand what services are included in the rental fee and what charges there will be for other services (see Table 14-3).

What is the quality of care? The level of sanitation can be determined by the cleanliness and neatness of the central refuse area (see Table 14-4). Prompt repairs are reflected in the condition of the equipment in the laundry areas and in the lighting systems; rust on plumbing fixtures suggests the contrary. A tenant survey can indicate the length of time required to obtain repairs and the relationships of the occupants both with one another and with the management.

What are the legal contingencies of the rental agreement? The agreement between the renter and the landlord may be as informal as a handshake or it may be a complicated legal document. Verbal agreements, though binding in many states, are often difficult to enforce. A

278

TABLE 14-4   Renter's Checklist for Health and
Safety Conditions

Item	Information	
	Type	Condition
Protection		
Insects and Rodents		
Fire Exits and Warnings		
Safety Measures		
Stairs		
Floors		
Glass Windows and Doors		
Other		
Lighting		
Public Areas		
Doorways		
Security		
Main Entrance		
Individual Entrance		
Public Areas		
Parking		
Structural Features		
Walls		
Ceilings		
Floors		
Windows		
Fireplace		
Wiring		
Outlets		
Circuits		
Plumbing		
Sink		
Lavatory		
Shower		
Tub		
Water Closet		
Outdoor Space		

written agreement or a lease dated and signed by both parties clarifies responsibilities and outlines remedies for noncompliance.

A lease is the name for the contract used to outline permission granted by the owner to a renter for use of a particular space for a specific period of time in return for a stipulated fee. It includes the name and address of the landlord and tenant, the amount of the rent and how it is to be paid, the beginning and terminal dates of the contract and a description of the property. The U.S. Department of Housing and Urban Development has developed a model lease to be used for all housing projects under its jurisdiction. The lease suggests that security deposits be limited to one month's rent and that no monetary penalties be assessed for late payment of rent. It stipulates that interest must be paid on the security deposit and specifies that the deposit be used only for default on rent or for repairing damages caused by the intention or negligence of the tenant. It requires repair of defects hazardous to life, health, and safety within 72 hours of the time they are reported to the management, if feasible. If the repairs are not made, the tenant's rent can be abated during the time the defect exists and the tenant remains. Other optional clauses can be included.

1. *Changes in rental fees.* In times of rising prices, one advantage of a lease arrangement to the renter is that the rental fee is established for the duration of the agreement. Some leases have a stipulation that under special conditions extra charges can be made to accommodate increases in taxes or assessments made against the building.

2. *Maintenance included in the rental fee.* The general assumption is that the landlord assumes responsibility for the care and maintenance of the building. Residential property maintenance codes vary. Representative basic amenities and services that are provided in apartment houses include hot water, heat, elevator service (if there are more than four floors), light and ventilation. Plumbing, drainage, and sewage systems must be kept in good working order and appliances installed by the landlord must be kept in good repair. Individual locked mailboxes are required, as well as adequate facilities for garbage disposal. Extermination services must be provided as often as necessary to keep the building free of insects and rodents. The building and sidewalks should be kept clear of snow, ice, and litter and each apartment should be painted every three years. Since housing codes are poorly and seldom enforced, it is helpful to have the lease spell out maintenance requirements.

3. *Termination or renewal requirements.* Some rental agreements do not end automatically with the termination date, but with notification that the renter intends to change residence when the lease ends. If such notice is not given, the lease may be automatically renewed. Just as important are the rules for continuing the rental arrangement and the landlord's responsibility if a fee change is extended at the conclusion of the current agreement.

4. *Escape clauses.* Many people rent because they enjoy the freedom or flexibility provided. Leases often have clauses that forbid the tenant to sublet the premises or charge him a fee for subletting.

5. *Use restrictions.* Some landlords place use restrictions on facilities. Pets, business activities, or children may not be permitted; carpeting and special equipment installed by the tenant may have to be left behind when the renter moves. A check with the tenants helps determine how rigorously such policies are enforced.

6. *Right of entry.* A landlord has the right to inspect the property to ascertain its condition. The renter has the right of privacy. Unless an emergency exists, the renter's rights usually take precedence. It is best to establish the landlord's right to enter as a part of the rental agreement.

7. *Liens on personal property.* Late payment of rents can result in the confiscation of personal property by the landlord, and the property may be held until the tenant's financial obligations are met. Under some conditions, such personal property can be sold by the landlord.

OWNING

The preparation of a place to live plays an important part in the growth of new families. In some societies, not until the house was ready for occupancy could the young couple receive final sanction. A "house of one's own" has been basic to the American concept of the good life. It was fostered by European governments in an effort to entice people to settle in the new colonies. It was perpetuated by the American government through the Homestead Act, which granted land in return for building and improving. Financial policies during the Great Depression encouraged people to pay off their mortgage debts. Each year more houses are built for ownership than for rental. The 1970 U.S. Census showed that an additional 7 million people had joined the ranks of homeowners since 1960, with nearly 63 per cent of all housing units occupied by owners.

Ownership suggests both financial and social status. Owners are considered more stable, more interested in the community. There is a belief that not until a man has something to lose does he become a mature, responsible citizen. Owners seem to live under consistently better conditions—fewer weeds, more flowers, and less debris. On the other hand, research has also shown that renters have a more positive attitude about their housing situation, consistently perceiving their housing conditions as good when, compared to those who own, they had fewer square feet, fewer rooms, and larger families. Ownership also brings the chance to remodel one's dwelling to fit personal taste and to possess an asset that is transferable to heirs.

Advantages of Owning

From the buyer's point of view, ownership offers many advantages.

1. *Freedom from rules and restrictions.* The owner of a home can alter his property (within the limits of the building code), hang pictures on the wall, or remodel the kitchen. He is free to express his individuality. The home can be decorated, furnished, remodeled or landscaped as desired, to fit the owner's whims or personal style of living.

2. *More living space.* Most owner-occupied dwelling units are single-family detached houses, larger than multifamily units and with more private outdoor space. This means more room in which to live, greater privacy for the total family as well as for each individual. Often it provides a better environment for children.

3. *Increased economic stability.* Although the investment aspect of owning is questionable, there are economic advantages. It provides a way to save that might not otherwise occur. Monthly payments on amortized loans help accrue principal. Although this equity is not available until the property is sold, it does represent an asset that can be used as security for other loans. This, in turn, may lead to financial independence or at least a good credit rating. Some value a house as a hedge against inflation. If market prices rise, the mortgage payment

will not. But there is always the possibility that the reverse might occur; when this happens, not only is the payment higher than necessary, but the property is worth less than the purchase price.

4. *Increased community spirit.* Neighbors with similar interests promote a sense of community. Frequently lifelong friendships are formed and often it is the girl or boy next door that becomes a marriage partner. As owners are interested in maintaining property values, projects that improve the quality of the neighborhood hold their interest. Because the tax rate affects their pocketbooks, they tend to respond to school bond appeals and street improvements that increase property valuations.

Disadvantages of Owning

There are major disadvantages that tend to deter home ownership or make it impossible. Owning a home requires time, effort, and money. Whenever something needs to be repaired or replaced, the owner must do it or have it done. To maintain property values, the owner must periodically refinish the interior or exterior, cut the grass, and shovel the snow. He is subject to varying monthly expenses for heat, maintenance, and repair—which makes budgeting and the control of household funds more difficult.

The owner risks overburdening the family financially or to tying himself to a building that may cease to serve its purposes, impairing other values the family deems important. Only those can purchase a house who can obtain a suitable mortgage arrangement, who save enough for a down payment, and calculate the other costs involved.

Often a house is purchased with the belief that it will provide a haven during one's declining years. Payments can be made while income is high, so that costs are reduced when income is lowered. More frequently, however, the rise in property taxes, insurance rates, or maintenance and repair costs more than compensate for the decreased mortgage payments. If the neighborhood declines, the house may depreciate in value even though it is well maintained. Nor does the owner control the real estate market. Conditions may not be favorable when it comes time to sell; mortgage money may not be available; interest rates may be so high that monthly payments exceed the potential buyer's ability to pay. In this case owners must sell at a loss or not at all.

Units Available for Ownership

The potential buyer has a wider choice in location, style, and type of dwelling than has the renter, simply because there are more units constructed for sale than for rent.

Single-Family Detached Dwelling. The conventional single-family house is the goal of the majority of American families. Statistics show that two out of every three buyers select an older house. A house in an already established neighborhood solves many problems. Taxes are usually stable. A more central location presents the possibility of shorter commuting distance to work and shopping. As much as 20–30 per cent more living area may be obtained because older houses have larger rooms and long-forgotten amenities such as a kitchen pantry, double-entry doors, entrance halls, and separate dining areas. These may also prove to have been poorly planned.

Bargains are often available because an older house may not be in prime condition. If the purchaser is not skilled, does not enjoy the challenge of remodeling, or has no cash reserve, what appeared to be a bargain may become a problem. New equipment may be costly. Extra maintenance or operational costs may be required.

A good compromise is a house that is approximately five years old. Such a house has been "broken in," but is not yet in need of modernization or extensive repair.

There are pitfalls in purchasing an existing house. There is the possibility of termite infestation, sagging floors, inadequate wiring or plumbing or insulation, defective heating, leaking roof or gutters or basements.

A new house may be purchased from the owner, a building company, a real estate firm, or a contractor. It will be fresh and clean, with modern fixtures and equipment, efficient heating and cooling systems, adequate light and wiring systems. A relatively small down payment can be made, sometimes as little as 10 per cent of the purchase price. But a new house is not without problems. The quality of workmanship, design, and materials varies. If the community is new, charges for lighting and paving the streets, installing water and sewer lines, and collecting trash may increase initially low taxes.

Many new houses are built and sold from a few display models. The purchaser selects a lot by looking at drawings, usually before access to exact locations is provided. The uninitiated can easily be overwhelmed by the appearance of the model home, assuming that all features in the model are part of the basic price, when in reality there is an extra charge for decorating and landscaping or for finishing the basement and attic.

Some people, though relatively few, may choose to have their homes built. They may purchase a stock house plan and hire contractors to build from it, use a builder's plan, buy a prefabricated house from a franchised dealer, purchase a shell house and have it completed, or have a house custom designed by an architect. Building one's own home can result in saving as much as 25 per cent of the purchase cost, but there is always the possibility that it will cost more than originally planned. One has the advantage of tailoring a dwelling to his individual needs, selecting the fixtures, colors, building materials, and floor coverings—a satisfying and rewarding experience but an enormous amount of work. It is necessary to find a suitable lot, obtain house plans and specifications, judge the house by sketches and blueprints, hire appropriate professionals and skilled workers, arrange adequate financing, and complete the landscaping. Enormous risks are involved. Borrowing money can be more difficult; interest is paid from the time of the loan, not from the time of occupancy, and while one waits for workmen or materials. Misunderstandings between workmen and owner may delay completion and further increase charges.

Multifamily Dwellings. Duplexes, townhouses, and apartments can be purchased either as separate units or as an entire structure. Commonly an individual purchases the entire building, lives in one of the units, and rents the rest. Cooperative and condominium plans involve purchasing an individual unit in an apartment complex or townhouse cluster. The owner of the individual unit has the right to the space described in the title and is responsible for its maintenance and upkeep. In addition, he has interest in the common elements such as the exterior, the hallways, utilities, land and recreational facilities.

Cooperatives have the longest history in the United States. Under the cooperative arrangement, buyers of units share ownership of the building (or buildings) and land. Each also has the privilege of using the land and sharing the common facilities. Shares can be sold or the apartment subleased but the new tenant must be approved by the board of directors. In addition to a down payment, the owner pays monthly rent to cover a share of the mortgage. If this payment cannot be met, the owner can sell, sublet, or simply move out after giving notice, thus forfeiting the down payment. If one moves out, the monthly charges of the remaining shareholders may increase until the apartment is sold to another party. Under this plan, the buyer has the advantage of helping to choose other occupants, enjoys reduced rental costs and the financial benefits of owning; but is not free to sell or sublease at will, or to increase the mortgage for the apartment, and must abide by majority decision.

Condominiums are new to the United States. Under the condominium plan, one purchases property rights for an individual dwelling plus a proportionate share of all the common facilities and ground under and surrounding the building or complex. Each buyer arranges a separate mortgage and pays individual taxes on a unit and contributes to a maintenance and service fund. The condominium is operated by a board of directors according to the bylaws described in a master deed. Actual day-to-day management of the property is usually the responsibility of a professional management team. Additional fees may be levied for use of recreational or service facilities.

Condominiums are popular in resort areas. Owners may maintain year-round residence, but it is likely they will be in residence only intermittently. When they are absent, arrangements can be made to rent the unit.

The prospective buyer must consider the practicality of the proposed assessment budget, the condition of the buildings and property, and resale rights and prospects. The master deed stipulates the

284

way the condominium will be administered; it should be fully understood prior to purchase. If the unit lacks provisions for a replacement fund, the purchaser may incur extra charges to replace roofing, paint the exterior, or repave drives, streets, and parking lots. Monthly dues may increase because of poor or unscrupulous management. (The owners' association may not be able to select another manager because of the terms in the original contract.) Additional fees may be necessary when common elements are not adequately insured, or for snow removal, rental services, parking, and use of recreational facilities. Unless the master deed stipulates otherwise, individual units can be used for offices and other purposes. Restrictions may be imposed regarding conditions of ownership and occupancy, remodeling, pets, and even children of certain ages. Since many condominium projects are purchased from models and blueprints, locations may prove disappointing, recreation facilities may not be completed within schedule, or insufficient interest in the project may slow its completion. Additional assessments may be made to complete recreational facilities; or the facilities may be opened to nonresidents to defray expenses or they may simply be abandoned. Lack of a prior agreement to void the sale in case the developer defaults can result in loss of the deposit. Sometimes, an existing rental structure is converted into a condominium. Such conversion offers buyers the opportunity to live in an established neighborhood, sometimes at a lower price than would be possible in a newly established project. In such cases, the prospective buyer should consider the extent and quality of any needed renovation for the building as a whole or for the individual unit, and the condition of mechanical and electrical systems. Special attention should also be given to reserves for capital expenditures and maintenance.

Mobile Homes.   Although mobile homes are portable, they are designed to be towed to a parking site, where they are connected to utilities. Low in cost, mobile homes are appropriate for recreational housing and appealing to young married couples and retired persons. Similar in atmosphere to the single-family detached dwelling, the mobile home is lower in initial cost, monthly rent, and maintenance cost.

One of the problems presented by mobile homes is not the lack of choice but the extensive range of manufacturers and styles available. There are also options for furniture, appliances, trim, details, and paint. Most mobile homes carry factory warranties but the buyer must be sure that the dealer will provide services. A second major problem is location. Although there are more than 15,000 mobile home parks in the U.S., there may not be one that the family considers desirable. Most parks offer adequate water, sewage, and electricity connections, but appearance, recreational facilities, transportation, and distances to shopping, religious, and educational facilities are also important. Rents range from $35 to $100 or more per month.

The financing of a mobile home is similar to the financing of an automobile. Dealers or salesmen are still responsible for many of the loans, but as mobile homes have become larger, more traditional mortgage financing through banks and saving and loan associations has become possible. There is no need for a title search or attorney fees to be sure that the person selling the unit possesses a clear title. Loan terms are much shorter, ranging from seven to ten years, partly because the loan is smaller than that for a conventional house. In theory a minimum of 10 per cent down payment is required. FHA and VA loans are available if the unit is immobilized on the lot (that is, if the wheels have been removed and the coach affixed to a solid foundation with a permanent hookup to all utilities). It is important to be sure that zoning codes do not exclude mobile homes on individual lots if this method of financing is obtained.

A frequent mistake in purchasing a mobile home is to forget the costs of the extras required (steps, handrails, skirting, foundation) before the unit is operable. In hurricane areas, it is also necessary to make certain that the home is properly anchored. These costs can be estimated at 15 per cent of the cost of the unit. Another common error is to consider only the loan repayments and not include fees for utilities and parking.

Recreational Homes. Vacation homes are seasonal in nature although they can provide an opportunity for year-round leisure. Most of them are described as permanent dwellings and may range from a tent camper located on a lot in a resort area to an elegant country home. In 1970, 4.6 per cent of the people who occupied their own homes had second homes.

A study of second homes in the State of Washington showed that 85 per cent were located along the seacoast, mountain lakes, or streams. The remainder were near a recreational activity enjoyed by the family—ski areas, riding stables, or golf courses. Forest and vacation lands are the most popular locations. Permits from the U.S. Department of Land Resources are still available in some areas. These run for twenty years and stipulate that buildings must preserve the natural character of the area. They tend to be requested by local residents rather than out-of-staters. If a better use for the land arises during the first ten years the permit is in force, notification can be given that there will be no renewal and the owner is reimbursed for any improvements. Resort developers are the major source of land for second homes. Although lots can be purchased and a tent or trailer home used for a limited period, it is usually necessary to build a permanent structure.

The growth in second homes has been a response to increase in leisure time, discretionary funds, interest in the environment and in outdoor recreation. The prime motive for purchase has been to assure an environmentally desirable place. A secondary motive is the hope that the dwelling can be converted to a permanent home after retirement. In this way, the trauma of moving in old age would be lessened.

Others see a second home as an investment or a hedge against inflation.

In general, the distance to a second home varies considerably. Urban dwellers are more likely than rural dwellers to have a second home, and they are more willing to travel greater distances. The site chosen depends upon the amenities available, the difficulty of reaching the location, the prestige of the natural environment, and the cost of land. But the danger of vandalism in unoccupied homes and the rising price of gasoline may tend to restrict future development. As Margaret Mead states,

> It is an expensive form of vacationing, for it is necessary to have a car . . . and yet less use is made of it. The family is pinned down in one spot dependent on the recreation activities of one locality, deprived of the variety which traveling vacationers can find . . .[1]

Financing Home Ownership

Criteria for the selection of a house vary because the house is an investment as well as a place to live. Professional advice is often solicited.

Value. The first indication of value is the neighborhood. Neat, attractive, well-designed houses suited to the surroundings are characteristic of a desirable location. Contact with the local planning board, the building inspector, the tax office, and the school board can reveal the attitude of residents toward improvements, school support, police and fire protection, the type of buildings and businesses in the area, and also future trends. Shopping in the local stores and visiting the local school can also be revealing.

A second indication of value is the quality of materials and construction. There should be no cracks in the walls; floors should be level and free of squeaks; doors and windows should fit closely. The prospective buyer should inquire whether or not the dwelling qualifies for an FHA insured loan, and should check the credentials and record of the builder. Building codes change from time to time, so an older house should be checked for inadequate wiring. It should also be checked for termite damage. Monthly costs can be estimated by examining the heating system, the insulation, and the type and capacity of the hot-water heater. If the buyer does not feel qualified to judge these items, it is possible to hire a professional inspector or to purchase insurance.

The house must be appraised before a loan can be obtained. The difference between the amount a financial institution is willing to lend

---

[1] M. Mead, "Outdoor Recreation in the Context of Emerging American Cultural Values: Background Considerations," *Trends in American Living and Outdoor Recreation,* Outdoor Recreation Resources Review Commission Study Report 22 (Washington, D.C.: U.S.G.P.O., 1962), p. 15.

TABLE 14-5 Checklist for Home Owners

Item	None Available	Good	Needs Repair	Cost	Remarks
Neighborhood					
Appearance of House					
Lawns					
Distance from School					
Church					
Shopping					
Recreation					
Fire Department					
Fire Hydrant					
Public Transportation					
Public Services					
Water					
Sewer					
Streets					
Street Lighting					
Private Services					
Gas					
Electric					
Telephone					
TV Cable					
Zoning Classification					
People and Families					
Income Average					
Interests					
Construction					
Exterior Conditions					
Siding or Walls					
Foundation					
Roof					
Insulation					
Doors and Windows					
Attic					
Basement					
Conditions Interior					
Walls					
Joints and Moldings					
Floors					
Basement					
Equipment					
Heating System					
Water Heater					
Light Fixtures and Outlets					
Other					

and the asking price is a good indication of value, and so is the tax appraisal, which is usually a percentage of market value. The sale price should be compared with that of other homes in the neighborhood. (It should be neither the highest nor the lowest.) There are several ways to make these comparisons. One method is to count the rooms and the special features that provide living space, such as the garage, swimming pool, basement, or patio. The total of the rooms and special features divided into the total price equals the cost per room. If the size of rooms and the space for storage in the two dwellings differ, the comparison is inappropriate.

Construction costs tend to set values for all houses. When they increase, the price of all houses tends to rise. The prospective buyer should multiply the number of square feet available for living by the current estimated cost of construction per square foot in the community where the house is to be purchased. The potential buyer should be able to justify any differences between the two sums.

Value is also indicated by the length of time the house has been for sale. The longer it has been on the market, the more likely it is that it can be purchased at a reduced price. The buyer should also remember that the value of the property is the selling price minus the realtor's commission (see Table 14-6).

Legal Information.   The legal documents required in the purchase of a house tend to increase initial costs. The purchase and sale of land is more involved than the exchange of any other property. The docu-

TABLE 14-6   Home Owner's Aid to Cost Comparisons

	Cost		
Item	#1	#2	#3
Selling Price			
Realtor's Commission			
Total Cost of House			
Cost per Room			
Cost per Square Foot			
Appraised Value			
Tax Value (— per cent of Total Value)			
Mortgage Loan Available			
Other Houses in Neighborhood			
Total Cost Range			
Cost per Room			
Cost per Square Foot			
Construction Costs per Square Foot			
Comparisons to			
Appraised Valuation			
Tax Valuation			
Other Houses			
Total			
Per Room			
Per Square Foot			
Construction Costs			

ments contain much technical language. A prospective buyer should become familiar with those phrases that commonly occur.

1. *Agreement to buy.* A written agreement between the parties informs the seller that the buyer has decided to purchase the property. Two forms exist. The first is an "option to buy." This does not commit the buyer to purchase the property, but it allows a specific period during which the buyer can investigate the property and make a decision, and it binds the owner to wait until the period expires before accepting another offer. The other form, more binding, is called a "contract of purchase," an "offer to buy," an "offer to sell," or a "contract for sale." It states the location of the property, the total purchase price, the amount to be placed in escrow, a description of the real estate (anything attached to the land), and any conditions that affect its use. It should also state that the sale will proceed only after the title is cleared and the buyer qualifies for a loan. Among the provisions should be conditions under which the earnest money can be returned. Usually a date of possession is established and the party responsible for paying current taxes and expenses is determined.

2. *Performance of completion.* This phrase is aimed at seeing that a house still under construction is completed by establishing a bond to cover remaining costs. Should the contractor be unable to fulfill the obligation, the bonding company assumes the responsibility.

3. *Earnest money.* Sometimes called "subscription money," this is a deposit given to the seller to show that the potential buyer has serious intentions. It is normally held by an intermediary or put in escrow until the sale is completed, when it becomes a part of the down payment. If the sale does not go through, through no fault of the seller, the buyer may forfeit the earnest money.

4. *Clear title.* The seller must establish a legal right to sell the property and show that there are no liens or debts against the property by contractors, subcontractors, workmen, or suppliers. An examination is made of previous titles of ownership of the land. A determination is made of whether there are any encumbrances—unpaid mortgage, taxes, assessments, or other claims that cannot be paid after the seller receives the money from the sale. As debts on the property become the obligation of the buyer, any arrangements related to them should be clearly defined in the purchase agreement. The document describing this history is called an "abstract of title." A quicker method of assuring a clear title is to purchase title insurance.

5. *Passing the title.* This term conveys that the property has been transferred from one person to another.

6. *Deed.* This is the document written to transfer the property from one person to another. It must be signed, delivered to the new owner, and registered by the proper government office. There are several types.

A warranty deed offers the greatest protection against legal challenge and is considered most desirable. It contains eight parts: (1) the date of the transaction; (2) the amount of the true sale price (consideration); (3) the legal description of the property; (4) the clause that permits the new owner to have and hold the property (*habendum* clause); (5) the covenant that holds the previous owner responsible for any loss incurred; (6) the other buildings, walks, plantings, etc. (included appurtenances); (7) confirmation that the seller owns the premises, has the right to sell, and is free of all except stated encumbrances; and (8) a testimonial by the persons involved, or the signatures of the seller, the buyer, and a notary public.

A quit-claim deed is used to transfer whatever interest a previous owner may have had in the property to another. The land may still be subject to mortgages, judgments, or unpaid taxes. It is normally used to relinquish inheritance rights or nullify an outstanding claim to an interest in the land. It is considered complete when the grantor and the grantee have signed it and it has been delivered to the new owner and recorded in the proper county office.

7. *Land contract.* Buyers who are not able to obtain financing through a lending institution because of insufficient money or a poor credit rating may be able to negotiate a land contract with the seller. Under this arrangement the buyer makes a small down payment and agrees to pay the remainder plus interest to the seller in periodic installments. The difference between land contracts and a mortgage is the point at which the title is passed. In a land contract, the seller retains title until the entire purchase price is paid or enough money can be borrowed from a financial institution to meet a mortgage, whichever is written into the contract. Such a contract is advantageous for the buyer with little savings. Its disadvantage is that the buyer does not actually have title to the property. Frequently the seller will agree to put the title in escrow or in the hands of a qualified agent who will see to the interests of both parties.

8. *Tenancy.* Tenancy concerns ownership rights, which differ with each state. Most of the confusion encompasses the rights of husbands and wives. When any property is purchased after the marriage, the form in which the couple's names appear on the deed affects the individual rights of the couple and the manner and cost of passing the estate should the marriage dissolve.

Most states make it possible for husbands and wives to act as if they were a single person, or in "tenancy by entirety." In such cases, the names would appear on the deed as "John Public and Mary Public, his wife." Neither spouse can separately destroy the tenancy and if one spouse dies the survivor automatically becomes full owner. If state law is based on the Napoleonic Code, community property provisions prevail. In this instance, husband and wife are regarded as a corporation. When either spouse dies the corporation is dissolved and half of the property descends to the legitimate children of that spouse. In order for the property to be owned by the survivor it is necessary for the couple to make mutual wills. When the clause "joint tenancy with the rights of survivorship" is added to the deed, the surviving spouse becomes sole owner.

Types of Financing.   When a house is purchased, the seller is entitled to be paid in full. Nearly all buyers must borrow money. Most obtain whatever is necessary from a lending institution, pledging the property as security and promising to pay taxes and insurance and to maintain the property in good condition. The mortgage obligates the borrower to repay the lender in regular payments (including interest on the amount borrowed) for specified number of years. If payments are not met, the lender may take the property. The borrower can lose both the equity (borrowed money that has been repaid) and a place to live. The repayment process is a complicated one, involving many charges in addition to the mortgage loan itself. The borrower should recognize both the obligations and the risks.

1. *Types of mortgages.* There are three basic types of mortgages. The most common is the conventional mortgage insured by the Federal Housing Administration or the Veterans' Administration, and loans from government agencies. The money provided by the lender is secured by the value of the property to be purchased and the financial integrity of the borrower. This investment is protected by a large down payment (5—35 per cent of the value of the property is required). Typically, about 75 per cent of the property value is borrowed for a period of twenty to thirty years. High-risk borrowers must be insured by either a private or a government agency. The cost of such coverage is about 0.025 per cent of the loan per year. Usually private agencies insure only during the loan's early years.

The government insures loans through the Federal Housing Administration. In the event of default by the borrower, the agency will honor the lender's claim after the mortgager has been foreclosed and the property conveyed. The FHA does not lend money, nor are loans paid should the borrower die. This system does permit a lower down payment because it grants a higher percentage of appraised value of the house and results in lower monthly payments because of the longer loan period. It is possible to receive as much as 97 per cent of the first $25,000 of the dwelling's appraised value, plus 90 per cent of the next $10,000 and 80 per cent of the remainder up to $45,000. Loans cannot exceed three quarters of the dwelling's estimated useful life. These loan limits can and do change.

To receive an FHA loan, the buyer must apply through an approved financial institution. A government appraiser determines the amount of mortgage loan it will insure. If the amount is agreeable to the lender, completed forms are forwarded to obtain the borrower's credit history, and FHA officials judge whether the plan would be reasonable indebtedness. If the plan is approved, the lender is notified and completes the transaction with the borrower. There is a maximum interest rate that can be charged.

Two problems exist: the current loan limit is too low to finance many of the houses on the market and FHA regulations forbid a second mortgage; the maximum interest rate is lower than that of the present market. Lenders qualified to make FHA loans do not care to because of the low yield. Because processing takes longer than it does for conventional loans, these loans are difficult to obtain.

The VA mortgage is very similar except that loans are guaranteed rather than insured. The government promises to repay up to a certain amount of an approved loan in case of default. The maximum level guaranteed is $17,500. There is no insurance premium to pay, no down payment is required and a repayment period of as long as thirty years can be obtained. Loans of this type are available only to qualified veterans, their widows, and other specified service personnel. Eighty per cent of the loans are given for previously occupied houses rather than for new ones.

Federal land banks, organized by the government just prior to World War I, continue to make loans on rural real estate. Under the supervision of the Farm Credit Association, these loans are made primarily to farmers and ranchers but any rural resident may apply. No loan can exceed 85 per cent of the appraised value of the real estate offered as security. The loans may range in term from five to forty years and be amortized, unamortized, or a combination of the two. In general they are twenty-year amortized loans designed to respond to current economic conditions. This is an advantage in that it results in the lowest current interest charges, which will decrease when the market rates go down, but it may be a disadvantage in times of increasing interest rates. Each borrower must also purchase stock in the Federal Land Bank Association equal to 5 per cent of the loan. This stock is pledged as collateral security for the payment of the loan and is retired when the loan is paid in full.

When the first mortgage and down payment do not meet the selling price, a second mortgage is needed. This places two claims on the property in case of default. The holder of the second mortgage can enforce his claim only after the first mortgage is paid in full. Because of the greater risk, interest charges for second mortgages are higher.

For buyers with little or no cash reserves, a package mortgage is advantageous. Typically these loans are arranged by builders who equip the house with appliances, fixtures, and equipment. The lender includes their cost as a part of the loan.

When inflationary costs of the late 1970s forced many people out of the housing market, innovative mortgage plans were needed. One, backed by the U.S. Department of Housing and Urban Development, has graduated mortgage payments. This would permit low payments during the early years of the loan when, presumably, the borrower is young and income low. Proposed California laws include a mortgage which would have interest payments only during the first year when "moving in" expenses are high. Another would create an annuity for retired persons by permitting them to borrow monthly on their equity in the house where they lived. Upon their death the loan would be paid out of the estate.

Favorable loan contracts are amortized and have prepayment privileges. Open-end contracts are open-ended, allow the borrower to in-

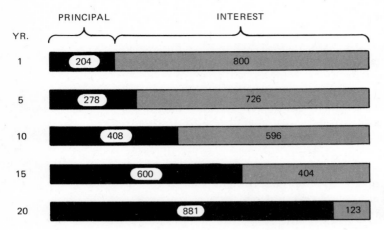

PRINCIPAL | INTEREST

YR.		
1	204	800
5	278	726
10	408	596
15	600	404
20	881	123

FIGURE 14-1 Level payment plan on a 20 year loan of $10,000 at an interest rate of 8 per cent.

crease the loan without rewriting the mortgage. When repair or remodeling is required, such improvements are facilitated by extending the time period for the existing loan or by increasing the monthly fee. Amortization permits repayment in a fixed amounts. These repayments are due at regular intervals (usually each month) for the lifetime of the loan. Often a proportion of the taxes and insurance is also collected so that sufficient funds are available when these charges become due. In an amortized mortgage arrangement each payment reduces the amount of money borrowed, thereby reducing the amount of interest in the next payment and increasing the amount of equity. During the early years, a large share of each payment is interest; during the terminal ones, a large share of each payment is principal.

The prepayment clause provides for repaying the loan at any time without penalty. The faster a loan is paid, the less interest is due. Some lenders permit a certain proportion of the loan to be repaid yearly; others accept prepayments only after a certain period of time.

2. *Sources of mortgages.* Loans can be obtained from a variety of sources. Home loans are the main business of the savings and loan institutions, which have accounted for the largest volume of mortgage credit since the passage of the Housing Act in 1934. Most loans are conventional. Mortgage companies are most likely to arrange government-insured or guaranteed loans by acting as brokers to bring borrowers and lenders together. Savings banks and a broad category of both private and commercial lenders (pension funds, insurance companies, credit unions, and even rich uncles) provide the remainder of the mortgage money and most secondary financing.

To obtain a loan, the potential borrower must first check at a financial institution where the person has had an opportunity to display a capacity for financial management—for example, a bank where the individual has a checking or savings account. Banks have a natural inclination to try to accommodate a customer whose credit rating is known. The buyer might also consider assuming the present owner's

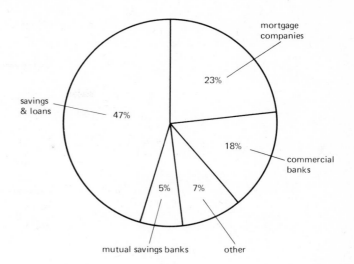

FIGURE 14-2 Sources of mortgage credit. Reprinted with permission from CHANGING TIMES Magazine, © 1975 Kiplinger Washington Editors, Inc., Sept. 1975.

mortgage. This has the advantage of resulting in a low interest rate on the assumed loan, but a large down payment or a second mortgage may be required. If a second loan is required, two payments each month may be arranged, one of which may make the total interest rate paid higher than that for a new loan for the full amount.

3. *Mortgage costs.* Costs vary according to the source of the loan, the kind of a loan, and the credit rating of the borrower. The highest rate currently permitted by the Federal Housing Administration or the Veterans' Administration is 8.5 per cent. In addition, the insurance charge of 0.05 per cent makes the total of 9 per cent for FHA loans. Interest rates for conventional loans depend primarily on market conditions. When the supply of money is plentiful and demand for loans is low, rates go down. When the supply is limited and demand high, rates go up but are limited by state usury laws. In early 1978, interest ranged from 8.75 to 9.25 per cent on uninsured conventional loans. Interest on second mortgages was even higher. To increase yield when money is scarce, a lender often charges a discount or points. This one-time charge equals up to 1 per cent of the loan. It may be charged against the buyer, the seller, or both. On FHA and VA loans, payment of points is restricted to the seller and the amount is included in the selling price.

The amount of interest paid affects the total cost of the house. Even a variation of 0.05 per cent makes a significant difference (see Table 14-7). In general, the lower the rate and the shorter the period, the lower the cost (see Table 14-8). Money can be saved by making a large down payment and paying off the loan in the shortest time possible (see Table 14-9).

Transfer Costs. When the property is officially transferred to the new owner, the note and mortgage for the financial arrangements must be signed, and the deed transferring title to the buyer must be

TABLE 14-7 Effect of Interest Rate on Cost of $20,000 Loan Over a 25-Year Period

Monthly	Total Interest	Total Cost
$141	$22,390	$42,390
148	24,330	44,330
154	26,280	46,280
161	28,200	48,200
168	30,220	50,220
175	32,370	52,370
182	34,460	54,460

Adapted from *Selecting and Financing a Home*, Home and Garden Bulletin No. 182, Agricultural Research Service, December 1970, p. 21.

TABLE 14-8 Effect of Repayment Period on Cost of $20,000 Loan at 9 Per Cent Interest

Payment Period (Years)	Monthly	Total Interest	Total Cost
5	$415	$ 4,910	$24,910
10	253	10,400	30,400
15	203	16,490	36,490
20	180	23,160	43,160
25	168	30,220	50,220
30	161	37,820	57,820

Adapted from *Selecting and Financing a Home*, Home and Garden Bulletin No. 182, Agriculture Research Service, December 1970, p. 21.

TABLE 14-9 Effect of Size of Down Payment on Cost of $20,000 Loan at 9 Per Cent Interest for 25-Year Period

Down Payment	Monthly	Total Interest (25 Years)	Total Cost of House (25 Years)
$ 0	$168	$30,220	$50,220
500	164	29,460	49,460
1,000	160	28,710	48,710
2,000	151	27,200	47,200
3,000	143	25,690	45,690
4,000	134	24,180	44,180
5,000	126	22,670	42,670

Adapted from *Selecting and Financing a Home*, Home and Garden Bulletin No. 182, Agriculture Research Service, December 1970, p. 22.

executed and recorded. This requires the services of both the government and other professionals, the cost of which averages about $560, but can be as much as $4,000. Variations are related to location, the price of the property, the kind of financing, and the type of institution involved. On the average, the buyer's costs for a conventional loan are greater than if the loan is secured through either the Federal Housing Administration or the Veterans' Administration. The seller's closing costs can be passed to the buyer in the form of a higher sales price. Certain charges characteristically appear on settlement statements.

1. *Title search.* Required by the lender, this service may be part of an attorney's fee or a separate charge.

2. *Title insurance.* This protects the lender's interest against loss owing to unforeseen occurrences that might be traced to legal flaws in previous ownerships.

3. *Attorney's fees.* Since everybody concerned with the transfer of property may be an expert—except the buyer and the seller—each should be represented by someone who knows the language. Even if an attorney is not hired, the lending institution may require a fee for its lawyer to handle the closing. Lawyers' fees vary with the location of the property, the number of duties required, the difficulties encountered in the course of the performance of those duties, the price of the property, and even the attorney's professional standing. Charges have ranged from as little as $105 to as much as $675.

4. *Survey.* This service determines the precise location of the house and property, affords protection against encroachments or overlapping of boundary lines. Charges may vary from $80 to $500, depending on the complexity of the survey.

5. *Preparation of documents.* The charge for this service may be a part of the attorney's fees but the service can be performed by a lender or realtor, in which case there will be a separate charge.

6. *Credit report.* A history of the buyer's financial circumstances and money management practices.

7. *Origination fee.* This service involves the processing of the loan application and the initiation of the loan. The fee charged for this service is usually a small percentage of the face value of the mortgage. The Federal Housing Administration and the Veterans' Administration limit this fee to no more than 1 per cent of the mortgage.

8. *Discount points.* This is a charge assessed by the lender to increase the yield of the loan.

9. *Appraisal fee.* The appraisal of the value of the property is required in the origination of a loan.

10. *Transfer tax.* This is a fee charged by state and local governments when property changes hands.

11. *Mortgage insurance premiums.* This is a fee to the company or government agency that guarantees the lender against loss if the borrower fails to make payments.

12. *Escrow fees.* This is the charge for having the funds or documents held in trust by a third party.

13. *Adjustment of prepaid items.* The taxes and special assessments for street or sewer are paid in advance. The seller is entitled to a refund of that portion of the year for which the buyer will own the house.

14. *Other miscellaneous fees.* These may include fees for a notary public, inspections for termites or other damage, photographs, and recording and processing fees.

The 1974 Real Estate Settlement Procedure Act was designed to take some of the mystery out of property settlements and to permit the buyer to make comparisons. It requires the lender to list closing costs or give a good-faith estimate of them prior to the day the property is to change hands. Much of this information is related to the credit processes of the financial institution. As the loan application is virtually completed when these charges are known, it is necessary for the consumer to initiate more than one loan application if he is to make comparisons without delaying property settlements.

Insurance. Insurance in the amount of the loan or the unpaid principal is required to protect the lender from damage to the property by

FIGURE 14-3 Relationship between various insurance plans.

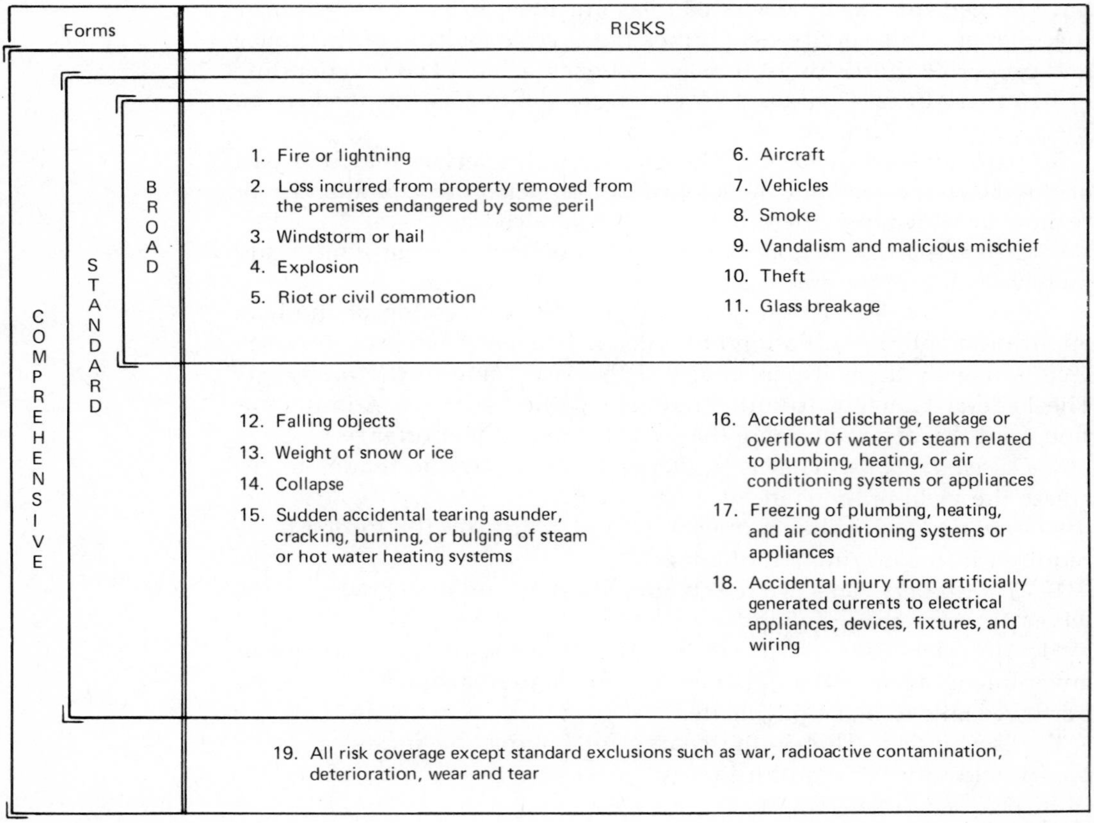
Forms
RISKS
COMPREHENSIVE
STANDARD
BROAD
1. Fire or lightning
2. Loss incurred from property removed from the premises endangered by some peril
3. Windstorm or hail
4. Explosion
5. Riot or civil commotion
6. Aircraft
7. Vehicles
8. Smoke
9. Vandalism and malicious mischief
10. Theft
11. Glass breakage
12. Falling objects
13. Weight of snow or ice
14. Collapse
15. Sudden accidental tearing asunder, cracking, burning, or bulging of steam or hot water heating systems
16. Accidental discharge, leakage or overflow of water or steam related to plumbing, heating, or air conditioning systems or appliances
17. Freezing of plumbing, heating, and air conditioning systems or appliances
18. Accidental injury from artificially generated currents to electrical appliances, devices, fixtures, and wiring
19. All risk coverage except standard exclusions such as war, radioactive contamination, deterioration, wear and tear

some hazard. The exact amount depends upon the lender and the price of the property. The full value need not be covered because the land and some parts of the building (foundation, walks, drives) are often not destroyed. In most instances, 80 per cent of the replacement value is sufficient. This should be adjusted yearly to accommodate changing construction costs and prevent the payment of only depreciated values should damage occur. Savings are available for those who shop around (see Table 14-10). Additional insurance may be desirable to protect the owner against personal liability in the event someone is injured on the property and against theft. There are policies that combine the various types of insurance; some include more protection than is needed; others do not contain all the protection desired. Finally, to protect the buyer's family in case something happens prior to the time the loan is repaid, the buyer sometimes purchases extra life insurance.

TABLE 14-10   Variation in Property Insurance Rates

Company	Cities				
	Marietta, Ga.	Mill Valley, Calif.	New Rochelle, N.Y.	St. Cloud, Minn.	Webster, Mo.
Aetna	127	105	125	131	140
Fireman's Fund	114	138	129	124	143
Geico	95	106	105	121	95
INA	122	121	124	112	150
Nationwide	95	130	130	*	*
State Farm	99	114	113	98	92

* Not sold in that location.

Adapted from *Money Magazine*, February 1974, p. 76, by special permission; © 1974, Time Inc. All rights reserved.

Taxes.   Property tax is the main source of income for the local community. The Douglas Commission tax study found that two thirds of local revenues come from this source. Assessments are also made against the owner of real estate for special improvements related to the property—streets, lighting, parks, fire hydrants, and the like.

All real property is appraised for tax purposes by the state or local government. Appraised value is usually a percentage or proportion of the market value. The tax rate is determined annually by adding the amount established for each governmental jurisdiction in which the property is located to the special assessments approved by the residents. Improvement districts vary, so that people living in the same town may have different tax rates. The effective rate should be approximately 1.75 per cent of the market value, but rates range as high as 4 per cent in some locations (see Table 14-11). A high tax rate places a heavy burden on the owner, and it most affects those who are least able to afford it. Exemptions are often given to veterans, the elderly, or

TABLE 14-11 Variation of Real Estate Taxes in Major U.S. Cities

City	Tax Rate Per Year	City	Tax Rate Per Year
Boston	$2,688	Detroit	$739
New York	1,503	St. Louis	713
Los Angeles	1,925	Denver	812
San Francisco	1,895	Cleveland	885
Chicago	1,286	Seattle	729
Washington	743	Dallas	408
Philadelphia	665	Houston	326

Adapted from *Business Week*, Nov. 3, 1973, p. 86.

to institutions supported by citizen donations. In addition, a property assessment may have been unfair or be in need óf readjustment as the value of the property changes. The effective tax rate, the community's past tax record, and any future developments that might incur special assessments or raise fees should be considered prior to purchase inasmuch as these considerations affect operating costs.

The current income tax policy subsidizes the housing industry by permitting owners to deduct interest charges on house loans from income before determining personal income tax. The Joint Economic Committee has estimated that such deductions cost the U.S. Treasury $2.6 billion a year. Unfortunately, the benefit from this hidden subsidy is directly proportional to the individual's tax bracket. Poor people are poor because they make little money and are in a low tax bracket. Even if they deduct all their interest payments for a house, their tax savings will be small. On the other hand, a person in the 20 per cent tax bracket who has borrowed enough to create yearly interest charges of $3,000 could realize an annual savings of $600.

When an owner sells a house, the taxes are only on that portion of the sales price that exceeds the original cost. Because it is classified as a capital gain, only half the profit is added to the income. If another house is purchased within a year or one of equal or higher price is built within eighteen months it eliminates the capital gain tax.

SUMMARY

The amount people spend on housing depends on the way they rank their other wants and needs, and upon the local housing supply. Some people prefer the flexibility and freedom inherent in renting whereas others believe ownership offers more advantages. The prospective buyer, however, has the larger selection from which to choose, with the single-family detached dwelling being most popular.

Legal and other professional services are often needed to clarify the conditions of purchase between renter and landlord or buyer and seller. Renters must consider the kind and quality of services, any ad-

300

ditional fees that might be charged, and the conditions of the rental agreement. For owners, the type of accommodation (new, existing, or built-to-order) is important, as well as financing obligations and risks. As very few people have sufficieint funds to pay for a house, it is especially important for a prospective buyer to know the types and sources of mortgages, the conditions of a favorable loan, and the various costs involved.

15

Consumer Assistance

N the United States, housing is purchased for an anticipated benefit. Most people are concerned about material and labor, but give
priority to the pleasure they expect from living in the house.
Housing is also a highly complex consumer product. Houses have
a more or less fixed location and a life frequently longer than the purpose for which they were intended. Housing is one of the more expensive consumer items. Even when rented, it represents a large proportion of the monthly budget. All of this makes housing a most
difficult problem with which to cope. There is, however, much public
and private assistance available.

GOVERNMENT AID

Federal Aid

The size and influence of the housing market has made it a target of
much federal legislation. Some contend that housing is a business,
and therefore has the right of private enterprise to solve its own problems. Others maintain that housing affects the public welfare, for
which the federal government is responsible. Research, experi-
mentation, and dissemination of resultant information are other
aspects of the government's responsibility.

Research and Information.   Research in the field of housing has had
a long history. Aid to education as well as business can affect the
housing industry. The Morrill Act of 1862 and the Hatch Act of 1887,
which provided land and support for agricultural colleges and experiment stations, also made provisions for housing research. As policies

for these agencies have changed, the research concerns have broadened. Current research emphasizes building materials and structures.

Special bills to gather information range from the Model Cities program to encourage local community development to Operation Breakthrough, designed to motivate the development of new technology and improvement of architectural design, site planning, and marketing procedures.

Economic aid to private housing is of the first significance. When stimulation of the housing market is required, federal legislation provides aid to private housing. Most of this legislation makes money available to lending institutions. When business reached a virtual standstill in the Great Depression, for example, legislation was enacted to try to suppress foreclosures on home loans. At first this was done by shoring up the faltering lending institutions. Lack of success caused the aid to be redirected to the individual owner, and the Home Owner's Loan Corporation (HOLC) was founded to refinance home loans.

A series of National Housing Acts was initiated in 1934. The early ones sought to enforce sounder lending practices. The Federal Housing Administration was established to reduce the risk of home mortgages for qualified lending institutions, making insurance available to those persons who were good credit risks and were purchasing housing meeting their minimum standards. The financial institution had to provide systematic monthly amortized payments, longer repayment periods, and low interest rates. Inspectors visit new construction sites to check for conformance with government standards, and appraisers are sent to establish values for ready-built housing. Subsequent legislation has been enacted to encourage financing of houses for sale, of rental units, and of the alteration, repair, improvement, and conversion of old homes.

Another boost given to the sale of homes after World War II was a section of the Servicemen's Readjustment Act designed to provide a more liberal basis for loans. Since many veterans had been unable to accumulate enough wealth to be eligible for conventional FHA loans, the Veterans' Administration was authorized to guarantee the difference. The peak of activity was in the 1950s, but though the expiration date of the original bill has now passed, veterans of more recent conflicts are still eligible.

Other methods of encouraging the private housing industry are not so visible. Basically designed to encourage and regulate business, these include the Home Loan Bank Board, which charters and supervises federal home savings and loan corporations, and the Government National Mortgage Association (GNMA). The former insures the accounts of participant members; the latter creates an adequate secondary market for mortgages for specific types of housing.

The private housing industry received other significant aid from the Community Facilities Administration, created by the 1959 Housing Act, which provides low-interest loans to finance housing for the elderly as well as assistance for college housing programs. Massive unemployment in the housing industry and large inventories of unsold houses led to a Tax Reduction Act in 1975 and 1976, which authorizes a 5 per cent tax rebate (not to exceed $2,000) to those purchasing new houses.

Aid to Public Housing. Public housing is another way the government assists citizens to acquire a decent home in a suitable environment. It is housing constructed by the government or built with government subsidy for specified groups, such as workers in defense industries, members of the armed services, farmers, or members of minority groups; most often it is housing for low-income families.

Legislation was enacted during both World Wars to provide homes for families of workers in defense industries and the military. That provided in 1917–18 arrived too late to be entirely allocated, but both temporary and permanent houses were built during World War II. Afterwards some of these structures were reclassified and transferred to local authorities to become part of low-income housing projects. Others were sold to individual owners to help supply low-cost housing to returning veterans. Many loan arrangements have been made available to rural and farm families, and current emphasis is on rental units for elderly people in rural areas.

Federal aid to low-income families began under the Emergency Relief and Construction Act of 1932. The Reconstruction Finance Corporation was authorized to make loans to corporations that would provide housing to low-income people. Because there was little response, the next year the Public Works Administration was given federal funds to finance low-cost housing, slum clearance, and subsistence homesteads. Although the goal was to create jobs, the result was the direct participation of the federal government in housing construction.

Many problems were encountered. The lack of success in meeting needs of low-income families or clearing slums led to the establishment of the United States Housing Authority, later to become the Public Housing Administration. This agency was authorized to grant loans and subsidies to local public housing authorities for low-rent housing and slum clearance.

Public housing has forced awareness that something must be done about substandard housing in slum areas. Not until the Housing Act of 1954 were there specific provisions for communities to establish minimum standards of health, sanitation, and safety for dwellings, establish a timetable and budget for carrying out the plan. Popularly called Urban Renewal, the plan included methods for relocating families and businesses, and for renewing and revitalizing existing structures as well as destroying those that were hopelessly deteriorated or incompatible with over-all land use. Subsequent modifications have been made to help prevent the spread of slums to other areas and to minimize renewal costs. One of the more significant additions has been aid for the preservation of historic sites, which tend to be located

304

in older parts of the city. While this program has been beneficial to a number of people, it has also been responsible for destroying 400,000 dwelling units.

The image of public housing that has evolved is one of endless rows of high-rise buildings or of buildings almost as bleak as those they replaced. New approaches are needed. One solution is to provide housing vouchers to assist people in securing housing. The recipient would decide the level of housing he desired—and the voucher would be used toward the payment. Several variations on this plan have been tried and are discussed in the following pages.

Subsidized Multifamily Housing.   Section 236 of the Housing Act of 1968, provides for the subsidizing of multifamily housing. Under its provisions, a basic rental, related to the cost of operation, is determined for each housing unit in a project. The tenants pay either the basic rental or 25 per cent of their monthly income, whichever is greater. (The tenant's payments cannot exceed the fair market rental.) When rent collections do not equal the cost of operation, federal subsidies make up the difference. Unspent subsidies are put in the Housing and Urban Development revolving fund to build a reserve for subsidy payments. Priority is given to low or moderate-income families, to individuals over 62, and to the handicapped who have been displaced by urban renewal or other government actions.

Rent Supplement.   The rent supplement program enables the family to rent new and rehabilitated housing financed with funds from Housing and Urban Development and the Federal Housing Administration. The federal government supplements the difference between 25 percent of the family income and the rent charged for the unit—paying up to 70 per cent of the actual rent.

Leased Housing.   Leased housing makes possible the leasing of private dwelling units by the Public Housing Authority for occupancy by low-income groups. The program is designed to disperse low-income families throughout the municipality rather than concentrating them in one place.

Subsidized Home Ownership.   Established under Section 235 of the 1968 Housing Act, subsidized home ownership permits low-income families to purchase homes by making possible mortgages of approximately 100 per cent.

The success of these programs has never really been evaluated. The housing scandals of the 1970s caused the Nixon Administration to place a moratorium on most federal housing and urban development in 1973. Later, many of these housing programs were terminated. Recently congress authorized a national housing allowance experiment that would provide low income people opportunity to select their own housing. Similar in concept to food stamps, it would incorporate a grant—either cash or by purchase of a certificate—which could be used to pay the rent or mortgage.

State Aid

Most state aid to housing is channeled through legislation that enables local governments to participate in federal programs. State laws supplement other legislation in setting standards and regulations concerning housing.

Safety Regulations for Public Buildings.   Safety regulations for public buildings are enforced through regular building inspections of structures for public use. Infractions incur fines and must be corrected. Although similar regulations are not mandatory for private housing, they often serve as guidelines for the work areas in the home.

Health Regulations.   Health Regulations are largely concerned with sanitation standards for public buildings, maintenance of pure water supply, prevention of water and air pollution, and proper disposal of waste.

Human Rights.   Civil rights legislation provides members of minority groups more housing choices by making it mandatory that all interested parties be advised of property for sale or rent, regardless of location. Builders and real estate agents are obliged to attract minorities to suitable housing and lenders must make loans available on the same basis to all.

Consumer Protection.   Consumer protection in housing is usually related to unfair leasing or rental arrangements. A Uniform Residential Landlord and Tenant Act forbids the separation of the tenant's obligation to pay rent from the landlord's obligation to maintain property, and grants tenants the right to make repairs at the landlord's expense when such repairs are not made by the landlord after a written request and within a reasonable length of time.

Local Aid

Public policies concerning housing in the United States began at the local level, in city planning and building codes. Early regulations concerned fire because major building materials were highly combustible. Of equal importance were sanitary regulations related to the location and construction of outdoor privies, the housing of animals, and the collection and disposal of garbage. Another early concern was the size and location of proposed housing, and as early as 1727 lot and house size were restricted. Planning commissions and building codes continue these restrictions to the present day.

City Planning. The purpose of city planning is to promote orderly growth. While striving to help maintain property values by designating various types of land use, city planners make recommendations for zoning, for street design, for surfacing and lighting, for location of highways, freeways, and shopping centers, as well as for availability of sewer and water systems, electric and gas lines, and storm drains. City planners also regulate building height, lot sizes, setbacks, and parking requirements.

Building Codes. The intent of building regulations is to assure that certain construction standards are met in order to protect the individual from fire and accidents. Construction plans are submitted for approval; a permit is issued; and inspections of the structure are made and certified at specified intervals. If plans fail to meet the code, recommendations are made. These may be accepted or alternate plans may be submitted. If construction fails to conform with the plan, a stop order is issued until the infraction is remedied. Building codes cover such items as the relationship of light and air to room size, the number of outside exits, fireplace construction, electric wiring, plumbing, roof pitch, foundations, framing, and other structural matters.

Housing Codes. Generally, housing codes are found only in larger communities. The purpose is to provide basic housing standards relating to the health and safety of the occupant and those residing in the vicinity. Included are descriptions of design and equipment; occupancy and use. Lack of adequate financing, human resources, and public interest often hamper code administration and enforcement.

PRIVATE AID

Within the housing industry are many entrepreneurs, professionals, and associations that offer information and services to the consumer. The type of aid required varies drastically from region to region, person to person. The average person requires information about housing only intermittently. This infrequency makes it impossible for each individual to develop expertise in the field or even in one aspect of housing. The aid of one or more specialists is often needed.

Occupations Related to Housing Design

The Architect. The service given by the architect includes conceiving the design, preparing the plans, and establishing the specifications for construction.

The architect's impact on housing is more significant when he works as an educator, an urban planner, a government employee, or a researcher than as a designer of houses for individuals.

The prospective buyer may seek the architect's help after making a decision to have a house built to order. The client indicates the amount of money to be spent and the size and inclinations of the family to be housed as well as providing a building site. The architect works out the best possible plan for the budget, the lot, and the family; giving advice about materials and supervising construction. Normally, the architect charges a fee ranging from 7 to 12 per cent of the building costs, although small projects may be handled for a flat fee. A formal, written agreement (one is available from the American Institute of Architects) should specify the services of the architect and list the fees for each. Payments are expected when the contract is signed, after the preliminary drawings are approved, upon completion of the working drawings, and when the building is completed. Often, the last 10 per cent is retained by the client until the final inspection, so there can be a time-and-use test.

Design and inspiration time usually requires about two months, during which the architect produces preliminary sketches of exterior and interior and a floor plan. At this point changes can be made rather easily. Working drawings and details follow; once these are accepted, building specifications for materials and workmanship are determined and submitted to contractors for bids. It is a wise procedure to have a basic plan and several alternates that can be bid on separately. Usually the lowest bid is accepted. Procedures for authorizing changes should be clarified for all concerned. The client, particularly, may not realize that a seemingly small change may affect the over-all design or total cost. Suggestions from workmen or other professionals may be well-intentioned, but the architect should have final authority. The architect usually assumes responsibility for supervising construction, making visits to the building site at reasonable intervals to approve various parts of the work, or withholding approval if the terms of the contract are not being met.

Many architects do not find house design profitable, and it is often difficult to locate one who will accept the challenge of designing individual houses. The local chapter of the American Institute of Architects or the nearest school of architecture may be helpful in suggesting qualified architects. References should be solicited from former clients concerning a given architect's ability to stay within proposed budgets and to organize.

Landscape Architect.   The landscape architect designs ground formations, plantings, and outdoor buildings and solves outdoor engineering problems. Some landscape architects are associated with architecture firms; others work independently. Most landscape architects charge fees on a percentage-of-cost basis, but some are willing to work on an hourly basis if the job is comparatively simple; still others operate in connection with the local florist or nursery.

Interior Designer and Decorator.   The interior designer, whose work is often an extension of the architect's, is responsible for designing or specifying furniture, built-in cabinets, or minor architectural features to meet individual needs. Like the architect, the interior designer can recommend craftsmen or manufacturers who can produce custom designs. The interior designer, with his knowledge of harmonious color schemes, helps in the selection of fabric, floor and wall covering, furniture, and lighting devices. He will also supervise painting and installation of carpeting and lighting equipment. Many interior designers are self-employed, charging a percentage of the cost.

Although the decorator is usually trained in the field of design, the main concern is with the interior furnishing of the house. Decorators are familiar with all types of household fabrics and coverings, furniture styles and trends. Some decorators act as buyer for the client; others will merely suggest solutions to interior furnishings problems. Decorators' services may be purchased separately, but often they receive a commission from the sale of retail or manufactured items.

Occupations Related to Housing Construction

The building industry is responsible for the construction of about three fourths of the new houses in the United States and for the renovation and remodeling of old ones. Many different organizations and individuals are involved; their common bond is membership in the National Association of Home Builders.

Developer. A developer sees potential in large tracts of land and divides them into smaller lots for home use. A full-scale developer obtains options for the land and arranges for its subdivision, secures financing, provides house plans, acquires any local government permits, and meets federal insurance commitments. On a modified scale, the developer plans rights-of-way for streets and utilities. Local governments generally insist that streets and roads be paved, that utility service to various lots be supplied, and that space for parks and common recreational areas, schools, and street lighting be provided.

Builder. The small-scale builder constructs 1–24 houses per year, employs 1–10 workers and assumes major responsibility for management and labor. The medium-scale builder completes 25–29 units per year, employing 10–19 persons. The main responsibility is for organization and supervision, and most of the time is spent coordinating the work of various employees and seeing that materials reach the building site as needed. The custom builder follows the specifications of the individual buyer. (Other builders are speculators who work from standardized plans and hope their houses will attract buyers.) The large-scale builder is an executive whose firm completes more than 100 homes a year, and employs 100 or more workers, many of whom are professionals and craftsmen. Sometimes an architect will be employed by a large-scale builder. Landscape architects are not often consulted, but the services of an interior designer are often solicited.

The importance of a building contract cannot be underestimated. It should describe construction time and contract sum. Final payment can be withheld until all guarantees, warranties, and operating instructions or other descriptive materials concerning equipment and materials are supplied.

Builder/Developers. Builders who develop or improve the land as well as construct houses are usually known as "tract builders." They produce thousands of dwellings a year near the fastest-growing portions of urban America. They work with one or two basic plans, so that they can mass purchase building materials and labor, use assembly-line techniques, and schedule labor and equipment efficiently. Because all the houses in a tract are of approximately the same size and age, the buyer has the advantage of knowing that neighboring houses will not quickly become obsolete. The prospective buyer can also see other houses in the development in various stages of construction, and thus judge the quality of construction.

Contractors. The primary responsibility for actual construction—for seeing that the house meets the plans, specifications, and terms of the contract—is the contractor's. A contractor can also provide estimates of the building costs or practicability of building or remodeling. Although such estimates are in no way binding, the contractor's reputation rests on their accuracy.

Methods of work vary. A good contractor will follow the house plans to the letter, use quality workmanship and materials, maintain high standards of integrity, and handle financial matters competently. Many contractors are affiliated with the Associated General Contractors of America. The names of local contractors can be supplied by the Better Business Bureau, financial institutions, or real estate brokers.

Contractors submit bids, or estimates, of the price to be charged for the completion of a particular job. The more detailed and specific the job description, the more accurate the estimate can be. Many different types of arrangements can be made. A "fixed" bid binds the contractor to a definite price for all work and materials described in the plans and specifications. In such a case the contractor assumes the risk that the cost of materials and labor may rise. A "cost plus" bid passes that risk to the consumer—but is not conducive to complete and efficient work by the contractor. If the job is small, an arrangement can be made whereby the consumer pays for materials while the contractor takes responsibility for labor: the contractor can't lose money on materials, yet has an incentive to do the work efficiently and quickly.

Contractor/Builders. Most contractors employ only a carpenter and a general laborer or two. Often they qualify as small-scale builders because they build a few houses on speculation as well as contract for specific projects. Some general contractors supply the materials and hire only labor and equipment, but the majority hire subcontractors who provide their own equipment and materials.

Subcontractors. The building industry includes many specialists in excavation, masonry, plumbing and heating, electrical work, plastering, and painting. No single project can offer steady employment to all. The largest subcontractors are suppliers or producers who install their own products. A subcontractor can offer valuable advice and assistance, ranging from an estimate of the costs of modernizing an old house to the performance of a simple task like installing a new appliance.

Occupations Related to Marketing of Houses

Real Estate Brokers. The realtor helps people find a place to live, specializing in matching wants of buyers with the local supply. Only those brokers who have passed competency examinations and belong to the National Association of Real Estate Boards may call themselves realtors. Essentially, the real estate agent deals in information. He establishes a selling or rental price, advertises the property (either alone or through an association of brokers), shows the property to prospective buyers, and negotiates sales agreements. The realtor also provides prospective buyers with information on the status of the local housing market as well as with an opportunity to compare all property available in the area.

The realtor usually represents the owner, who pays the agent a fee or commission based on the sales price or rental fee. The size of the fee may also vary with market conditions: during poor periods in the housing market, the broker may reduce his fee in order to facilitate a sale.

Financial Institutions. The average person who decides to build or purchase a house needs financing. There are different types of lending agencies. Lending agencies come under greater governmental supervision than almost any other type of private business. This supervision is even more rigorous for agencies associated with the Federal Reserve or Home Loan Bank systems. Charges for financing vary according to the type of loan, the risk involved, the size of the down payment, the length of the repayment period, and the availability of capital.

Almost every bank, savings and loan association, or mortgage company employs someone to advise the prospective buyer on the financial aspects of owning a home. They will help in determining the market value of a house the individual wants to purchase. Any charge for this service is negligible.

Service Occupations

The Appraiser. The value of a house is determined by the appraiser, who is familiar with trends in the local market and in the industry (appraisals are also useful in establishing a base for property tax or establishing an inheritance). The appraiser may be an agent of a financial institution or of the local or state government, or he may be an independent broker. Those employed to establish tax valuations are salaried; independent appraisers charge a set fee or a percentage of the appraised value. Financial institutions or real estate brokers often absorb the appraisal fee as part of overhead.

Inspectors. Many banks and loan companies require an inspection report before granting a mortgage. Inspectors can help identify potential problems as well as any current defects. Their reports can be used as a basis for price bargaining.

There are inspectors for plumbing, wiring, roofing, insulation, termites and heating, as well as for the over-all soundness of the structure. The service is available from many manufacturers or suppliers of special equipment (termite control companies, for example, provide inspection service). The Nationwide Real Estate Inspectors Service, Inc., provides inspectors skilled in all aspects of housing. Inspection fees may range from a few dollars to as much as $200, depending upon the extent of the service requested and the complexity of the structure.

Insurance Agents. Insurance protection is an important aspect of housing. Some types of mortgage loans require insurance against property damage from fire, natural causes, man-made disasters. Personal liability insurance protects the owner from the expenses incurred if someone is injured on the property. Protection from crime, especially burglary, is increasingly necessary. An insurance agent can recommend the type of insurance that will provide the best possible protection most economically. Large insurance companies may be more stable than smaller ones because they are able to spread their risk over more people and property. It is wise, however, to select a company with a local office so that help is quickly available in the event of trouble.

Lawyer. Many legal documents are involved in housing. The lawyer can warn a prospective purchaser of legal entanglements and assure that the client has the necessary legal protection in papers and agreements drawn up by others. A lawyer can trace the history of a property to make certain that there are no outstanding claims against it, or may certify that the records have been examined and that, in his or her opinion, there are no such claims. A lawyer should be a member of the local, state, or national bar association as well as being knowledgeable about real estate law. Financial institutions, real estate agents and, in some cities, the local bar association, will recommend qualified attorneys.

Home Economist. Home economists are intermediaries between the consumer and the builder or the manufacturers of housing products. Manufacturers, utility companies, and consumer magazines employ home economists to research consumer needs—and this information is then used in the evaluation of house designs. Home economists also can be helpful in explaining the use and care of the product to the consumer. Sometimes, when home economists are part of the sales team, their responsibility is to emphasize the advantages of a particular product, to encourage customers to use additional products or to be more satisfied with their buying decisions. A few home economists are available on a consultant basis; their fees are based on the services rendered.

Other Aids. An important consumer aid is the information provided about products by a third party through the award of a "seal" or "certificate of approval."

In this way, products are promoted by award-granting organizations such as consumer magazines, independent testing companies, professional organizations, and government agencies as well as by retailers and manufacturers. Those most closely associated with housing industry products are Underwriters Laboratories and American Gas Association. The consumer should investigate the basis for such awards or endorsements to determine if products are tested, inspected, approved, or guaranteed by the agency.

SUMMARY

The complexity, expense, and various measures used to evaluate housing success make housing decisions difficult for the average consumer. Local, state, and federal government agencies, and private industry as well as professionals and skilled craftsmen are available for assistance. It is important to know what aid can be expected from each. In general, the government has aided citizens in achieving a healthful, safe dwelling. Minimum property standards, building codes, amortized loans, and public housing are some of the results of government efforts. Private industry is interested in the promotion of products or services that are an integral part of the housing industry; although such promotion is profit-motivated, the resulting product improvement, instruction on the correct use and care of products, and specialized service provided can lead to a more satisfactory housing situation. In addition, various professionals are available to give advice to the consumer.

the future of housing

If you can look into the seeds of time
And say which grain will grow and which will not
Speak then to me. . . .

Shakespeare
Macbeth

16

The Future of Housing

O F critical concern for housing policy in the future is the number of people to be housed. If current population trends continue, additional space will be needed for housing construction, more materials for buildings, and more energy for their operation. At present, birth rates are increasing by 1.1 per cent per year, and the growth is expected to continue for sixty to seventy years.

Another factor that will influence housing policy is population mix. The current increase in the proportion of single adults, newly married couples, and elderly citizens creates a demand for smaller housing units.

Density of population is another concern. It can affect the mental and physical health of the individual as well as the use of natural resources. Demographers indicate that people have been moving to large urban centers in search of high incomes, more job opportunities, and more and better public services. If the American dream of owning a single-family house on an individual plot of land prevails, it could result in the merging of what are now discrete metropolitan areas. The spreading megalopolis in California threatens to wipe out half of the state's best agricultural acreage by the year 2020. A shift in value patterns would permit a change in building codes, smaller lots, the elimination of setbacks; it might lead to an emphasis on houses with interior patios instead of exterior gardens or an increase in multifamily structures. These changes would free land for other uses. Acceptance of higher housing densities might also change the composition of the basic social unit—the family. Many people already find the nuclear family inadequate and are experimenting with different family patterns. Communes, for example, require less space because the size of private areas is reduced and work and leisure areas are shared. Others

317

suggest it would be more efficient to use living space in shifts, as we do factory work space. The following pages explore housing systems that have been proposed for the future. The final decision will not be made by the architects and engineers who have formulated or created the sytems, but by those who accept and use them as their environment for living.

HABITATION SETTLEMENTS

Unlike the rectangular boxes clustered and stacked in today's cities, scattered over the suburbs, or isolated in rural areas, housing in the future will be a composition of systems. Five highly complex systems will be integrated—nature, the individual, society, the house, and the networks through which interaction with other systems can take place (transportation, communication, and service or utility pathways). One way to accomplish this would be to build large public buildings and surround them with smaller residential units. This would provide a setting of calm and serenity for family life and orderly civic development.

Others predict an effort to transform sprawling cities into manageable wholes, to provide mass-produced housing in better environments with less labor, materials, and land. That was the goal of Safdie's Habitat in Montreal. Marina City in Chicago, the Embarcadero Center of San Francisco, and Rockefeller Center in New York City indicate that higher living densities can be achieved and networks of communication, transportation, and service integrated. Omnibuildings would provide space for all human activities, enabling people to live from birth to death within their walls. Tunneling into the earth for major streets, as is being done in Japan, is another way to accommodate burgeoning population, to reduce energy demands, and to alleviate visual pollution. Soleri's "arcologies," which combine both tunnel and high-rise, are designed so that residential units encircle a central core of utility networks: no individual is more than fifteen minutes (via elevators and escalators) from the furthest extremity of the community.

Efforts to control pollution and climate may lead to new housing concepts. Solar energy would be utilized for temperature control and traffic would be routed underground. Smaller vehicles, without wheels and perhaps without engines, would clip on to automated highways or guiderails. Pollutants would be expelled, and computerized lighting could give a continuous flow of light. Such theorists as Buckminster Fuller believe such a system would be energy-efficient, removing the need for air conditioning, snow removal, and street cleaning.

Another interesting proposal synthesizes cybernetics and yoga. A spiral macrostructure with artificial levels to accomodate 25,000 people, it contains pathways on both land and water to provide a never-ending succession of discoveries and perspectives. Walkways wander through residential areas, landscaped gardens, and fountained

A. Habitat Montreal (above)

B. Habitat Israel

FIGURE 16-1 Safdie's concept of high density housing. Courtesy of Moshe Safdie and Associates.

CHAPTER 16
THE FUTURE OF HOUSING

squares. At the center of the structure a lake supplies water for canals and fountains.

A constellation city of business and industry accommodating 600,000 people in its core would be surrounded by smaller, special-purpose satellites for education, culture, or sports. Green areas could separate the constellations, and the use of cars could be restricted to intercity travel.

Housing resources in the future will be found in currently wasted land. Residential sites could be located under the seating areas of sports arenas and under the cloverleaf interchanges on highways. Individual house shells could be simply connected to a central core containing the various services needed—safe drinking water, a method to dispose of waste, power for cooking and heating, and transportation to and from sources of food, medical and legal aid, and municipal services. People could provide their own shell from the waste products of a technological society or purchase a plug-in module from a department store. Already in use in Hong Kong are steel uprights and beams supplied with poured-in-place concrete slabs and built-in utility networks, which are rented to people who have their own exterior.

The sea also holds possibilities. Given a way to conquer the problem of decompression, marine biologists foresee colonies of underwater farms and mines or recreation centers.

More immediately possible is the use of large ships to provide housing. Omnibuildings on ocean platforms, much like oil-drilling rigs or floating coastal islands, could absorb some of the population of sea-

FIGURE 16-2 A sea structure. Buckminster Fuller Archive.

320

coast regions. Sea cities could be anchored on ocean reefs or placed on platforms. Modular construction would permit growth without construction noise or interference: small-sized modules could be constructed elsewhere and attached as necessary. These might even be detached and towed to a new location when desired, eliminating the problem of empty living units or the strain of packing household goods when moving from place to place. Anchored in relays across the ocean, these megastructures could provide safe harbors for ships and smaller crafts.

Others envision bridge structures, operated by a system of service towers with connecting girders and cables, spanning long distances. Individual cells or capsules would be attached to both primary towers and bridge supports. Such a design is already under construction in Tokyo Bay.

The space program may be the catalyst for living environments in the atmosphere, freed of such earthly constraints as gravity, weather, and building codes. Inflatable structures—easy to transport, erect, and discard—might be used as components, floating in the air surround-

FIGURE 16-3 An illustration of the exterior of a giant wheel that might be used for a permanent community in space. Courtesy NASA.

ing the earth. The land could become available for other uses, and "link-on" connectors would make possible endless growth.

Man-made satellites, other planets, and planetoids also present possibilities. Some envision space islands that use solar energy, with air, rock, and water manufactured from asteroids. Their lower gravity might simplify transportation, because people could fly with paddle-like wings from place to place. Other scientists conceive a wheel-like structure for outer space settlements. A tube, 130 meters in diameter, used as the rim for a wheel 1790 meters in diameter could provide space for 10,000 people. Space colonists could choose any type of earth environment for the interior and artificial gravity would be created by revolving the wheel. Modular construction would be used for individual habitats. When terraced in clusters up the curved wall of the tube, a feeling of spaciousness, even in high density residential areas could be achieved. Unlike present dwellings designed to protect humans from weather, the chief function of space habitats would be to assure privacy. Light, strong, sound absorbent materials with fire resistive properties would be important. Dwarf fruit trees would provide both food and ornamentation.

Just emerging is the theory of biostructures, which emulate the biological processes of growth and reproduction. Fuller's geodesic dome is one variant. Another is an exoskeleton or "second skin" (whose

FIGURE 16-4 Artist's concept of the interior living level. Courtesy NASA.

forerunner is the space suit), which eventually could enable people to walk around with their homes on their backs.

HABITATION UNITS

Just as important as the vast urban complexes of the future are the shells for individuals and families. Because most people turn to books and magazines when converting dreams into reality, they are locked into traditional ways of thinking. When structures are thought of as a process instead of as a building, new ways of thinking—and living— become possible.

Design

The number of designs for any individual shelter seems almost unlimited. Information concerning all possibilities and their ramifications

FIGURE 16-5 Sectional view of the proposed space wheel. Courtesy NASA.

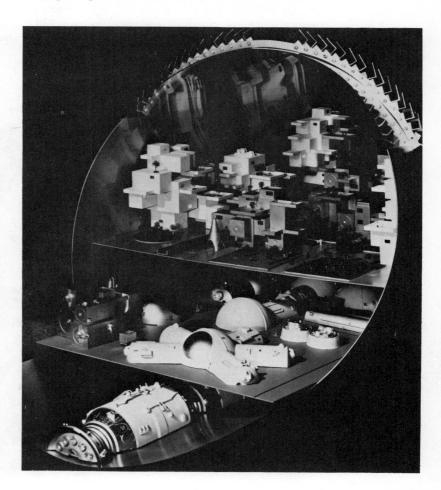

can be stored in computers. Data banks already permit designers to juggle the merits of cost, quality, and aesthetics. If all possible design alternatives were stored, the entire range of solutions would be provided the individual when preferences were programmed into the computer.

Living units in the future are likely to be smaller and more efficient than current ones. This requires a reconsideration of basic shapes. Most man-designed housing is based on squares and rectangles. Nature, on the other hand, for high-density colonies such as those of bees and hornets, produces hexagons. Round or oval structures have less exterior exposure through which heat and cool air can escape, and are more easily prefabricated.

Fuller predicts the use of the dome for enclosing space. The building materials for domed structures cost substantially less than those for conventional rectangular houses of equal floor area. Domes make possible an airier and more imaginative interior because of their spaciousness and unmatched illumination. Glass domes, and metalized Mylar components that have one-way vision and a utility core, would make possible comfort and privacy as well as a panoramic view. Domed structures, however, require open-plan designs. When space

FIGURE 16-6 Trees, grassy parks, birds—even streams and ponds to help obtain a familiar environment for the space colonists. Courtesy NASA.

A. Circular

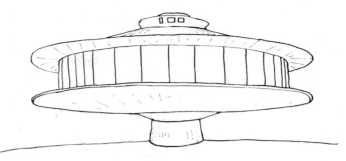

B. Pyramid. Courtesy
Simpson Timber Com-
pany

C. Dome. (below)
Courtesy Temcor

FIGURE 16-7 Shapes of habitats of the future.

is subdivided, rooms tend to end up pie-shaped with ceilings that are too high.

Space can be consolidated by centralizing cooking areas, heating and cooling systems, and storage and leisure facilities. Meals could be ordered from central storage and common facilities could be used for preparation. When greater privacy is desired, a utility cassette similar to those now found in boats and camping trailers could be utilized. Or it might be possible to purchase a standard living package containing the necessities of life—shelter, food, and energy—and do away with permanent structures, leaving nature untouched. This might destroy feelings of place and identity, the total effect of which cannot be assessed.

Materials

Although materials that require little maintenance are currently valued, technology can produce maintenance-free recyclable materials and remodel them to fit new needs. Most are lighter in weight than lumber or bricks and could be transported more easily and at less cost. Fiber glass, for example, has already proved successful for boat hulls. Another promising material is urethane foam, from which any shape can be produced. Even seating surfaces, tables, and cabinets could be molded into place. Pleasing to the touch, urethane foam has better insulation qualities than fiber glass, and its rough texture provides good sound absorption. It can be prefabricated or poured on location. Balloons, wire mesh, wood, or cardboard would form the base; plumbing and wiring could be installed and foamed over. Urethane foam can also be extruded through a steel mold mounted at the end of a truck boom, which can be moved along the area in which the wall is to be placed, producing walls that can stand without support. Foam's

FIGURE 16-8 A house of foam.

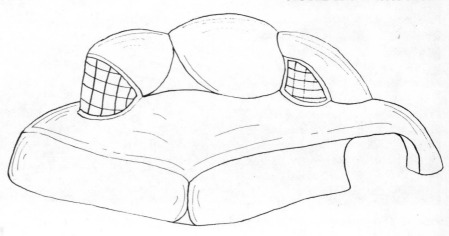

superior tensile strength enables it to carry the roof load. Window openings can be cut into walls as desired and fitted with acrylic or glass panes. Foam also has disadvantages. At 600°F. (315.5°C) the material flashfires with a thick, black smoke that might be poisonous, and it deteriorates if left unprotected in sunlight. Concrete or special fireproof coating is recommended for exteriors and plaster for interiors.

Construction

People tend to build for as long as possible but they buy for the short term. More efficiency might be possible if structures were built to last for a relatively few years. It might be less costly to replace old houses than to remodel them.

Portability could become a highly valued characteristic. Accordionlike structures have already been designed of aluminimum and bondolite or plastic. These can be flattened and stored until needed, or transported to a new site when required. As parts wear out they can be replaced. Lightweight and weather-resistant, they can be transported by plane or truck at less cost than the present mobile home.

Curves and built-in features are possible if a house is premolded. Completed modules can be used alone, hooked together, or stacked on top of one another. Maintenance-free materials in a wide range of colors are currently available.

The most advantageous systems approach is likely to be prefabrication, but changes in building codes and in labor and government regulations would be required. Modern plastics and adhesives could be used in the prefabrication of future living quarters. These finished structures would resist moisture, fire, and wear—and be easy to repair. Units can be stacked or joined to form split-level, single-storied, or multiwinged homes.

Livability

Moderation of climate was a prime motive for shelter. During the twentieth century, Americans have depended on fossil fuels for power to operate equipment and control indoor climate. The energy crisis of 1973 led to exploration of alternate fuel sources such as sun, wind, and water. Research into solar energy suggests that, because the sun is not a constant source of energy, there will be a need for solar energy reservoirs. Individualized systems are highly sophisticated and costly. The solution may be in the development of sun cells stationed in outer space to collect sun power and transfer it to earth as needed.

Hydrogen is one of the cleanest burning fuels. If it could be economically separated from water, it could replace fossil fuels for heat and electricity. If households were provided with cleaner air, the need for storage space for cleaning supplies and equipment might be reduced. More even temperatures could reduce the need for bed cover-

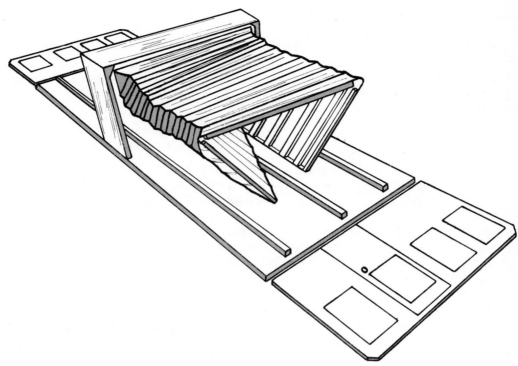

A. Ready for erection

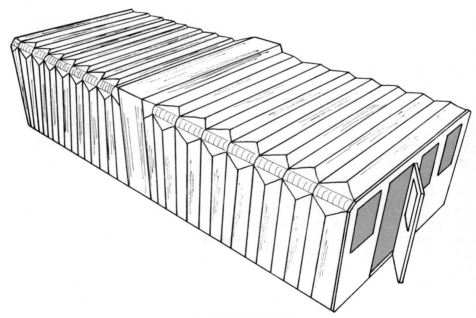

B. Ready for occupancy

FIGURE 16-9 An accordian house.

328

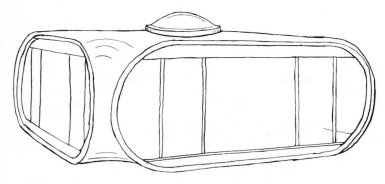

FIGURE 16-10 A molded house of fiber glass.

ings—and, therefore, the need for storage space for linens. Sleeping pallets could then substitute for both beds and living room couches, reducing the need for separated sleeping areas.

The use of computers and improved delivery systems could revise work and leisure activities, thereby reducing space needs. Computerized systems would make possible for an item in storage to be located, retrieved, and replaced as needed. The time and effort required to prepare and serve meals could be reduced. Microwave cooking would reduce power requirements and change cooking utensils. Thermoelectric appliances that have no moving parts could reduce the need for noise insulation. Refrigerated compartments or heating units of various sizes and shapes could decentralize the cooking area. The possibility of flipping a switch to change a unit from a cooling to a heating appliance is intriguing. Piping both heat and cold to various locations of the house rather than having separate units at several locations has been suggested. The acceptance of any or all of these would have far-reaching implications for space requirements.

In the last analysis, the most important function of any future habitat is to produce space for a healthy, happy life. Safdie suggests that the most appropriate way would be to have a magic housing machine that would plop out houses at the push of a button after each individual's requirements had been programmed into it.[1]

The question of whether this will ever be possible or desirable will be answered in the future. In the meantime, the process of change will be hardly discernible: only 2 per cent of the housing supply is replaced or increased each year. The readers of this book, by making thoughtful decisions, can play an important role in the future of housing design.

[1] "New Architecture: Building for Man," *Newsweek*, Apr. 19, 1971, p. 37.

Sources of References

Many books, bulletins, journals, newspapers, and unpublished materials were used as background for this book. Only books and journals that can be obtained through routine library channels are included in this bibliography. Those that were used in more than one chapter are listed under "General References." Those related to a specific topic are listed under the various chapters.

General References

AGAN, T., and E. LUCHSINGER. *The House: Principles/Resources/Dynamics.* New York: J. B. Lippincott Company, 1965.

ALEXANDER, H. H. *Design, Criteria for Decisions.* New York: Macmillan Publishing Co., Inc., 1976.

ANDREWS, W. *Architecture, Ambitions and Americans.* New York: Harper & Row, Publishers, 1955.

BEITLER, E. J., and B. LOCKHARD. *Design for You.* New York: John Wiley & Sons, Inc., 1961.

BEMIS, A. F., and J. BURCHARD. *The Evolving House: History of the Home.* Cambridge, Mass.: Massachusetts Institute of Technology Press, 1933.

BEYER, G. H. *Housing and Society.* New York: Macmillan Publishing Co., Inc., 1972.

CHERMANOFF, S. I., and C. ALEXANDER. *Community and Privacy: Toward a New Architecture of Humanism.* Garden City, N.Y.: Doubleday & Company, Inc., 1963.

COOPER, C. *Easter Hill Village: Some Implications of Design.* New York: The Free Press, 1975.

———. *The House as a Symbol of Self.* Berkeley, Calif.: University of California Press, 1973.

CRAIG, H. *Homes with Character*. Lexington, Mass.: D. C. Heath & Company, 1970.

DORIADIS, C. A. "The Housegroup," *Ekistics,* June 1975, pp. 361–64.

FABUN, D. *Shelter: The Cave Re-examined*. Beverly Hills, Calif.: Glencoe Press, 1970.

FOOTE, N., et al. *Housing Choices and Housing Constraints*. New York: McGraw-Hill Book Company, 1960.

FRIEDMANN, A., et al. *Interior Design: An Introduction to Architectural Interiors*. New York: American Elsevier Publishing Co., Inc., 1976.

GARRETT, P. *Consumer Housing*. Peoria, Ill.: Charles A. Bennett Co., 1972.

GIEDION, S. *Mechanization Takes Command*. New York: Oxford University Press, Inc., 1948.

GOTTLIEB, L. D. *Environment and Design in Housing*. New York: Macmillan Publishing Co., Inc., 1965.

GUTMAN, R. *Neighborhood, City to Metropolis: An Integrated Reader in Urban Sociology*. New York: Random House, Inc., 1970.

HALL, E. T. *The Hidden Dimension*. Garden City, N.Y.: Doubleday & Company, Inc., 1966.

HARRISON, H. S. *Houses: The Illustrated Guide to Construction, Design and Systems*. Chicago, Ill.: National Institute of Real Estate Brokers of the National Association of Realtors, 1976.

HARRISON, M. *The Kitchen in History*. New York: Charles Scribner's Sons, 1972.

HELPER, D., and P. I. WALLACH. *Housing Today*. New York: McGraw-Hill Book Company, 1965.

HEMPHILL, F. M., and C. J. VELZ. *Investigation and Application of Home Injury Survey Data in Development of Prevention Procedures*. Ann Arbor, Mich.: University of Michigan School of Public Health, 1953.

HOWARD, M. S., and W. R. PARKER. *Planning Bathrooms for Today's Homes*. Home and Garden Bulletin No. 99, Washington, D.C.: U.S. Government Printing Office, January 1967.

KENNEDY, R. W. *The House and the Art of Its Design*. New York: Van Nostrand Reinhold Company, 1953.

KIRA, A. *The Bathroom*. New York: The Viking Press, Inc., 1976.

KIRKPATRICK, W. A. *The House of Your Dreams*. New York: McGraw-Hill Book Company, 1958.

LIFSHEY, E. *The Housewares Story: A History of the American Housewares Industry*. Chicago, Ill.: National Housewares Manufacturers Association, 1973.

The Light Book. Nela Park, Cleveland, Ohio: General Electric Residential Lighting Specialists.

LINKE, R. A. "Development Housing and Family Needs," *Forecast for Home Economists,* October 1959, pp. 12–14, 34.

MAAS, J. *The Gingerbread Age*. New York: Bramhall House, 1957.

McCULLOUGH, H. E. *Space Design for Household Storage*. University of Illinois Agricultural Experiment Station. Urbana, Ill.: August 1952.

Manual of Acceptable Practices to the HUD Minimum Property Standards. Vol. 4, U.S. Department of Housing and Urban Development. Washington, D.C.: U.S. Government Printing Office, 1973.

MICHELSON, W. "Most People Don't Want What Architects Want." *Transaction*, July–August 1968.

Minimum Property Standards for One- and Two-Family Dwellings. Vol. 1. U.S. Department of Housing and Urban Development. Washington, D.C.: U.S. Government Printing Office, 1973.

MUMFORD, L. *Culture of Cities.* New York: Harcourt Brace Jovanovich, Inc., 1938.

NATTRASS, K., and B. M. MORRISON. *Human Needs in Housing: An Ecological Approach.* Milburn, N.J.: R. F. Publishing Co., 1975.

NELSON, G., and H. WRIGHT. *Tomorrow's House: A Complete Guide for the Home Builder.* New York: Simon & Shuster, Inc., 1945.

NEUTRA, R. *Survival Through Design.* New York: Oxford University Press, Inc., 1954.

PANERO, J. *Anatomy for Interior Designers: How to Talk to a Client.* New York: Whitney Library of Design, 1962.

PICKERING, E. *Shelter for Living.* New York: John Wiley & Sons, Inc., 1941.

Population and the American Future. Report of the Commission on Population Growth and the American Future. Washington, D.C.: U.S. Government Printing Office, 1972.

Proceedings of the Housing Conferences. American Association of Housing Educators, 1957–75.

RAPOPORT, A. *House Form and Culture.* Englewood Cliffs, N.J.: Prentice-Hall, Inc., 1969.

ROGERS, K. E. *The Modern House, U.S.A.: Its Design and Decoration.* New York: Harper & Row, Publishers, 1962.

ST. MARIE, S. S. *Homes Are for People.* New York: John Wiley & Sons, Inc., 1973.

SCHORR, A. L. *Slums and Social Insecurity.* U.S. Department of Health, Education, and Welfare, Social Security Administration Division of Research and Statistics. Research Report No. 1 Washington, D.C.: U.S. Government Printing Office, October 1963.

Selecting and Financing a Home. Home and Garden Bulletin No. 182, Consumer and Food Economics Research Division, Agricultural Research Service. Washington, D.C.: U.S. Government Printing Office, December 1970.

SHERWOOD, R. F. *Homes Today and Tomorrow.* Peoria Ill.: Charles A. Bennett Company, 1972.

Small Homes Council Circular Series. University of Illinois Bulletins, Urbana, Ill.

Space Standards for Home Planners. Western Cooperative Series, Research Report No. 2. Western Region Agricultural Experiment Stations.

STEPHENS, G. *Remodeling Old Houses Without Destroying Their Character.* New York: Alfred A. Knopf, Inc., 1974.

U.S. Bureau of the Census. *Census Population, 1970. Vol. 1: Characteristics of the Population, Part 1.* U.S. Summary Section 2. Washington, D.C.: U.S. Government Printing Office, 1973.

———. *Census of Housing, 1970. Vol. I.: Housing Characteristics for States, Cities and Counties, Part I.* U.S. Summary. Washington, D.C.: U.S. Government Printing Office, 1972.

VON ECKHART, W. *A Place to Live.* New York: Delacort Press, 1967.

We Americans: Our Homes. U.S. Department of Commerce, Social and Economic Statistics Administration, Bureau of the Census. Washington, D.C.: U.S. Government Printing Office, October 1972.

WEDIN, C. S., and L. G. NYGREN. *Housing Perspectives: Individuals and Families.* Minneapolis, Minn.: Burgess Publishing Company, 1976.

WHITE, B. J. *Readings for Family House Planning.* Fort Collins, Colo.: Colorado State University, 1974–5.

The Yearbooks of Agriculture: 1968, 1971, 1972, 1973. U.S. Department of Agriculture. Washington, D.C.: U.S. Government Printing Office.

Preface

PACKARD, V. *The Status Seekers.* New York: David McKay Co., Inc., 1959.

Chapter 1

AGAN, T. "People and Their Housing," *Journal of Home Economics,* October 1972.

ARONI, R. "The Ecology of Housing," *Ekistics,* June 1975, pp. 372–76.

BUCKLEY, W. (ed.). *Modern Systems Research for Behavioral Scientists.* Chicago: Aldine Publishing House Company, 1968.

CARSON, R. *The Silent Spring.* Boston: Houghton Mifflin Company, 1962.

DICE, L. R. *Man's Nature and Nature's Man.* Ann Arbor, Mich.: University of Michigan Press, 1955.

HOOK, H. C., and B. PAOLUCCI. "The Family as an Ecosystem," *Journal of Home Economics,* May 1970, pp. 315–18.

WAGNER, R. *Environment and Man.* New York: W. W. Norton & Company, Inc., 1971.

Chapter 2

"Anchoring Mobile Homes Against Wind Damage." *Management Guides 450.1.* Cooperative Extension Service. Montana State University, Mont., January 1972.

BLAIR, T. A., and R. C. FITE. *Weather Elements.* Englewood Cliffs, N.J.: Prentice-Hall, Inc., 1965.

BROWN, D. F. *Homesite Considerations.* Pacific Northwest Cooperative Extension Publication No. 137. Cooperative Extension Service. Oregon, Washington, and Idaho, January 1974.

DANZ, E. *Sun Protection: An International Architectural Survey.* New York: Praeger Publishers, Inc., 1967.

DOBER, R. P. *Environmental Design.* New York: Van Nostrand Reinhold Company, 1969.

Environmental Quality 1973. The Fourth Annual Report of the Council on Environmental Quality. Washington, D.C.: U.S. Government Printing Office, September 1973.

Homebuyers: Soil Surveys Can Help You. Soil Conservation Service, Program Aid No. 1050. Washington, D.C.: U.S. Government Printing Office, 1974.

InResidence Shelters from Extreme Winds. Texas Tech University, Department of Civil Engineering and the Institute for Disaster Research, Lubbock, Tex.

KAHN, L. "A Statement by Louis Kahn," *Arts and Architecture,* February 1961, p. 29.

NEUTRA, R. J. *Richard Neutra on Building: The Mystery and Realities of the Site.* Scarsdale, N.Y.: Morgan and Morgan, 1951.

Solar Dwelling Design Concepts. U.S. Department of Housing and Urban Development, Office of Policy Development and Research, Washington, D.C.: U.S. Government Printing Office, May 1976.

STEIN, R. G. "Design for Climate." *Harper's,* June 1974, p. 8.

TREWARTHA, G. *Introduction to Climate.* New York: McGraw-Hill Book Company, 1968.

WAHLWILL, J., and D. H. CARSON (eds.). *Environment and the Social Sciences.* Washington, D.C.: American Psychological Association, 1972.

WOOD, A. L., et al. *The Effects of House Orientation on Interior Temperature and Light Quality.* Washington Agricultural Experiment Station, College of Agriculture, Washington State University, Pullman, Wash., April 1971.

Chapter 3

AGAN, T. et al. "Adjusting the Environment for the Elderly and the Handicapped," *Journal of Home Economics,* May 1977, pp. 18–20.

ARDREY, R. *The Social Contract.* New York: Atheneum Publishers, 1970.

BARKLEY, J. D. "Room Space and Its Relationship to Mental Health, Some Observations of a Relocation Officer," *Journal of Housing,* March 1973, pp. 132–33.

BERENSON, B. *Aesthetics and History.* Garden City, N.Y.: Doubleday & Company, Inc., 1953.

BEYER, G. H. and F. H. J. NIERSTRASZ. *Housing the Aged in Western Countries.* New York: Elsevier Publishing Company, 1967.

BOHANNON, P. *Social Anthropology.* New York: Holt, Rinehart and Winston, 1963.

BREEN, L. Z. "Aging and Its Social Aspects," *Journal of Home Economics* October 1962, pp. 685–89.

BRENNFELS, W. "Institutions and Their Corresponding Ideals," *Quality of Man's Environment.* Washington, D.C.: Smithsonian Institute Press, 1968.

BROADY, M. *Planning for People.* London: Bedford Square Press, 1972.

CANTER, D. *Psychology for Architects.* New York: John Wiley and Sons, Inc., 1974.

CHAPMAN, D. *The Home and Social Status.* London: Routledge and Kegan Paul, 1955.

CHATFIELD-TAYLOR, A. "Hitting Home," *Architectural Forum,* March 1973, pp. 58–61.

Check List for Retirement Houses. Small Homes Council, University of Illinois, Urbana, Ill., 1958.

CRULL, S. R. "Cultural Aspects of Housing Consumption," *Illinois Teacher,* November/December 1976, pp. 73–76.

334

CUTLER, V. F. *Personal and Family Values in the Choice of a Home*. Cornell University Agricultural Experiment Station Bulletin 840. Ithaca, N.Y., November 1947.

DONAHUE, W., and C. TIBBETS (eds.). *Aging in Today's Society*. Englewood Cliffs, N.J.: Prentice-Hall, Inc., 1960.

DUVALL, E. M. *Family Development*. Philadelphia: J. B. Lippincott Company, 1967.

Family Life Education: A Cause for Action. American Social Health Association, Family Life Education Project, New York, 1966.

FLEMMING, C. M. *Adolescence*. New York: International Universities Press Inc., 1949.

FOOTE, N. "Family Living as Play," *Marriage and Family Living*, November 1955, pp. 296–301.

GOODE, W. J. *A World Revolution and Family Patterns*. New York: The Free Press, 1963.

HALFSTROM, J. L., and M. M. DUNSING. "Level of Living Factors Influencing the Homemaker's Satisfaction," *Home Economics Research Journal*, December 1973, p. 126.

HALL, E. T. "The Anthropology of Space," *Architectural Review*, September 1966, p. 835.

HOCART, A. M. *Progress of Man*, London: Metheun and Co., Ltd., 1933.

J. C. Penny Forum. New York: J. C. Penny Company, Spring/Summer, 1976.

JOHNSON, R. J., and M. A. POND. "Health Standards of Housing for the Aging Population," *Journal of Gerontology*, April 1952, pp. 254–58.

LANG, J., et. al. (eds.). *Designing for Human Behavior: Architecture and the Behavioral Sciences*. Stroudsburg, Pa.: Dowden Hutchenson & Ross, Inc., 1974.

LANGFORD, M. *Community Aspects of Housing the Aged*. Ithaca, N.Y.: Center for Housing and Environmental Studies, Cornell University, 1962.

LOPATA, H. Z. *Marriages and Families*. New York: D. Van Nostrand Company, 1973.

LUKESHOK, A., and K. LYNCH. "Some Childhood Memories of the City," *Journal of American Institute of Planners*, Summer 1956, pp. 146–52.

MASLOW, A. H., and N. L. MINTZ. "Effects of Aesthetic Surroundings. I: Initial Effects of Three Aesthetic Conditions Perceiving 'Energy' and 'Well Being' in Faces," *Journal of Psychology*, April 1956, pp. 247–54.

MAY, E. E., et al. *Independent Living for the Handicapped and the Elderly*. Boston: Houghton Mifflin Company, 1974.

McCRAY, J. W. and S. S. DAY. "Housing Values, Aspirations and Satisfactions as Indicators of Housing Needs," *Home Economics Research Journal*, June 1977, pp. 244–254.

MEAD, M. (ed.). *Cultural Patterns and Technical Change*. United Nations Educational Scientific and Cultural Organization. New York: The New American Library, 1955.

MEEKS, C. B., and R. E. DEACON. "Values and Planning in the Selection of a Family Living Environment," *Journal of Home Economics*, January 1972, pp. 11–16.

MICHELSON, W. *Man and His Urban Environment: A Sociological Approach.* Reading, Mass.: Addison Wesley Publishing Co., Inc., 1970.

MILLSPAUGH, M., and G. BRECKENFIELD. *Human Side of Urban Renewal.* Babemore, N.Y.: Fight Blight, Inc., 1958.

MONTGOMERY, J. E. "Housing and Its Effects on Behavior," *What's New in Home Economics,* February 1969, pp. 53–55.

MOORE, B. M., JR. "Thoughts on the Future of the Family," in *Political Power and Social Theory.* Cambridge, Mass.: Harvard University Press, 1958, pp. 160–78.

MORRIS, E. W., and M. A. WINTER. "Theory of Family Housing Adjustment," *Journal of Marriage and the Family,* February 1975, p. 82.

NEEDHAM, D. L. *Housing Conditions and Housing Problems Perceived by Families in Selected Low-Income Areas of Georgia, Texas and Virginia.* School of Home Economics, University of Georgia, College of Agriculture Experiment Station, Athens, Ga., September 1973.

NEWMAN, O. *Defensible Space.* New York: Macmillan Publishing Company, Inc., 1972.

NICHOLSON, E. "Physical and Psychological Adequacy," *Journal of Home Economics,* October 1962, pp. 700–05.

Planning Homes for Occupancy. Public Service Administration, Chicago, Ill., 1950.

"The Psychological Dimension of Architectural Space," *Progressive Architecture, April 1965, pp. 159–63.*

RAGLAN, L. *The Temple and the House.* London: Routledge and Kegan Paul, 1964.

RAVEN, J. "Sociological Evidence on Housing: The Home Design," *Architectural Review,* September 1967, pp. 236–40.

————. "Sociological Evidence on Housing: Space in the Home," *Architectural Review,* July 1967, pp. 68–72.

REDFIELD, R. *The Little Community.* Chicago: University of Chicago Press, 1958.

RUTHERFORD, R., and A. J. HOLTS (eds.). *Architectural Designs: Homes for the Aged, The European Approach.* Peoria, Ill.: Howard C., 1963.

SKOLNICK, A., and J. H. SKOLNICK. *Intimacy, Family and Society.* Boston: Little, Brown and Company, 1974.

SOLIEN DE GONZALES, N. L. "Household and Family in the Caribbean," *Social and Economic Studies,* September 1960, p. 106.

SOMMER, R. *Personal Space: The Behavioral Basis of Design.* Englewood Cliffs, N.J.: Prentice-Hall, Inc., 1969.

STEPHENS, W. N. *The Family in Cross-Cultural Perspective.* New York: Holt, Rinehart and Winston, 1963.

"This is How It was in 1775," *Changing Times,* July 1975, p. 4.

TIBBETS, C. "Economic and Social Adequacy of Older People," *Journal of Home Economics,* October 1962, p. 695.

VAN SCOYOC, M. R., and J. L. DEVINE. "Group Instruction in Homemaker Rehabilitation," *Journal of Home Economics,* October 1970, p. 616.

VEBLEN, T. *The Theory of Leisure Class.* New York: The Viking Press, Inc., 1943.

Wedin, C. S. "The House and Its Social-psychological Aspects," *Illinois Teacher*, September/October 1976, pp. 32–35.

Wilner, D. M., et al. *The Housing Environment and Family Life*. Baltimore, Md.: The Johns Hopkins University Press, 1962.

Winter, M. and E. W. Morris, "The Housing We Would Like," *Journal of Home Economics*, May 1977, pp. 7–10.

Zey-Ferrell, M. et. al. "Consumer Preferences and Selected Socio-economic Variables Related to Physical Adequacy of Housing," *Home Economics Research Journal*, June 1977, pp. 232–43.

Chapter 4

"Cheaper by the Panel," *Agricultural Research*. Washington, D.C.: U.S. Government Printing Office, March 1974, p. 9.

Current House Construction Practices. Small Homes Council, Building Research Council, University of Illinois, Urbana, Ill., 1974.

Feedback: Operation Breakthrough. U.S. Department of Housing and Urban Development. Washington, D.C.: U.S. Government Printing Office, August 1974.

Horning, W. *Architectural Drafting*. Englewood Cliffs, N.J.: Prentice-Hall Inc., 1966.

"Industrialized Housing: What Is It Really and Where Is It Going?" *House and Home*, November 1973, pp. 64–71.

McHarg, I. L. *Design with Nature*. Garden City, N.Y.: Doubleday & Company, Inc., 1971.

Oliver, P. (ed.). *Shelter and Society*. New York: Praeger Publishers, Inc., 1969.

Price, C. M. *The Practical Book of Architecture*. Philadelphia: J. B. Lippincott Company, Inc., 1966.

Rudofsky, B. *Architecture Without Architects*. Garden City, N.Y.: Doubleday & Company, Inc., 1964.

————. *The Prodigious Buildings*, Harcourt Brace Jovanovich, Inc., N.Y., 1977.

Salvadori, M., and R. Heller. *Structure in Architecture*. Englewood Cliffs, N.J.: Prentice-Hall, Inc., 1963.

Chapter 5

"The Attack on Snob Zoning," *Environment: The Lender's Role*. U.S. Savings and Loan League, 1972.

Brennan, T. *Midland City*. New York: Dennis Dobson, 1948.

"Building Codes," in *Building the American City*. U.S. National Commission on Urban Problems (Washington, D.C.: U.S. Government Printing Office), Chapter 3.

Burchard, J. E. "The Urban Aesthetic," *The Annals of American Academy of Political and Social Science*, November 1957, pp. 112–22.

Carter, D. G., and K. H. Hinchliff. *When You Build or Remodel Your Farmhouse: A Guide to Planning*. Regional Publication 8, Circular 620. University of Illinois, College of Agriculture, Urbana, Ill., January 1948.

DANIELS, C. "The Filtering Process and Its Implications for Housing Policy," *Human Ecology Forum,* Winter 1974, pp. 18–20.

ELDREDGE, H. W. (ed.). *Taming Megalopolis. Vol. I: What Is and What Could Be.* New York: Praeger Publishers, Inc., 1967.

FISH, T. "Who Will Live in the New Communities?" *Human Ecology Forum,* N.Y. State College for Human Ecology, Cornell University, Ithaca, N.Y., Winter 1972.

GOWANS, A. *Images of American Living.* Philadelphia, Pa.: J. B. Lippincott Company, 1964.

HOWARD, E. (ed.). *Garden Cities of Tomorrow.* London: Faber & Faber, Ltd., 1946.

LEINWAND, G. (ed.). *The City as a Community.* New York: Washington Square Press, 1970.

LERNER, M. *America as a Civilization.* New York: Simon and Shuster, 1957.

MEEKS, C. B. and E. OUDEKERK. A Review of Housing Codes in N.Y. State, Consumer Economics and Public Policy, N.Y.S. College of Human Ecology, Cornell University, Ithaca, January 1977.

MOWERER, E. R. *The Suburban Community.* New York: G. P. Putman's Sons, 1958.

Planning the Electric Water System and Plumbing for Your Farmstead. U.S.D.A. Misc. Publication 674. Washington, D.C.: U.S. Government Printing Office, 1961.

Planning a Home in the Country. Extension Bulletin 547, Cooperative Extension Service, College of Agriculture, Washington State University, Pullman, Wash., September 1969.

SORENSON, D. M. and H. H. STOEVENER (eds.). Economic Issues in Land Use Planning, Western Rural Development Center, Special Report No. 3, Oregon State University Agricultural Experiment Station Corvallis, April 1977.

"Take a Fresh Look at Townhouses," *Changing Times,* August 1973, pp. 35–36.

"Trek Back Toward the Cities," *U.S. News & World Report,* Oct. 16, 1972.

TUNNARD, C., and B. PUSHKAREV. *Man-Made America: Chaos or Control?* New Haven, Conn.: Yale University Press, 1963.

WEISS, S. F., et al. "Selected Preliminary Findings/Evaluation of New Communities, U.S.A.," *Ekistics,* June 1975, pp. 423–28.

WINSLOW, D. E. A. *Provision of Housing Codes in Various American Cities,* National Housing Conference, 1950.

Chapter 6

BURCHARD, J., and A. BUSH-BROWN. *The Architecture of America.* Boston: Little, Brown and Company, 1969.

DAVIDSON, M. B. *Notable American Houses.* New York: American Heritage Publishing, Inc., 1971.

FERGUSSON, J. *A History of Architecture in All Countries from Earliest Times to the Present Day.* London: John Murray, 1874.

HAMLIN, T. *Greek Revival Architecture In America.* New York: Oxford University Press, Inc., 1944.

Lancaster, C. *Architectural Follies in America.* Rutland, Vt.: Charles E. Tuttle Co., 1960.

Mumford, L. *Sticks and Stones.* New York: W. W. Norton & Company, Inc., 1924.

Newcomb, R. *Architecture of the Old Northwest Territory.* Chicago: University of Chicago Press, 1950.

Pratt, D., and R. Pratt. *A Guide to Early American Homes—North.* New York: McGraw Hill Book Company, 1956.

———. *A Guide to Early American Homes—South.* New York: McGraw Hill Book Company, 1956.

Violet leDuc, E. *The Habitations of Man in All Ages.* London: Sampson Low Marston, Searle and Rivington, 1876.

Whiton, S. *Interior Design and Decoration.* Philadelphia: J. B. Lippincott, Company, 1974.

Chapter 7

Design Considerations in Mobile Homes. Pacific Northwest Cooperative Extension Services. Oregon, Washington, and Idaho, January 1974.

Edwards, C. The History and Development of the Recreational Vehicle and Mobile Home Industries. East Lansing, Mich.: Carl Edwards and Associates, 1977.

Evans, H. M. *Man the Designer.* New York: Macmillan Publishing Co., Inc., 1973.

Fransblau, R. N. "You, Psychology, and Your Home," *Psychological Planning: The New Dimension in Home Decorating.* Houston, Tex.: Mastic Tile Corporation of America.

Gries, J., and J. Ford (eds.). *Publications of the President's Conference on Home Building and Ownership.* Washington, D.C.: U.S. Government Printing Office, 1932.

Itten, J. *The Art of Color.* New York: Van Nostrand Reinhold Company, 1973.

"Nader's Men Tag Mobile Homes as Fire Trap and Industry Cries Foul," *House and Home,* December 1972, p. 34.

Mobile Homes: Current Housing Subject Reports (HC7-6). U.S. Bureau of the Census. Washington, D.C.: U.S. Government Printing Office, 1972.

"Professional Builders National Consumer Builder Survey on Housing," *Professional Builder,* January 1975, pp. 81–97.

Rasmussen, S. E. *Experiencing Architecture.* Cambridge, Mass.: Massachusetts Institute of Technology Press, 1959.

"Tyranny in Mobile Home Land," *Consumer Reports,* July 1973, pp. 440–42.

Chapter 8

Belcher, J. C., and P. B. Vazquez-Calcerrada. "A Cross-Cultural Approach to the Social Functions of Housing," *Journal of Marriage and the Family,* November 1972, p. 754.

Beyer, G. H., et al. *Houses Are for People: A Study of Home Buyer Motivations.* Ithaca, N.Y.: Cornell University Housing Research Center, 1955.

DREYFUS, H. *Measure of Man.* New York: Whitney Library of Design, 1959.

GALLOGLY, F. D. "Housing Decisions in Selecting a Residence in Planned Townhouse Development," *Home Economics Research Journal,* June 1974, p. 258.

GALLUP, G. "The Woman's Mind," *Ladies Home Journal,* April 1962.

GUTMAN, E. M. *Wheelchair to Independence: Architectural Barriers Eliminated.* Springfield, Ill.: Charles C Thomas, 1968.

Ideas for Planning Your New Home. Menlo Park, Calif.: Sunset Books, Lane Publishers, March 1975.

Ideas for Storage. Menlo Park, Calif.: Sunset Books, Lane Publishers, February 1976.

NEWMAN, S. J. *Housing Adjustment of Older People.* Ann Arbor, Mich.: Institute for Social Research, University of Michigan, March 1975.

REIMER, S. "Architecture for Family Living," *Journal of Social Issues,* January–February 1951, p. 148.

——. "Maladjustments to the Family Home," *American Sociological Review,* October 1945, pp. 646–48.

ROSSI, P. H. *Why Families Move.* New York: The Free Press, 1955.

What People Want When They Buy a House. Washington, D.C.: U.S. Government Printing Office, 1955.

Chapter 9

Bedroom Planning Standards, Small Homes Council Circular Series C5.6. University of Illinois, Urbana, Ill., 1974.

"Biography of the Bath. Part III: The Bath Comes to America," *Cleanliness Facts,* Soap and Detergent Association, November/December 1975, pp. 11–12.

BLUM, M., and B. CANDEE. *Family Behavior Attitudes and Possession.* Pierce Foundation, 1944.

HOWARD, M. S., and W. R. PARKER. *Planning Bathrooms for Today's Homes,* Home and Garden Bulletin No. 99, U.S.D.A. Washington, D.C.: U.S. Government Printing Office, January 1967.

JESSE, J. "The Bath: Luxury of Luxuries." *Givaudanian,* II (1974), p. 7.

KIRA, A. *The Bathroom: Criteria for Design.* Center for Housing and Environmental Studies, Cornell University, Research Report No. 7, Ithaca, N.Y.

NEUTRA, R. *Life and Human Habitat.* Stuttgart: Verlagsanstalt Alexander Koch GMBH, 1956.

Planning and Remodeling Bathrooms. Menlo Park, Calif.: Sunset Books, Lane Publishing Co., 1975.

Space Standards for Home Planners. Western Cooperative Research Report No. 2. Western Region Agricultural Experiment Stations.

Chapter 10

ALLEN, L. "Kitchen Planning Combines Efficiency and Beauty," *What's New in Home Economics,* March 1970, p. 41.

Better Kitchen Storage. Pacific Northwest Extension Service, #47, Extension Consumer Service Publications. Oregon, Washington, and Idaho, January 1975.

BEYER, G. H. (ed.). *The Cornell Kitchen.* Ithaca, N.Y.: Cornell University Press, 1955.

COOK, G. A. *How to Remodel Your Kitchen and Save $$$.* Garden City, N.Y.: Doubleday & Company, Inc., 1975.

Creative Kitchens and Laundries. General Electric, Appliance Park, Louisville, Ky.

FULLER, M. (ed.). *The Maytag Encyclopedia of Home Laundry.* Popular Library Edition, Maytag Co., Newton, Iowa, 1965.

HABEEB, V. "Speaking Out; Noise Pollution and the Kitchen," *Maytag Kitchen Merchandiser,* 1972.

HOLBROOK, H. S., et al. *Your Farmhouse, Planning the Kitchen Workroom,* U.S.D.A. Home and Garden Bulletin No. 12. Washington, D.C.: U.S. Government Printing Office, December 1951.

HOWARD, M., and G. K. TAYLOR. *Space Requirements for Home Food Preservation.* Technical Bulletin 1143. Washington, D.C.: U.S. Government Printing Office, April 1956.

KEISER, M. B., and B. J. SANEHOLTZ. *Laundry Practices and Procedures of Homemakers in Northern Ohio.* Kent State University. Technical Bulletin 104. Kent, Ohio, 1964.

Kitchens: Planning and Remodeling. Menlo Park, Calif.: Sunset Books, Lane Publishing Co., September 1976.

McCULLOUGH, H., et al. *Space Standards for Household Activities.* Bulletin 686 University of Illinois Agricultural Experiment Station, May 1962.

McCULLOUGH, H. E., and M. B. FARNHAM. *Kitchens for Women in Wheelchairs.* University of Illinois, College of Agriculture Extension Service in Agriculture and Home Economics, Circular 841, November 1961.

Maytag Home Laundry Idea Center. Bulletin #2, Home Service Department, The Maytag Co., Newton, Iowa.

Plan a Workroom. Extension Bulletin 562, Cooperative Extension Service, College of Agriculture, Washington State University, Pullman, Wash., November 1973.

STEIDL, R. E. *Arrangement of Kitchen Centers.* Cornell Extension Bulletin 1028, State College of Home Economics, Ithaca, N.Y., April 1961.

————. *Trips Between Centers in Kitchen for 100 Meals.* Cornell University, Agricultural Experiment Station Bulletin 971, State College of Home Economics, Ithaca, N.Y., January 1962.

WILSON, M., et al. *Standards for Working Surface Heights and Other Space Units of the Dwelling.* Agricultural Experiment Station Bulletin 348, Oregon State University, Corvallis, Ore., 1937.

Chapter 11

Leisure Rooms. Menlo Park, Calif.: Sunset Books, Lane Publishers, 1975.

MANSFIELD, E. A., and E. L. LUCAS. *Clothing Construction.* Boston: Houghton Mifflin Company, 1974.

Sewing Centers. Cooperative Extension Service, College of Agriculture, Washington State University, Pullman, Wash., November 1973.

Space and Place for Leisure, Part I: Living Room. Extension Service, University of Nebraska, College of Agriculture, Lincoln, Nebr.

Space and Place for Leisure, Part II: Activity Rooms. Extension Service, University of Nebraska, College of Agriculture, Lincoln, Nebr.

Chapter 12

Garages and Carports. Small Homes Council Circular Series C5.9. University of Illinois, Urbana, Ill., 1954.

Chapter 13

Air Conditioning and Home Management. Carrier Corporation, Syracuse, N.Y., 1960.

ALEY, J. "The Nagging Problem of Noise," *House and Home*, February 1963, pp. 98–101.

Attic Fan Arrangement and Operation for Summer Cooling. Cooperative Extension Service, College of Agriculture, Washington State University, Pullman, Wash., February, 1970.

BLACK, R. W. "Desirable Temperatures in Offices," *Institute of Heating and Venting Engineering*, July 22, 1954, pp. 319–28.

Book of Successful Fireplaces. Cleveland, Ohio: Donley Bros., 1965.

BRAGDON, C. R. *Noise Pollution: The Unquiet Crises.* Philadelphia: University of Pennsylvania Press, 1971.

COSGROVE, J. J. *History of Sanitation.* Pittsburgh, Pa.: Standard Sanitary Manufacturing Company, 1909.

Designing for Home Safety: Training Guide. Housing Production and Mortgage Credit, Federal Housing Administration, U.S. Department Housing and Urban Development. Washington, D.C.: U.S. Government Printing Office, January 1975.

"Efficient, Economical, Affordable," *Agricultural Research*, April 1977, pp. 1–11.

Fiberglass Insulation for Light-Frame Construction. Denver, Colo.: Johns-Manville, 1975.

FRIGGENS, P. "What You Should Know About Solar Heating," *Reader's Digest* June 1976, pp. 137–42.

FRANKLIN, B. H. "How Safe Is Safe?" *What's New in Home Economics* Jan. 20, 1975, p. 3.

GATELY, W. S., and E. E. FRYE. *Regulation of Noise in Urban Areas.* A Manual Prepared for Public Officials, Managers and Environmental Engineers, Department of Mechanical and Aerospace Engineering, University of Missouri, Rolla, Mo., October 1973.

GUILFORD, J. S., et al. *An Experimental Study of Home Accident Behavior.* American Institute for Research, Los Angeles, Calif., 1965.

Heart of the House. Better Heating and Cooling Council, New York.

342

Heating Systems for the Home. Cooperative Extension Service, College of Agriculture, Washington State University, Pullman, Wash., June 1975.

How to Build and Plan Fireplaces. Menlo Park, Calif.: Sunset Books, Lane Publishing Co., August 1974.

"Humidifiers for the Home," *Consumer Reports,* February 1976, pp. 101–106.

KELLY, R. "Forward," *How to Work Wonders with Light.* Jersey City, N.J.: Lightolier, 1958.

"Noise: How to Control Noise in the House," *House and Home,* April 1958, pp. 128–37.

Planning Your Home Lighting. House and Garden Bulletin No. 138. Washington, D.C.: U.S. Government Printing Office, April 1968.

Public Hearings on Noise Abatement and Control. Vol VII: Physiological and Psychological Effects. U.S. Environmental Protection Agency, Washington, D.C.: U.S. Government Printing Office, 1971.

"Solar Power for Your House—How Practical Now?" *Changing Times,* March 1976, pp. 43–46.

SPIES, B. "Solar Energy: Fuel of the Future?" *Forecast for Home Economists,* February 1976, pp. 41, 42, 74.

STALLONES, R. A. "Theory and Methods of Epidemiologic Study of Home Accidents," *Annuals, New York Academy of Science,* 1963.

Standard Method for Determining Residential Humidification Requirements for Appliance Humidifiers. Association of Home Appliance Manufacturers, AHAM No HU-1-A, Chicago, Ill.

"Will an Attic Fan Cut Your Air Conditioning Costs?" *Changing Times,* June 1976, pp. 27–29.

WOODWARD, W. E. *The Way People Lived.* New York: E. P. Dutton & Co., Inc., 1944.

Chapter 14

"Buy a House or Rent? A Fresh Look at the Options," *Changing Times,* April 1975, pp. 12–16.

Condominium Buyer's Guide. National Association of Home Builders, Washington, D.C., 1975.

"Eight out of Ten Potential Homebuyers Out of Luck," *Billings Gazette,* March 20, 1977.

FEISS, C. *Second Homes in Washington.* Interagency Committee for Outdoor Recreation, Cooperative Extension Service, College of Agriculture, Washington State University, Pullman, Wash., September 1971.

GARVEY, W. W. *The Role of House in Developing Countries.* Subcommittee on Housing Publication Committee on Banking and Currency, U.S. Senate, March 1963.

"Getting a Home Loan These Days," *Changing Times,* September 1975.

"A Guide for Renters: Parts I, II, and III." *Consumer Reports,* November 1974, January 1975.

HANNA, S. "Predicting Family Housing Expenditure," *American Association Housing Educator's Newsletter,* Apr. 1, 1973.

The Home Buyer's Estimator of Monthly Housing Cost. Washington, D.C.: U.S. Government Printing Office, 1976.

"Housing: It's Outasight," *Time*, September 12, 1977, pp. 50–57.

Johnson, A. F. *Consolidated Securities of the Farm Credit Banks.* Fiscal Agency for Farm Credit Banks, New York, 1976.

Joint Economic Committee, *The Economics of Federal Subsidy Programs.* Washington, D.C.: U.S. Government Printing Office, 1972.

"The Legal Side of Owning a House," *Changing Times*, July 1970, p. 56.

Lunner, M. *Comparing Costs of Housing.* Pacific Northwest Extension #139. Oregon, Washington, Idaho, January 1974.

Mead, M. "Outdoor Recreation in the Context of Emerging American Culture: Background Considerations," *Trends in American Outdoor Living and Outdoor Recreation.* Outdoor Resources Review Commission Study Report #22. Washington, D.C.: U.S. Government Printing Office, 1962.

Morris, E. W., et al. "The Measurement of Housing Quality," *Land Economics*, November 1972.

Parkinson, T. L. "The Role of Seals and Certification of Approval in Consumer Decision Making," *Journal of Consumer Affairs*, Summer 1975, pp. 1–4.

Paxton, E. T. *What People Want When They Buy a House.* Washington, D.C.: U.S. Government Printing Office, 1955.

Rand, E. T. "The Consumer as Renter," *Human Ecology Forum*, Spring 1974, pp. 14–15.

Rapkin, C. "Rent–Income Ratio," *Urban Housing.* New York: The Free Press, 1966.

Starr, R. *Housing and the Money Market.* New York: Basic Books, Inc., 1972.

"Suppose Your Apartment Goes Condominium," *Changing Times*, October 1974, pp. 45–47.

Tombaugh, L. W. "Factors Influencing Vacation Home Locations," *Journal of Leisure Research*, Winter 1971, p. 56.

Watkins, A. M. *How to Judge a House.* New York: Hawthorn Books, Inc., 1972.

Winter, M. "Renters: Numbers and Choices," *Human Ecology Forum*, Spring 1974, pp. 16–17.

Wise Home Buying. U.S. Department of Housing and Urban Development Publication #267. Washington, D.C.: U.S. Government Printing Office, 1972.

Woman's Congress on Housing. Housing and Home Finance Agency, Washington, D.C., 1956.

Chapter 15

Clawson, M. (ed.). *Modernizing Urban Land Policy.* Baltimore, Md.: The Johns Hopkins University Press, 1973.

Encyclopedia of Career and Vocational Guidance. Vol. 1. Chicago: Ferguson Publishing Co., 1975.

A Guide to Fannie Mae. The Federal National Mortgage Association, Office of Corporate Relations, Washington, D.C., June 1975.

Maisel, S. J. *Housebuilding in Transaction.* Berkeley and Los Angeles, Calif.: University of California Press, 1953.

Meeks, C. B. "Review of the Housing Allowance Program," Journal of Consumer Affairs, Winter 1976, pp. 208–23.

Miller, R. L. Economic Issues for Consumers. New York: West Publishing Co., 1975.

Miller, S. M. "Shaping Your Future Living Space," What's New in Home Economics, October 1974, pp. 34–36.

Occupational Outlook Handbook. Bulletin 1875, U.S. Bureau of Labor Statistics. Washington, D.C.: U.S. Government Printing Office, 1976–77.

Runge, N. "What Do Architects Do?" Newsletter. Oklahoma Home Economics Association, Tulsa, 1973.

Sullivan, L. Kindergarten Chats. New York: George Wittenborn, Inc., 1947.

Chapter 16

Beckwith, B. P. The Next 500 Years: Scientific Predictions of Major Social Trends. New York: Exposition Press, 1967.

Brown, E. L., and W. R. Nelson. "Effects of a Changing Environment on Human Happiness and Welfare," Agricultural Science Review, Third Quarter 1971, pp. 27–30.

Cole, D., and D. Cox. "Islands in Space," The Futurist, June 1973, p. 133.

Helman, H. The City in the World of the Future. Philadelphia: J. B. Lippincott Company, 1970.

Hu, S. M. "Housing Today and Tomorrow," Forecast for Home Economists, Teachers Edition, March 1972, pp. F24–28, F45–48.

Jencks, C. Architecture 2000; Predictions and Methods. New York: Praeger Publishers, Inc. 1971.

Johnson, R. D. and C. Holbrow (eds.). Space Settlements: A Design Study. Scientific and Technical Information Office, National Aeronautics and Space Administration, Washington, D.C.: U.S. Government Printing Office, 1977.

Joseph, E. C. "What Is Future Time?" The Futurist, August 1974, p. 178.

Marks, W., and R. Skirkanich. "Ocean Platforms: Extending Man's Domain into the Seas," The Futurist, August 1973, pp. 159–65.

Mason, R. "Beyond 2000 Architecture," The Futurist, October 1975, pp. 235–46.

"A Mushrooming of Domes," Life, July 14, 1972, pp. 60–66.

Nervi, P. L. Aesthetics and Technology in Building. Cambridge, Mass.: Harvard University Press, 1965.

"New Architecture: Building for Man," Newsweek, Apr. 19, 1971, p. 87.

"Newest Housing Ideas: Some for Today and Some for the 12th of Never," House and Home, April 1969, pp. 16–17.

Ogg, E. Population and the American Future. Public Affairs Pamphlet No. 503, Public Affairs Committee, Inc., January 1974.

Petrullo, L. "Review of the New Utopias," Contemporary Psychology, March 1967, pp. 165–167.

Soleri, P. Arcology: The City in the Image of Man. Cambridge, Mass.: Massachusetts Institute of Technology Press, 1967.

STONNER, D., et al. "The American Dream! Really?" *Interaction "Eco,"* Department of Family Ecology, Michigan State University, College of Human Ecology, East Lansing, Mich.

WOLF, P. *The Future of the City.* New York: Whitney Library of Design, 1974.

"Your Own Home: A Fading Dream," *U.S. News & World Report,* Oct. 14, 1975, p. 54.

346

Index

350

354

356